EPIC TO NOVEL

THOMAS E. MARESCA

Epic to Novel

OHIO STATE UNIVERSITY PRESS

Portions of the chapter entitled "Dryden" appeared in the summer 1974
issue of *ELH* under the title "The Context of Dryden's Absalom and Achitophel."

Library of Congress Cataloging in Publication Data

Maresca, Thomas E
Epic to Novel

Bibliography: p.
1. English fiction — Early modern, 1500–1700 — History and
criticism. 2. Epic poetry, English — History and criticism.
I. Title.
PR769.M3   823'.03   74-19109
ISBN 0-8142-0216-0

FOR DIANE

CONTENTS

This book attempts to trace the process by which the novel replaced the epic as the major literary form in English. It explores the hows and whys of this process by an analysis of the subject matter of epic rather than its form or manner; that is, it attempts to find out what post-classical readers understood when they read epic by examination of major commentaries on Virgil's *Aeneid* from the early Middle Ages through the Renaissance. After that it proceeds to the same goal by close reading of major English literary works that bear a parodic relation to epic. I understand the epic tradition this book talks about as a heterogeneous body of materials growing from a single root, always changing and transforming themselves, but changing in ways and directions indicated by their earliest shaping. What I think I am describing is an organic growth toward the novel, observing its own inner laws and rhythms; it is as if the genre of epic possessed a kind of autonomy that pushed its practitioners into channels and branches already potential within it. Innovations within the epic tradition seem almost always the product of internal realignments or mutation, almost never the result of grafting.

In working method and critical position, I have chosen to follow Aristotle's example rather than his conclusions; I try to proceed from the critical description of a single text outward to more general conclusions, gathering evidence as I go. Generally speaking, the book is cumulative. Rather than overburden it at the outset with theory, I have left many things to be clarified and elaborated throughout. I hope that by its conclusion all of my sweeping assertions and cryptic phrases will have been supported and explained. Similarly, in the arrangement of chapters

I have occasionally disregarded chronology for the exposition of a clear logical development. Terminology I found a maddening problem, not yet resolved to my own satisfaction. In some cases, I invented or purloined useful words; in others, old and somewhat weak-hammed warhorses were trotted out for another go-round. This is particularly true of "form and content" — a distinction I find more and more artificial, but which seems rhetorically necessary to the clarity of my arguments.

Beyond all this, this study because of its scope produces a great deal of fallout: it has something to say about the Medieval distinction between the allegory of the poets and the allegory of the theologians, about the meaning of *ut pictura poesis,* about poetic imagery and the seventeenth-century revival of atomic theory, about the meaning of narrative or plot in novels. I would call it an idiosyncratic book; others may think it merely cranky. Certainly I do not claim to be right in my conclusions in the sense of being exclusively right. What this book adds up to in my mind is one satisfactory mode of dealing with all of the factors I have examined. That there are other modes of so doing I have no doubt, but this one pleases me: it answers for me the basic questions of how and why the novel supplanted the epic, and it explains their essential relation — and those are the questions that pushed me to undertake this study in the first place.

I am grateful to many institutions and individuals for support and encouragement: to Ohio State University for a quarter of assigned research duty; to the Humanities Center of Johns Hopkins University for the fellowship that enabled me to do the basic research for this book; to the State University of New York Research Foundation for two Summer Grants-in-Aid that allowed me to write it; to two (to me unknown) readers for Ohio State University Press, for numerous pertinent and helpful suggestions; to good friends, whose names would read like a litany of my colleagues at Stony Brook, for advice and occasional consent; and to the late Earl Wasserman, for help and for friendship over many years. My greatest debt I acknowledge in the dedication.

I N ABSALOM AND ACHITOPHEL, Dryden created the last traditional verse epic of any merit written in the English language. By the strictest canons of neoclassical criticism, it *must* be considered an epic poem — or, making allowance for its brevity, an epyllion. Dryden labels it *Absalom and Achitophel: A Poem* in the same succint fashion in which Milton called his work *Paradise Lost: A Poem in Twelve Books*. Indeed, Dryden's poem much more closely approximates contemporary notions of epic than does Milton's. It is tightly organized around a single great end, presented under the guise of historical truth; Le Bossu's definition of epic fits it exactly:

> The Epopea is a Discourse invented by Art, to form the Manners by such Instructions as are disguis'd under the Allegories of some one important Action, which is related in Verse, after a probable, diverting, and surprising Manner.[1]

Generic definitions of this sort have no intrinsic importance; their value lies rather in what the properly identified particular example can tell us about the development of the form, and Dryden's poem, both in its excellences and in its limitations, provides a great deal of information about the crisis of epic poetry at this time. *Paradise Lost* had already contained the germ of serious mock epic (as opposed to epic burlesque) in the parodic relation in which Satan stands to God: in particular, his fraudulent self-examinations and false or mistaken recognitions of his "mission" offer the base on which Dryden builds the shaky edifice of

Absalom's self-created mission, to establish the "dominion of grace" that grotesquely and profoundly parodies David's merciful rule. From this to the full-blown inversions of Pope's *Dunciad* is a short step ideologically but a great one literarily and culturally. Before we get there, we will have to examine in some detail exactly what Dryden accomplishes in *Absalom and Achitophel.*

I

With very few exceptions, *Absalom and Achitophel* maintains a narrative integrity that few political allegories ever reach; its fable (in our terms, its vehicle) achieves a kind of autonomy that renders it complete and satisfying in itself and perfectly transparent as a vehicle for other things. These very qualities hide the real achievement of the fable of *Absalom and Achitophel* by cloaking it with an inevitability that it by no means possesses. We are sufficiently aware of the frequency with which seventeenth-century political writers compared Charles to David to accept without demur the appropriateness of the biblical tale to the English situation. If we remember piously that Dryden has really reversed the roles of the biblical Absalom and Achitophel, the fact does little to alter our acceptance of Dryden's fable as *donnée* rather than *aperçu*, semi-fact rather than full-fiction. Yet the imaginative reordering of history, both Jewish and English, constitutes the excellence of Dryden's poem, and the "fabulous" (in the root sense) nature of Dryden's narrative makes it so inevitable a vehicle of his meaning.

In general terms, the most significant change Dryden has made in the biblical narrative lies in his radical transformation of its temporal and conceptual contexts, both of which he wrenches into a rich ambiguity. To clarify this, we shall have to examine the much-worked-over opening lines of the poem:

> In pious times, e'r Priest-craft did begin,
> Before *Polygamy* was made a sin;
> When man, on many, multiply'd his kind,
> E'r one to one was, cursedly, confind:

When Nature prompted, and no law deny'd
Promiscuous use of Concubine and Bride;
Then, *Israel's* Monarch, after Heaven's own heart,
His vigorous warmth did, variously, impart
To Wives and Slaves: And, wide as his Command,
Scatter'd his Maker's Image through the Land.

(1–10)

Let us put aside at the outset the idea that this passage serves only as a witty justification for, or palliation of, Charles's promiscuity; that is certainly true, but I doubt that Dryden needed ten lines for only that. The passage establishes an explicit temporal and conceptual context for the whole poem, a context that the remainder of the poem will treat with the same irony and ambiguity that Dryden provides for the biblical narrative on which the poem as a whole is based. "Pious times, e'r Priest-craft did begin" were technically the patriarchal period before the establishing of the Levitical priesthood, the period between God's covenant with Abraham and the more explicitly codified covenant established with the people of Israel through Moses.[2] Obviously, chronological difficulties present themselves from the beginning: the biblical David did not live in those pious times, and Dryden's "Before *Polygamy* was made a sin" ignores the pointed injunction of Deuteronomy 17:17 that kings should not multiply horses, wives, or concubines. Indeed, before the end of this same first verse paragraph Dryden also indicates that priestcraft of some sort already had begun:

Gods they had tri'd of every shape and size
That God-smiths could produce, or Priests devise

(49–50)

Later sections of the poem of course confirm this fact:

This set the Heathen Priesthood in a flame,
For Priests of all Religions are the same

(98–99)

> Hot *Levites* Headed these; who pul'd before
> From the'*Ark,* which in the Judges days they bore,
> Resum'd their Cant, and with a Zealous Cry.
> Pursu'd their old belov'd Theocracy.
>
> (519–22)

The solution to these apparent contradictions can be found in careful consideration of the first lines of the poem. Pious times contrast with those after priesthood began. Priesthood itself Dryden associates with the institution of law and consequently of sin: polygamy is *made* a sin; man is *cursedly* (the word has links with the Fall that we cannot now discuss) confined; laws deny nature's promptings. The conception of law herein contained, particularly the conception of the law of Moses, would have been quite familiar to Dryden's audience, since it is Saint Paul's conception of the nature and function of the Mosaic law as he lengthily argues it in the Epistle to the Romans. Here is a brief extract of his argument:

> What shall we say then? Is the law sin? God forbid. Nay, I had not known sin, but by the law: for I had not known lust, except the law had said, Thou shalt not covet. But sin, taking occasion by the commandment, wrought in me all manner of concupiscence. For without the law sin was dead. For I was alive without the law once: but when the commandment came, sin revived, and I died. (7:7–9)

Dryden's appropriation of this conception at the beginning of his poem forces a revaluation, a relocation of the conceptual context in which we understand David. By placing him firmly in "pious times," Dryden leads us to see him as sharing the same sort of direct relationship to God as the patriarchs and Moses possessed; the language of the opening lines, with their emphasis on David as the monarch "after Heaven's own heart" (7), reinforces this. In fact, Dryden depicts David's sexuality as analogous to God's own creativity: it is his maker's image, not his own, that he scatters through the land.[3] Dryden here exploits a distinction familiar to his readers as the difference between the dominion of law, as exemplified by the Mosaic code, and the dominion of grace, as established by the crucifixion of Christ.[4] The pivotal point that allows him to turn this neat inversion is the traditional conception of David as a type of Christ, a conception that Achitophel recalls for us at a crucial point in the poem (line 416; cf. John 11:60) and that Dryden obviously exploits as a careful counterpoint to the dominion of grace his conspirators and Levites — and English puritans — hope to attain. David lives under the dominion of grace, in a kind of golden world where what nature prompts is after God's own heart: he embodies the conception of the divinely appointed king to whom law is irrelevant, who founds his dominion in God's will, in grace, and in his literal and metaphoric paternity of his people. David's own comments, at the end of the poem, make quite explicit this dichotomy between the dominion of law and the dominion of grace, and argue moreover that in rejecting him his rebels reject grace itself and demand the rigor of the law — which as Saint Paul says, is death.

> Law they require, let Law then shew her Face;
> They could not be content to look on Grace,
> Her hinder parts, but with a daring Eye
> To tempt the terror of her Front, and Dye.
>
> (1006–9)

And these lines also complete the conception of David as a patriarchal king possessing direct access to the Deity by their overt allusion to Moses' vision of the hinder parts of God, whose face no man can look upon and live (Exodus 33:18–23)

Into this context Dryden has fitted the action of *Absalom and Achitophel*. All of his rebels oppose not just kingship but grace; monarchy and divinity are at least parallel and probably interchangeable terms. "No King could govern, nor no God could please" (48) the Jews; they are called "a Headstrong, Moody, Murmuring race" who try, not the limits of law, but "th' extent and stretch of grace" (45–46). David becomes in their minds "An Idoll Monarch which their hands had made" (64), and they think to "melt him to that Golden Calf, a State" (66). Achitophel's temptation of Absalom adopts the form of the satanic temptation of Christ because it is simultaneously a temptation from grace, from filial devotion, and from political loyalty. But Achitophel and the other rebels do not reject the grounds of David's authority; rather, they seek to imitate them. Achitophel thus tempts Absalom to accept the role of Messiah, to falsely assume the guise of a bringer of the new and full dispensation of grace. The "Hot *Levites*" who head the "*Solymaean* Rout" parody exactly the basis of David's reign:

> Hot *Levites* Headed these; who pul'd before
> From th'*Ark*, which in the Judges days they bore,
> Resum'd their Cant, and with a Zealous Cry,
> Pursu'd their old belov'd Theocracy.
> Where Sanhedrin and Priest inslav'd the Nation,
> And justifi'd their Spoils by Inspiration;
> For who so fit for Reign as *Aaron*'s Race,
> If once Dominion they could found in Grace?
>
> (519–26)

Shimei, "who Heavens Annointed dar'd to Curse" (583), grotesquely parodies Christ's promise of abiding grace:

> When two or three were gather'd to declaim
> Against the Monarch of *Jerusalem*,
> *Shimei* was always in the midst of them.
>
> (601–6; cf. Matthew 18:20)

Corah, too, among all his other accomplishments, manages a travesty of Christ: Dryden applies to him the imagery of the brazen serpent set up in the desert to preserve the Israelites (633–35) — the image, of course, was traditionally accepted as a type of the crucifixion of Christ. All of these distortions of the true reign of grace simply repeat in David's kingdom the same sort of satanic parody of God's dominion that Milton described in *Paradise Lost*; the devil's party constantly tries to reproduce God's power, and constantly lapses into vulgar burlesque. This is the essential basis of serious mock epic; Satan is the paradigm mock-epic hero. *Paradise Lost* already contains the seeds of mock epic; the triumph of "Satan's party" on earth provided the soil for their germination, as we will see when we come to discuss *MacFlecknoe*.

Within the overall framework of the dichotomy between the dominion of law and the dominion of grace, the opening lines of the poem establish a subsidiary dialectic of grace, law, and nature. Nature prompts, and no law denies "Promiscuous use of Concubine and Bride" (5–6). While in Absalom alone "'twas Natural to please" (28), still "His motions" were "all accompanied with grace; / And *Paradise* was open'd in his face" (29–30). And the Jews, though minimally bound by law, still "led their wild desires to Woods and Caves, / And thought that all but Savages were Slaves" (55–56). This threefold battery of themes, grace, law, and nature, governs the ideological progression of the poem: "Religion, Common-wealth, and Liberty" (292) form, as Achitophel says, the general cry.

This dialectic operates in the poem in curious and often paradoxical ways. For David, to follow nature is to follow grace; at nature's prompting he scatters his maker's image through the land. His "native mercy" (939) Absalom admits is "God's beloved Attribute" (328). Yet even for him conflict occurs, especially when law and justice enter the case:

> If my young *Samson* will pretend a Call
> To shake the Column, let him share the Fall:
> But oh that yet he would repent and live!
> How easie 'tis for Parents to forgive!
> With how few Tears a Pardon might be won
> From Nature, pleading for a Darling Son!
>
> (955–60)

Dryden presents David as torn between two natures, between the king's two bodies, if you will:[5] as man, he grieves for his wayward son; as king, he punishes his wayward subject. The beginning of the poem schematized this paradox of kingship brilliantly. Initially, "Godlike *David*" (14), prompted by nature, scattered his maker's image through the land. The lines immediately following transform the procreative process from the semi-divine imparting of warmth it had been to a more earthy and natural — in a lesser sense — husbandry through an extended farming-seed metaphor. At the end of this, Dryden for the first time introduces Absalom and offers the following rationale for his physical beauty:

> Whether, inspir'd by some diviner Lust,
> His Father got him with a greater Gust;
> Or that his Conscious destiny made way
> By manly beauty to Imperiall sway.
>
> (19–22)

The contrast between Absalom's "manly beauty" and David's eminence as "*Israel's* Monarch, after Heaven's own heart" (7) explains itself, while the concise oxymoron "diviner Lust" sums up both David's dilemma and what is wrong with Absalom's conception. Dryden then makes of Absalom a baser — a more natural — version of David; he too follows nature, and his motions are "all accompanied with grace" (29), but what David and the reader see in him is not his maker's image, but rather

> With secret joy, indulgent *David* view'd
> His Youthfull Image in his Son renew'd
>
> (31–32)

Absalom bears the image of David as man, not of David as king; he is, as was the Duke of Monmouth, a *natural* son, an illegitimate — one born according to the order of nature rather than the order of law or grace. Dryden needs nowhere to stress either the irony of the unnatural conduct of this natural son or the paradox that the illegtimate should call for law.

Flawed human nature, as epitomized in the poem by Absalom, provides the possibility for the disruption of the dominion of grace in David's kingdom, just as it did in the garden:

> But, when to Sin our byast Nature leans,
> The carefull Devil is still at hand with means;
> And providently Pimps for ill desires.
>
> (79–81)

The brief paradox of the devil's providential pimping reminds us of the overarching dominion of divine law and grace within which human nature acts out its "ill desires"; it recalls an ultimate law, nature, and grace that are not in conflict but are in fact identical — but in the world of fallen nature, these are only hints. More immediately apparent in this world is the "natural Instinct" by which the Jews every twenty years rebel (218–19). Achitophel appeals shrewdly to this baser nature when he urges Absalom to set aside filial regard for David—

> Nor let his Love Enchânt your generous Mind;
> 'Tis Natures trick to Propagate her Kind.
> Our fond Begetters, who woud never dye,
> Love but themselves in their Posterity.
>
> (423–26)

And again when he urges him to open rebellion:

> Resolve on Death, or Conquest by the Sword.
> Which for no less a Stake than Life, you Draw;
> And Self-defence is Natures Eldest Law.
>
> (456–58)

And I presume Dryden refers ironically to this same nature when he ends Achitophel's speech with "He said, And this Advice above the rest, / With *Absalom's* Mild nature suited best" (477–78). Yet even within this generally sinful context paradox occurs, and this same "byast Nature" also works to ironic good among the poem's villains:

> But far more numerous was the herd of such,
> Who think too little, and who talk too much.
> These, out of meer instinct, they knew not why,
> Ador'd their fathers God, and Property:
> And, by the same blind benefit of Fate,
> The Devil and the *Jebusite* did hate:
> Born to be sav'd, even in their own despight;
> Because they could not help believing right.
>
> (532–40)

Dryden focuses all of these paradoxes in his disquisition on the social contract, where he raises a whole series of questions about the nature of governor and governed and the scope of law (753–810). Men are naturally prone to rebellion against both kings and god; but isn't something to be said for their natural rights, "their Native sway" (760)? May kings abrogate law? If not, are kings only trustees? If so, how can any man claim any natural right other than what can be defended by brute power? The result of such a process must be a Hobbesian state of nature "where all have Right to all" (794), and that is anarchy. Alteration of existing social structures always ends that way:

> To change Foundations, cast the Frame anew,
> Is work for Rebels who base Ends pursue:
> At once Divine and Humane Laws controul;
> And mend the Parts by ruine of the Whole.
>
> (805–8)

Dryden has carefully suppressed overt mention of grace from this argument to present fully the dilemma into which unaided nature and merely human law lead; as Dryden argues it, the political problem of the one and the many is unresolvable in human terms.

The poem, however, does offer a solution to this problem in terms of its major metaphor. *Absalom and Achitophel* contains an image cluster that sums up fully all the ramifications of this dialectic of grace, law, and nature: the relations of fathers and sons operate simultaneously in all three categories, and the images of fathers and sons, the metaphors of paternity and sonship, offer the key to the totality of the poem. The poem specifically labels kings as "the Godheads Images" (792) and consistently describes David in particular as "Godlike." The beginning of the poem explicitly links David and God through David's sexual potency: the "vigorous warmth" he indiscriminately imparts makes him the sun of the human world, analogous to the creative warmth of the sun in the physical universe and the overflowing being of God in the metaphysical. David the King and God the Father stand in almost one-to-one relation to each other, and this analogous relationship provides the resolution of the problem of government. Dryden signals us that this is the case when, near the beginning of his discussion of the problem of government, he makes choosing heirs for monarchs and decreeing for God parallel and almost cognate acts (758). He undercuts his own question about the contractual nature of kingship by referring to it as a "resuming Cov'nant" (767), and so linking it with God's covenant with the Israelites and implying the consequent parallel between God's dominion and the king's — and since the poem has argued from the very beginning that David's kingship constitutes the dominion of grace, this necessarily implies also that David's authority is as irrevocable as God's. Dryden clinches his argument by appeal to Adam's sin, a stock argument of the theorists of patriarchal government:[6]

> If those who gave the Scepter, coud not tye
> By their own deed their own Posterity,
> How then coud *Adam* bind his future Race?
> How coud his forfeit on mankind take place?
> Or how coud heavenly Justice damn us all,
> Who nere consented to our Fathers fall?
>
> (769–74)

Dryden's rhetorical questions amalgamate all three areas of the poem's dialectic and convict the rebels of the heresy of challenging divine justice. Adam's simple status as the natural father of the human race nullifies all questions of the people's "Native sway" (760): they have none, since it was all vested in him as the father of human nature. His rebellion against the kingship of God is symbolically reenacted in the poem in the temptation and fall of Absalom, an act that, like Adam's, will once again bring mankind under the dominion of law and death until the second Adam can restore the dominion of grace. David thus stands in the poem as God's vice-regent, king by divine right and patriarchal descent — a fact even Achitophel admits in his sneering reference to David's "Successive Title, Long, and Dark, / Drawn from the Mouldy Rolls of *Noah's* Ark" (301–2). Dryden's whole argument throughout this section of the poem draws heavily upon the patriarchal theorists and constantly employs their language. He states the basic problem in terms of the rights of fathers and sons:

> What shall we think! can People give away
> Both for themselves and Sons, their Native sway?
>
> (759–60)

And his citation of Adam uses the same terms of reference — tying posterity, binding one's future race, consenting to our father's fall (769–74). His subsequent critique of the problem of individual rights in a democracy follows quite closely the arguments of Sir Robert Filmer's *Patriarcha* and other similar tracts.[7] His implicit conclusion is inescapable: David exercises authority just as does a father in his family or God in the universe. Rebellion against him equals apostasy from God — setting up the golden calf of a state (66). Logically then, when "Godlike *David*" speaks at the end of the poem, "His Train their Maker in their Master hear" (938); and the paternal, creative David of the opening lines brings forth one more image of his maker in the land. And equally logically, the final lines of the poem harmonize grace, law, and nature in the restoration of "Godlike *David*" as "Lawfull Lord" presiding over "a Series of new time" (1026–31); Dryden alludes to Virgil's supposedly messianic eclogue, with its promise of the birth of the wonder child, the restoration of a golden world, and the reestablishment of the reign of justice and grace. The end of the poem fulfills its beginning; David's kingship and paternity are transformed into symbols of the reestablishment of universal order and the undoing of Adam's fall. The paradise that was metaphorically opened in Absalom's face (30) reaches its fulfillment in the advent of the second Adam who is to be born of David's line; the dominion of grace his rebels mistakenly seek through the son of his mortal body will be established by the son of his divine body.

Given the paramount importance of the idea of paternity in this scheme, the sort of son produced becomes a major index of the rightness or wrongness, the morality or immorality, of the father and his activities. The poem juxtaposes and contrasts the sons of its various actors for the purpose of illustrating the presence of proper hierarchical order or the absence of it. The comely Absalom, ambiguously graceful, starkly contrasts with the ugly, unformed progeny of Achitophel, the physical image of his father's mind.

>   . . . that unfeather'd, two Leg'd thing, a Son:
>   Got, while his Soul did hudled Notions try;
>   And born a shapeless Lump, like Anarchy.
>
>   (170–72)

Immediately after presenting the essentially patriarchal argument about government that we have already discussed, Dryden illustrates it by his encomium of Barzillai's son, who fulfilled all parts of the parallel duties "of Subject and of Son" (836). Such acceptance and fulfillment of the obligations of a hierarchical and patriarchal state produce another, metaphoric, image of the maker:

>   Oh Narrow Circle, but of Pow'r Divine,
>   Scanted in Space, but perfect in thy Line!
>
>   (838–39)

This encomium of Barzillai's son thus forms an integral unit in the poem's imagistic structure, point by point damning Absalom for his dereliction of the duties "of Subject and of Son." David himself places this image in its most important perspective when he refers to his rebellious subjects as Jacob and Esau:

>   True, they petition me t'approve their Choise,
>   But *Esau's* Hands suite ill with *Jacob's* Voice.
>
>   (981–82)

Jacob, the younger son and inferior by the order of nature, achieved priority according to the order of grace; as Bishop Hall expressed it, "Esau got the right of nature, Jacob of grace."[8] These two sons, contending for a paternal blessing, sum up the image of sonship in the poem: nature and grace struggle for dominion, nature with Esau's hands, simple power and bodily strength, grace with Jacob's voice, reason and prayer.

Dryden characterizes all of the poem's Esaus by marked physical descriptions; this process makes them primarily corporeal, while leaving the poem's Jacobs relatively untouched by the taint of fallen bodily nature. *Absalom and Achitophel's* villains exist in our imaginations primarily as physical entities — "that unfeather'd, two Leg'd thing," Achitophel's son (170); Achitophel himself,

> A fiery Soul, which working out its way,
> Fretted the Pigmy Body to decay:
> And o'r informed the Tenement of Clay;
>
> (156–58)

Corah,

> Sunk were his Eyes, his Voyce was harsh and loud,
> Sure signs he neither Cholerick was, nor Proud:
> His long Chin prov'd his Wit; his Saintlike Grace
> A Church Vermilion, and a *Moses's* Face;
>
> (646–49)

and even "The well hung *Balaam*"(574). Corporeal imagery marks all the rebels and their activities, dragging them down from the realm of spirit they would usurp to the world of matter, much as Satan's rebellion in *Paradise Lost* degraded him to the material form of the serpent. Images of eating and of food particularly abound in the poem, frequently in semi-blasphemous contexts. Jewish rabbis and Jebusites agree that it is their duty "T'espouse his Cause by whom they eat and drink" (107). The plot itself is "swallow'd in the Mass, unchew'd and Crude" (113). Dryden describes the beliefs of the Jebusites as follows:

> Th'*Egyptian* Rites the *Jebusites* imbrac'd;
> Where Gods were recommended by their Tast.
> Such savory Deities must needs be good,
> As serv'd at once for Worship and for Food.
>
> (118–21)

Nadab, in addition to canting, "made new porridge for the Paschal Lamb" (576). Dryden even uses such imagery negatively, and paradoxically corporealizes even his most abstemious villain, Shimei:

> And, that his nobel Stile he might refine,
> No *Rechabite* more shund the fumes of Wine.
> Chast were his Cellars, and his Shrieval Board
> The Grossness of a City Feast abhor'd:
> His Cooks, with long disuse, their Trade forgot;
> Cool was his Kitchen, tho his Brains were hot.
>
> (616–21)

This whole image pattern culminates in Absalom's offering himself to the mob:

> Th'admiring Croud are dazled with surprise,
> And on his goodly person feed their eyes.
>
> (686–87)

Naturally enough, Dryden also metamorphoses his speech into one more meal: his words are "More slow than Hybla drops, and far more sweet" (697). But the final transformation of the image, and its ideological climax in the poem, occur in David's speech: the process of corporealization to which the rebels have all been subjected here reaches its nadir in a symbolic cannibalism:

> Against themselves their Witnesses will Swear,
> Till Viper-like their Mother Plot they tear:
> And suck for Nutriment that bloody gore
> Which was their Principle of Life before.
>
> (1012–15)

Dryden binds his rebels together with still other material links; an ubiquitous pattern of references to blood, humors, lakes, and seas ties leaders and mob together in a common allegiance to the moon, which governs the motions of all such changeable bodies.

> For, govern'd by the *Moon*, the giddy *Jews*
> Tread the same track when she the Prime renews:
> And once in twenty Years, their Scribes Record,
> By natural Instinct they change their Lord.
>
> (216–19)

Zimri, "in the course of one revolving Moon, / Was Chymist, Fidler, States-Man, and Buffoon" (549–50). Sanhedrins and crowds are "Infected with this publick Lunacy" (788); both lack stability: they flow to the mark and run faster out (786). Achitophel hopes that David's power, "thus ebbing out, might be / Drawn to the dregs of a Democracy" (226–27). But the most important use of the image occurs quite early in the poem; it links Absalom even then with the fickle mob and sets up a loose parallel between his warm excess in murdering Amnon and the people's feverish propensity to rebellion. Absalom's "warm excesses" (37), Dryden tells us, "Were constru'd Youth that purg'd by boyling o'r" (38). He shortly after employs the analogy of the human body and the body politic to apply this same image, in much greater detail, to the consequences of the Popish Plot in the mob:

> This Plot, which fail'd for want of common Sense,
> Had yet a deep and dangerous Consequence:
> For, as when raging Fevers boyl the Blood,
> The standing Lake soon floats into a Flood;
> And every hostile Humour, which before
> Slept quite in its Channels, bubbles o'r:
> So, several Factions from this first Ferment,
> Work up to Foam, and threat the Government.
>
> (134–41)

This last use of the image once again forces a more serious revaluation of Absalom's excesses, and at the same time degrades him by linking him with the mob in a common subservience to passion and irrationality, to the lowest common denominators of human nature. All of these images of food, eating, and humors achieve a common effect in the poem: they constitute the symbolic enactment, in the moral and individual realm, of the public rebellion. They debase the image of his maker that David bears by reducing that image in the individual and in society to a mere physical effigy — they are, if you will, simply other versions of the golden calf to which the rebels would reduce David and God.

II

As opposed to the striking corporeality of the rebels, David and his party seem somewhat ethereal. Dryden employs no physical description whatever in his catalogue of the royalists, and his opening encomium of Barzillai's sainted and angelic son casts a protective cloak of spirituality and immateriality over all the members of the group. Indeed, Dryden does not even have the royalists *do* very much; in contrast to the rebels, who slide, rush, ebb, flow, and so on, the royalists merely stand and speak — thereby making a minor but effective imagistic point about stability and motion that David capitalizes upon in the very final lines of his speech (1018–25). But speech itself figures as the most important attribute of David's followers — honest speech as opposed to Achitophel's lies, rational argument as opposed to the rebels' propaganda, poetry as opposed to the fictions of Corah, Jacob's voice versus Esau's hands. The rebels curse and cant; the heroes pray and reason. This whole final section of the poem, from line 811 to the end, centers itself upon the right use of language as a criterion of loyalty, intelligence, and morality. The poem climaxes in David's speech precisely because only the enunciation of clear truth can conclude such a parade of lies and misrepresentations as the rebels have enacted. In a precisely parallel way, Dryden at this point in the poem begins emphasizing the fictive and artificial nature of *Absalom and Achitophel* itself, reminding us that it *is* a poem and exploiting the paradox of discovering truth through falsehood and fiction. The personality of the poet, as a kind of magical recorder of praise or blame for all future time, appears at the very beginning of this section; speaking of David's friends, Dryden says

> Yet some there were, ev'n in the worst of days,
> Some let me name, and Naming is to praise.
>
> (815–16)

He sustains this emphasis on the personal role of the poet and his personal involvement in his fiction all through the section on Barzillai and Barzillai's son:

> His Edlest Hope, with every Grace adorn'd,
> By me (so Heav'n will have it) always Mourn'd,
> And always honour'd . . .
>
> (831–33)

The apostrophe to the dead hero, beginning at line 838 with "Oh Narrow Circle" continues this tone, allowing us to hear the narrator's personal grief paradoxically set within the artificial framework of formal eulogy — a point reinforced by the poet's address to his muse and reference to what he has just spoken as "this Verse / To hang on her departed Patron's Hearse" (858–59). Barzillai himself Dryden praises for his discrimination and generosity in honoring "The Fighting Warriour, and Recording Muse" (828). He similarly commends "Him of the Western dome" for sense and eloquence (868–69), and pointedly adds the following:

> The Prophets Sons by such example led,
> To Learning and to Loyalty were bred:
> For *Colleges* on bounteous Kings depend,
> And never Rebell was to Arts a friend.
>
> (1870–73)

Dryden likewise distinguishes Adriel as "the Muses friend, / Himself a Muse" (877–78). He lauds Jotham for his ability "To move Assemblies" (884) and Amiel for his skill in leading the Sanhedrin —

> So dexterous was he in the Crown's defence,
> So form'd to speak a Loyal Nation's Sense,

That as their band was *Israel's* Tribes in small,
So fit was he to represent them all.

(904–7)

Dryden's long satiric portrait of Corah offers the best perspective from
which to view this concern with language, since Corah commits the
poem's greatest perversion of words. Dryden contrasts him tellingly with
Saint Stephen, who bore witness to the truth with his life; the bilingual
pun on *martyr* and *witness* enables him somewhat less than covertly to
warn Corah of the fate that awaits him:

Who ever ask'd the Witnesses high race,
Whose Oath with Martyrdom did *Stephen* grace?

(642–43)

And again, later in the passage:

Let *Israels* foes suspect his heav'nly call,
And rashly judge his Writ Apocryphal;
Our Laws for such affronts have forfeits made:
He takes his life, who takes away his trade.

(664–67)

But other aspects of Stephen's story serve Dryden's purposes as well;
certainly the fact that the protomartyr was brought to trial in the first
place by the suborned testimony of false witnesses bears heavily on
Dryden's irony here. In another way, too, Stephen provides a norm
against which to judge Corah: he enjoys a vision of Christ in glory (Acts
7:55–56) that Corah's lies grossly parody —

Some future Truths are mingled in his Book;
But, where the witness faild, the Prophet Spoke:
Some things like Visionary flights appear;
The Spirit caught him up, the Lord knows where.

(654–57)

Dryden's mention of Corah's *"Moses's* Face" (649) and Stephen's actual citation of Moses in his defense provide further clues to the significance of this passage. Stephen described Moses as a precursor of Christ, and as such he has already appeared in *Absalom and Achitophel;* Achitophel initially hailed Absalom as the Jews' "second *Moses,* whose extended Wand / Divides the Seas, and shews the promis'd Land" (234–35). Moses as the leader of the exodus from Egypt has of course been subliminally present in the poem from the first mention of the golden calf in line 66, or perhaps even from the first line of the poem, with its implicit reference to the founding of the Levitical priesthood under Moses' direction. However that may be, the figure of Moses as a divinely appointed ruler having direct access to the Deity has operated up to this point in the poem as a minor analogue to David. Here Dryden chooses to make this analogue explicit and important. The final lines of the passage on Shimei, which immediately precede the portrait of Corah, start the process in motion:

> And *Moses's* Laws he held in more account,
> For forty days of Fasting in the Mount.
>
> (628–29)

The fact of God's dispensing law to the Israelites obviously has in itself considerable importance to *Absalom and Achitophel,* but I want to concentrate for the moment upon the idea of Moses' vision of God on the mount, since Corah bears a parodic version of the outward effects of that vision in his *"Moses's* Face":

> And it came to pass, when Moses came down from mount Sinai with the two tables of testimony in Moses' hand, when he came down from the mount, that Moses wist not that the skin of his face shone while he talked with him. (Exodus 34:29)

Corah too has his visions, but they sound oddly more like Saint Paul's than Moses': "The Spirit caught him up, the Lord knows where" (657). The line recalls Paul's famous account in 2 Corinthians:

> I knew a man in Christ above fourteen years ago, (whether in the body, I cannot tell; or whether out of the body, I cannot tell: God knoweth;) such an one was caught up to the third heaven. And I knew such a man (whether in the body or out of the body, I cannot tell: God knoweth;) How that he was caught up into paradise, and heard unspeakable words, which it is not lawful for a man to utter. (12:2-4)

And there, I think we have the crux of the matter: he "heard unspeakable words, which it is not lawful for a man to utter." Corah debases that vision with his imaginary plots and malicious lies; he perjures himself, quite literally speaking "words, which it is not lawful for a man to utter." Dryden's description of him as the brazen serpent raised in the desert continues and completes the travesty: Corah, like Absalom, plays false prophet, false Moses, false Messiah. He leads not to the dominion of grace that the brazen serpent tokens but only to the same sort of parody of it that Absalom and Achitophel offer, and ultimately to the oblivion from which he rose. Corah, as a *"Levite"* and one of "Godalmightys Gentlemen" (644–45), pursues what Dryden has earlier described as "their old belov'd Theocracy" (552),

> Where Sanhedrin and Priest inslav'd the Nation,
> And justifi'd their Spoils by Inspiration;
> For who so fit for Reign as *Aaron's* Race,
> If once Dominion they could found in Grace?
>
> (523–26)

The parody is perfect and complete, for the biblical Corah — also a Levite — rebelled against Moses for precisely the same reasons:

> And they gathered themselves together against Moses and against Aaron, and said unto them, Ye take too much upon you, seeing all the congregation are holy, every one of them, and the Lord is among them: wherefore then lift ye up yourselves above the congregation of the Lord? (Numbers 16:3)

Needless to say, the predictive value of historical allusion would once again warn this Corah about the exemplary punishments God visits upon those who challenge his appointed rulers, even in the name of grace.

Dryden draws Corah as a total hypocrite, one who perverts the offices of priest, prophet, and witness to his own ends by base lies. His first couplet of direct address to Corah

> Yet, *Corah*, thou shalt from Oblivion pass;
> Erect thy self thou Monumental Brass
>
> (632–33)

seems to me to recall the famous opening of the last ode of Horace's third book, "Exegi monumentum aere perennius," "I have built a monument more lasting than brass."[9] The conception of Corah as anti-poet, as one who uses language to deceive and disorder, contrasts coherently in the poem with the emphasis Dryden will later place, and which we have already partially discussed, upon himself as poet: opposed to Corah stands, as loyal member of the king's party, the king's poet laureate (more accurately, and more to the point, the historiographer royal), who employs words to impose order, who uses fictions only for their inherent truth. Corah's lies constitute another debased image of the maker; Dryden, as a lesser maker in his own right, creates a true image of reality. So too does David, when he promises the speedy advent of law:

> Law they require, let Law then shew her Face;
> They could not be content to look on Grace
> Her hinder parts, but with a daring Eye
> To tempt the terror of her Front, and Dye.
> By their own arts 'tis Righteously decreed,
> Those dire Artificers of Death shall bleed.
> Against themselves their Witnesses will Swear
> Till Viper-like their Mother Plot they tear:
> And suck for Nutriment that bloody gore
> Which was their Principle of Life before.
>
> (1006–15)

His reference to the hinder parts of grace returns us to Moses' vision on the mount of the glory of God; now David, like Moses, acts as the bringer of divine law to men who have fallen from grace to depraved nature. In "Viper-like their Mother Plot they tear" we see the inevitable end to which unaided nature leads, as well as the end of that part of the paternal and filial images of the poem: nature can only turn upon itself; it can never rise above itself to law or grace, both of which are the free dispensations of God and his anointed kings. But the reference to the hinder parts of grace implies more than this. If David is now functioning properly as an intermediary between God and man, as the second Moses Achitophel claimed Absalom to be, then he is not merely imposing law upon his unruly subjects but offering them access to grace as well — that is, at the very moment when the operations of grace seem about to be suspended in the face of the "curst Effects of necessary Law" (1003), God and David paradoxically offer fresh gifts of grace. David stands as a hinge between the two great dispensations, that of law in Moses and that of grace in Christ. The dominion of law contains, in embryo, the dominion of grace. What Moses saw on the mount when he viewed the hinder parts of God most biblical commentators of Dryden's time agreed upon: he saw an image of the glory of God — the Shechinah some called it, others the Word, others Christ.[10] But it amounts to the same thing: at the moment of receiving the law, which brings death, Moses received a vision of the grace that brings life and of which he himself served as a type. That image of God's glory that he saw David here reproduces in himself and in his speech, using words as the agent of the divine will to create an image of the divine justice and mercy, just as the poet Dryden employs words to create yet another image of divine providence and just as the divine Word himself *is* that justice and mercy. And God himself guarantees the veracity of these images and words — not just by his consenting nod and thunder, but in the "Series of new time" (1028) that here begins. These new times will witness the divine birth, as Virgil's eclogue tells us: "iam nova progenies caelo demittitur alto" (4.7). The event there described Dryden and his audience knew to be the birth of Christ, the advent of the dominion of grace, the incarnation of the Word. That entrance of the eternal Word into human time establishes both the historicity and the essential truth of Dryden's fiction. It confirms the validity of God's own poem, which is creation in general and David in particular, and provides the ground for the human maker John Dryden's partial image of that creation. *Absalom and Achitophel* goes full circle, and "Godlike *David*" at the end of the poem is once more reproducing his maker's image in the land. Even the metaphor of paternity is restored to honor through the divine paternity and the divine sonship that will flow from David's line. Language too is restored after the abuse heaped on it by Absalom, Achitophel, and Corah: in the laconic "He said" that concludes David's speech, to which "Th'Almighty, nodding, gave Consent" (1026), and in the birth of the Word lie the restitution of all words and the vindication of all poetry — including this present fiction — as a true image of realtiy.

III

Absalom and Achitophel concludes as Fielding's *Amelia* concludes, with freedom from law and renewed access to grace, because both are works written in the epic tradition. That tradition is not just a vague group of themes and devices but a precise body of subject matter and form capable of manifesting itself in many guises. *Absalom and Achitophel* incarnates it for the last time, in English, as serious verse composition. After this, it will metamorphose itself into many parodic forms, both verse and prose, before Fielding once again seriously gives it flesh in his last (what we call) novel. To begin to understand those transformations, and to grasp the reasons for the necessary death of epic's poetic body, we must first comprehend the changes epic underwent before Dryden used it. What happened to the idea of epic between Virgil and Dryden — between the *Aeneid* and *Absalom and Achitophel* — accounts in may ways for its protean avatars afterward.

The *Aeneid* forms the core of the English epic tradition. From it sprout all of the ramifications of that tradition, in prose or verse, whether labeled romance or epic or novel. The *Iliad* and the *Odyssey*, no matter how largely they may figure in an individual writer's imagination, remain in comparison to the *Aeneid* peripheral to the growth and development of the genre in English. Even in the works of Pope, who was probably more familiar with the Greek epics than any major English writer before or since, the *Aeneid* provides the essential material upon which his imagination primarily works wherever he approaches the precincts of epic. This does not deny that Homer is important to the development of epic; it only says that in the English tradition he is less important than Virgil. This book will offer many occasions to speak of Homer; it will demand on many more that I talk of Virgil.

There are good reasons for this, the primary ones obviously being linguistic. Latin was the uniform language of learned men; Greek was not. The Middle Ages largely lost contact with Greek language and learning, and even after the Renaissance, knowledge of Greek belonged to the few among educated men rather than to the mass of them. Greek texts were published with Latin translations and Latin notes, and it is probable that it was through the Latin rather than directly from the Greek that most readers who encountered Greek literature at all made their contact. The second, and I think equally important, reason lies in the elaborate and prestigious body of commentary that gathered around the *Aeneid* and that found in that poem the paradigm of its genre.

I propose to discuss here a chronological selection of what strike me as key commentaries on the *Aeneid* — interpretative commentaries, not philological scholia. By so doing, it is not my intention to give the impression that there ever existed a uniform, unvarying, and never-broken tradition of Virgilian exegesis — a great chain of Virgil. Rather, I simply want to demonstrate the existence, ubiquity, and persistence of certain attitudes toward Virgil and his poem along with what seem to me the important qualifications and modifications of those attitudes. Particular attitudes toward epic poetry, particular ideas about the *Aeneid*, occur in strikingly similar forms in commentators from Macrobius to Le Bossu. That in itself is important, but the light such ideas cast upon the fate of epic is even more so.

In a very real sense, Macrobius presents whatever "Virgilian tradition" there is already fully formed.[11] His notion of Virgil and his poem contain already all of the attitudes that the Renaissance will see in poets and epic poetry. Let me, for the sake of illustration, simply juxtapose a passage from the *Saturnalia* with one from Tasso's *Discourses of the Epic Poem:*

> You see — do you not? — that the use of all these varied styles is a distinctive characteristic of Vergil's language. Indeed, I think it not without a kind of foreknowledge that he was preparing himself to serve as a model for all, that he intentionally blended his styles, acting with a prescience born of a disposition divine rather than mortal. And thus it was that with the universal mother, Nature, for his only guide he wove the pattern of his work — just as in music different sounds are combined to form a single harmony. For in fact, if you look closely into the nature of the universe, you will find a striking resemblance between the handiwork of the divine craftsman and that of our poet. Thus, just as Vergil's language is perfectly adapted to every kind of character, being now concise, now copious, now dry, now ornate, and now a combination of all these qualities, sometimes flowing smoothly or at other times raging like a torrent; so it is with the earth itself, for here it is rich with crops and meadows, there rough with forests and crags, here you have dry sand, here, again, flowing streams, and parts lie open to the boundless sea. I beg you to pardon me and not charge me with exaggeration in thus comparing Vergil with nature, for I think that I might fairly say that he has combined in his single self the diverse styles of the ten Attic orators, and yet not say enough.[12]

> Yet for all that, the world, which includes in its bosom so many and so diverse things, is one, one in its form and essence, one the knot with which its parts are joined and bound together in discordant concord; and while there is nothing lacking in it, yet there is nothing there that does not serve either for necessity or ornament. I judge that in the same way the great poet (who is called divine for no other reason but that, because he resembles in his works the supreme architect, he comes to participate in his divinity) is able to form a poem in which as in a little world can be read in one passage how armies are drawn up, and in various others

there are battles by land and sea, attacks on cities, skirmishes, duels, jousts, descriptions of hunger and thirst, tem-
pests, conflagrations, prodigies; there are a variety of celestial and infernal councils, and the reader encounters sedi-
tions, discords, wanderings, adventures, incantations, works
of cruelty, audacity, courtesy, and generosity, and actions of
love, now unhappy, now happy, now pleasing, now causing
compassion. Yet in spite of all, the poem that contains so
great variety of matter is one, one is its form and its soul; and
all these things are put together in such a way that one has
relation to the other, one corresponds to the other, the one
necessarily or apparently so depends on the other that if one
part is taken away or changed in position the whole is destroyed. And if this is true, the art of composing a poem is like
the nature of the universe, which is composed of contraries,
such as appear in the law of music, for it there were no
multiplicity there would be no whole, and no law, as Plotinus
says.[13]

This exalted vision of the poet corresponds in Macrobius to the
canonization of Virgil as philosopher and source of truth. Macrobius (in
his commentary on the *Somnium Scipionis*) links Virgil and Homer
with Cicero and Plato as "doctrinal authorities."[14] (The association with
Plato will be lengthily exploited by Cristoforo Landino a thousand years
later.) At roughly the same historical moment, Servius, in his commentary on the *Aeneid,* pictures Virgil as the same sort of polymath and
warns at the beginning of the sixth book that "All Virgil is full of wisdom,
but especially this book, the chief part of which is taken from Homer.
Some things in it are stated simply, others are taken from history, many
from the exalted sciences of Egyptian philosophy and theology, so that
several passages of this book have had entire treatises devoted to them."
Admittedly, this is not specific. Servius, although filled with admiration
for Virgil's wisdom, rarely and seemingly reluctantly allegorizes or
expounds that wisdom (his explanation of the golden bough is an important exception). Neither did Macrobius compile a systematic exegesis of
the *Aeneid,* although he does in the course of the *Saturnalia* expound

many specific points. What is important about the work of these men is the kind of attitude they set up toward, and the sort of expectations they generate about, Virgil and his *Aeneid*. The poet is a kind of demigod, and builds his poem with the same sort of wisdom that built the greater creation in which we dwell. It stands to reason then — especially since the poet is also a teacher of the order of Cicero and Plato — that in his poem we can, if we look rightly, discover profound moral and philosophical truths about that larger creation.

Later commentators addressed themselves directly to the specific nature of those truths. The commentary of Fulgentius (*De Continentia Virgiliana*) may strike us as crude and even silly, but it established patterns (or simply followed patterns already established) in Virgilian exegesis that persisted through and after the Middle Ages. Its expectations about the *Aeneid* remain, with some differences in terminology, the expectations of the seventeenth century. In Fulgentius's view, Virgil's minor poems allegorically reveal the secrets of the physical universe; the *Aeneid* concerns itself with "the condition of human life."[15] The subject matter of the poem is the acquisition, management, and perfection of wisdom. The shade of Virgil kindly explains to Fulgentius that this corresponds in human development to birth, learning, and happiness. (At this point in Fulgentius's commentary, Virgil compares these stages to the corresponding stages in the educational process. This link between the epic and the process of formal education is a facet of the genre that also figures largely in the commentary of Bernardus Silvestris and less prominently but still importantly in almost all subsequent readings of the *Aeneid*.) The kind of wisdom in question Fulgentius's Virgil very clearly defines as a philosophical rather than a theological virtue; Virgil himself was, as Fulgentius several times has him point out, a pagan and not a Christian. This explicit denial of Christian content offers an important clue not just to the understanding of epic (that seems bound up in the notion of wisdom and its affiliations with the educational process) but to the medieval approach to secular or profane poetry generally. Fulgentius several times interjects to draw parallels between Virgil's exegesis of his own poem and some Christian doctrines; in each case, Virgil firmly denies that the specific doctrine was known to him. The parallels remain only parallels, not coincidences or foreshadowings; and what ought to be discussed in profane poetry, Virgil implies, is not Christian dogma but the highest philosophic and scientific knowledge of the pagan world.

From this point on, Fulgentius's interpretation of the *Aeneid* — or rather, the interpretation he puts in Virgil's mouth — sets a pattern from which later commentaries will scarcely deviate. The philosophical core of the *Aeneid* begins not *in medias res* but *ab ovo,* with the birth of man into the storms and dangers of the temporal world (the storm and shipwreck of book one). The first, second, and third books describe the various vagaries and physical and mental imperfections of infancy and childhood, up to the point at which Anchises dies. The burial of Anchises represents Aeneas's release from parental control and his entrance into the life of the passions, symbolized by hunting, the storm (violent emotional disturbances), and his affair with Dido. At the urging of intelligence (Mercury), he abandons love, which then falls to ashes (Dido on the funeral pyre). Having reached a more prudent age, he follows the memory of parental example and engages in exercises proper to a cultured man (the funeral games). In the sixth book, Aeneas approaches the temple of Apollo, that is, he begins to study the mysteries of wisdom. He buries Misenus at this point because Misenus etymologically means vainglory, and this false pride must be abandoned before he can acquire the secrets of wisdom. The entrance of the underworld is his entrance into knowledge; here he contemplates the punishments of evildoers, the rewards of good men, and the follies of youth. Later, in seeing Dido among the shades, he reflects upon his former lust and is moved to repentance. He sees many being punished for the dreadful sin of pride. His planting the golden bough at the entrance of Elysium indicates that when the task of learning is accomplished, it must be planted forever in the memory. Elysium means release, a life freed from the fear of teachers.

> In the Elysian fields he sees Musaeus first. Musaeus means the gift of the Muses, the best poet of them all, who points out to him his father and the river, Lethe; the father, that is to say, that he may adopt a habit of seriousness, and Lethe, that he

may forget childish levity. Just reflect on the name itself of Anchises; in Greek Anchises is *ano scenon,* that is, inhabiting the fatherland. Now there is one God who is the father and the king of all, dwelling alone in the heavens who is known with the aid of the gift of knowledge. For note what Anchises teaches his son: "First, the heaven and earth, and the watery plains, the shining globe of the moon and Titan's star."[16]

In the seventh book, he arrives at Ausonia (growth in virtue) and chooses Lavinia (the way of labors) for his wife. In the eighth book, he seeks the help of Evander (the good man or human goodness) and arms himself against the attacks of evil. The ninth book describes his struggle with Turnus, who represents a violent mind (*turos nus*). Juturna is the sister of Turnus and represents destruction (which lasts long: *diuturna*), both of which Aeneas must overcome. Generally speaking, the second six books show the good man, having acquired wisdom, actively struggling against vice. (For this reason, in commentaries such as Landino's, where the wisdom acquired by the hero is defined as an essentially contemplative virtue, the last six books have no real place. Landino almost totally ignores them and concentrates his attention and the emphasis of his interpretation on Aeneas's journey, culminating in the achievement of contemplative wisdom in the sixth book.)

Thus badly condensed and baldly stated, Fulgentius's reading of the *Aeneid* must sound far more absurd than it actually is. His ignoring of narrative causality and sequence and his consequent treatment of each book as a self-contained unit account for the greatest divergences between his interpretation and Virgil's text; but the ages-of-man theory, the view of epic as a step-by-step examination of the growth and maturation of man, that he derived from this method persuaded and satisfied most of the Middle Ages — including such eminent minds as Petrarch's and Dante's — no doubt because he is not entirely wrong. Tracing the growth process from infancy on up may be a distortion, but it is a distortion of a process of intellectual maturation that is genuinely present in Virgil's text. The *Aeneid* is most definitely about — among many other things — growth in wisdom, and Fulgentius in linking that growth with formal education and with the ages of man simply expressed a sound insight in terms congenial to his times. Moreover, though his commentary may wander fairly far from the literal meaning of Virgil's text, it is still tied to it by two main facts. The first is the assumption, shared by late classical culture and the Christian Middle Ages, that Virgil was indeed a polymath, and that consequently the *Aeneid* covertly incorporated a great deal of esoteric knowledge that the man seeking true wisdom was under every obligation to unearth in every way possible. The second is Fulgentius's consistently etymological mode of procedure. For him, names — proper names particularly — provide the clues to the deeper meaning of the poem, and by etymological analysis (some farfetched in the extreme, some sound) he works out the allegory of the poem. A small example: the storm in book one is stirred up by Juno through the agency of Eolus. Here is Fulgentius's Virgil's explanation of that event.

> I introduced a shipwreck to represent the danger of birth in which there is a risk for the mother in giving birth and a danger for the infant in birth itself. The human race is universally involved in this necessity. And that you might understand this more clearly, this shipwreck was stirred up by Juno who is the goddess of birth. She sends Eolus; in Greek Eolus is *eon olus,* that is, destruction of life.[17]

Similarly, Fulgentius explains Palinurus as "wandering vision," Misenus as "vainglory," Anchises as "the inhabitor of the fatherland," and uses all of these etymologies as clues to the real meaning of the episode.

It seems important to point out here that, unlike the allegory of Scripture, the allegory of the poets, as Fulgentius explains it, is a self-enclosed linguistic system. God's word is polysemous, because God in effect speaks things as well as words, so that for the interpretation of Scripture one can appeal to the nature of the thing as well as to the meaning of the word. For poets, only the meaning of the word is available, and they must build their microcosms, and critics must pursue their meanings, through the shadow of language.[18] Narrative, the story, is the *fictum*, the made-up; the meanings of words are the real — and in poetry at least there is an intrinsic and essential continuity between the name and the thing, between the shadow and the body casting the shadow, between *verbum* and *verum*. For this reason, the hinge of the comparison Macrobius draws between the *Aeneid* and the world turns on Virgil's eloquence — his style recreates the variety of the world, and that worldly variety itself is implicitly understood to be God's rhetoric of things.

Fulgentius both insists on, and struggles against, the linguistic enclosure of epic. Virgil's earliest remarks in his commentary violate most of the rules of grammar and logic to isolate individual words as atoms of meaning, the essential seeds of the significance of the whole poem.

> And to satisfy your curiosity more fully on this point, I say that there are three stages in human life, the first is to have, then to rule over what one has, and thirdly to adorn what one rules. Therefore notice that these three stages are set down in the one line of ours, that is, *arma, virum,* and *primus. Arma,* that is, strength, refers to the bodily substance; *virum,* that is, wisdom, refers to the intellectual substance and *primus*, that is, prince, refers to the judging substance. Thus you have the three in their proper order, having, ruling, and adorning. Therefore under the figure of a narrative (*sub figuralitatem historiae*) I have shown the full condition of human life; first, being born, then learning, and finally happiness.[19]

Bernardus Silvestris's commentary will do the same thing to Virgil's sixth book: there Bernardus sets out to explain every word of the text, so that his work becomes almost an allegorical lexicon. But both commentators also push against the trap of language and attempt to break through the enclosure of epic to the reality outside it. Bernardus tries this by using analogy — of which more later — and Fulgentius by his frequent appeals to the spectral Virgil to admit cognates with the truths of revelation — that is to say, with Scripture. In either case, the poem would then be susceptible of analysis according to the methods of biblical allegoresis, and the linguistic trap would be successfully sprung.

The trick is not a contemptible one: Dante in his *Commedia* makes the claim for his poem that Virgil here implicitly rejects for his, and the results prove that the game is worth the candle. This kind of self-consciousness about its limitations — its style, its rhetoric, its form, its dependence on so inadequate a vehicle as language — seems to me absolutely characteristic of epic. As the supreme genre of classical and neoclassical literary theory, it is the most literary genre in its consciousness of its materials and its desire to transcend them. What epic seems always to want to do, and what the writers of epic always to try, is not to manipulate words but to shape reality. At least half of the works I am going to talk about in this book concern themselves with the way literature spills over into life — the way art transmutes itself into reality and in the process transforms reality.

The most important and extensive commentary on the *Aeneid* produced in the Middle Ages, that of Bernardus Silvestris, continues quite clearly the attitudes and techniques of Fulgentius.[20] Bernardus's mode of reading the *Aeneid* bears close relation to Fulgentius's (and to Prudentius's *Psychomachia*). The name of the character, place, or object furnishes the primary clue to its essence; its role in the poem is thus examined in this light, and its meaning almost invariably located (as in Fulgentius) in a kind of psychomachy — Aeneas the human soul, and everything else its affections, virtues, vices, or the temptations or maturational stages through which it must pass. The subject matter of epic is still, roughly, "the condition of human life." This is by no means to belittle Bernardus's work; on the contrary, it is a thoroughly sophisticated piece of literary criticism that shows tact and insight, respect for the literal meaning of Virgil's poem, and a consistent logic of exegesis. It may be the most important literary critical document of the Middle Ages for what it tells us about poetry and the way it was read. The commentary is really a tractate on education (cf. the educational concerns of Fulgentius's commentary), filled with remarks on the parts and functions of the trivium and quadrivium, with special attention devoted to the character and office of poetry.

Since Bernardus's commentary seems to me so crucial a document, I propose to discuss it here in some detail.[21] I will not attempt to point out all the lines of indebtedness to Fulgentius and Macrobius; it is enough to know that Bernardus borrowed freely from them and apparently felt few qualms about reshaping their ideas for his own purposes. He will quickly reveal himself as a further expositor of their general attitude and approach to Virgil. Bernardus's tone — at least initially — is that of an experienced teacher or lecturer expounding familiar or basic material: he is jocular, orderly; he makes transitions easily and clearly. One could speculate that his *Commentum* is compiled from lecture notes without being at all false to its tone or uncomplimentary to Bernardus. He was clearly an excellent teacher.

He begins by citing Macrobius to the effect that we are to observe two kinds of doctrine in the *Aeneid*, the truth of philosophy and the poetic fiction *(figmentum)*. He proceeds to investigate "whence it proceeds and how and why [unde agat et qualiter et cur]." *Unde* provides the poet's intention, in this case to tell the story of the Trojan exiles, not according to the truth of history (which is found in Dares), but in order to please Augustus. He also writes to imitate Homer, book 2 being the equivalent of the *Iliad*, books 1 and 3–12, the *Odyssey*. *Qualiter* explains the mode of the narration: Virgil employs artificial *(in medias res)* rather than natural (sequential) order. To explain *cur*, Bernardus remarks that poets write for the sake of utility (satirists) or delight (comic poets) or both (historic poets). We delight in seeing human experiences imitated, and we learn from these examples to seek *honesta* and to flee *illicita*. For example: from the labors of Aeneas we draw an example of endurance, from his love for Anchises and Ascanius, an example of piety; from the veneration he shows toward the gods and from the oracles he seeks, from the sacrifices he offers, from the vows and prayers he pours out, we are invited to religion. Through his immoderate love for Dido we are recalled from desire for illicit things. It is worth noting that for Bernardus these form the overt moral of the *fictum* and explain why the poet is narrating these events in the first place; Bernardus has not yet begun talking about the covert allegory.

These three items also serve the office of proem (to both the poem and the *Commentum*, apparently): *unde* renders the reader docile, *qualiter* benevolent, *cur* attentive. This accomplished, Bernardus turns his attention to the philosophic truth of the *Aeneid,* which is about the nature of human life. The mode of procedure is this: *sub integumento,* Virgil describes what the human spirit, temporarily placed in the human body, does or suffers. In this writing, he employs natural order and thus observes both orders in his work, the poetic using artificial, the philosophic natural — as, seemingly, is appropriate to each. "Integumentum vero est genus demonstrationis sub fabulosa narratione veritatis involvens intellectum, unde et involucrum dicitur [In fact, the integument is a kind of presentation that wraps the significance of the truth under a fabulous narrative, whence it is also called the envelope]" (p. 3.17–20). We find the usefulness of such a work according to our knowledge of ourselves, for as Macrobius says, it is of great utility for a man to know himself. These facts explain for Bernardus the "unde et qualiter et cur" of the philosophic doctrine of the poem, and he now announces his intention of opening the integument of the twelve single books in sequence (in point of fact, his *Commentum* as we now have it breaks off in the middle of book 6).

Bernardus's mode of procedure is to begin his discussion of each book by a summation of the narrative content and to follow that by a summary statement of the philosophic content, in a manner similar to Fulgentius's Virgil's demands for a summary of the content of each book before his exposition of it. Bernardus then goes into greater or lesser detail in his explanation according to no pattern that I have been able to discover. Indeed, his treatment of book 6 varies even from the simple formal pattern just described: it contains little summation of any kind and takes the form of an examination of almost every important word of the text. A few generalizations are safe however. Bernardus's exegetical technique, though refining on Fulgentius's in thoroughness, subtlety, and literary sensitivity, resembles the latter's both in ignoring the causality and sequence of the plot and in being primarily etymological. The word, the name, still furnishes the essential clue to meaning. And like both Fulgentius and Macrobius, Bernardus has a strong tendency to platonize Virgil and to interpret the poem in the light of Neoplatonic conceptions. It will not be possible to reproduce here all or even a large part of Bernardus's exegesis, but I will try to give samples of his working method and his critical bias. I hope, too, to demonstrate the extreme sophistication of Bernardus's criticism: the *Commentum* is no naïve document but (always granting its basic premises) an extremely supple piece of analysis.

For Bernardus, the first book of the *Aeneid* tells of man's first age. Through Eolus, the king of the winds who here evokes the storm at sea, we are brought to understand the birth of the child. He is called Eolus (*eon olus = seculi interitus*) because at the birth of man, *seculum*, that is, the life of the soul (*vita animae*) perishes, while depressed by the heaviness (*gravitas*, but used by Bernardus throughout with the obvious etymological connection with pregnancy, *gravidus*) of the flesh it descends from its divinity and assents to fleshly desire (*libidini carnis*). Thus Eolus sends forth the winds because the birth of man begets commotions, that is, vices. With these he attacks the sea, that is, the human body, which is a gulf of trackless and uncrossable humors. Here already Fulgentius's techniques have been subtilized and refined. The whole phenomenon of birth has been worked out linguistically by a group of verbs possessing a common sense of producing, begetting, bringing forth, which are in turn linked to the entrance of the soul (*anima, spiritus*) into the flesh (*carnis, humor, mare*) that Bernardus expresses succinctly by the meaningful *gravitas-gravidus* pun. Moreover, Bernardus reinforces the purely linguistic link by employing a whole body of analogies, the most prominent of which in this section of the *Commentum* is that of the four elements of the universe to the four humors of the body — thus the *humor* of the sea is the *humor* of the body, and the whole seemingly farfetched allegoresis is linked finally to Virgil's text by the touchstones of wind and sea, *spiritus* and *humor*, present in the text itself. By means of this sort of interpretation, the whole poem becomes, in effect, a giant synechdoche, and Bernardus in interpreting simply enlarges from part to whole, from particular to general. Allegory does not impose itself from without but generates itself from within: because for the Middle Ages analogy is true, allegory is necessary. That is to say, allegory is simply the rhetorical mode that embodies the dialectical mode of analogy; the two are literary and philosophical avatars of each other and are properly fused in a work like the *Aeneid* that is both literary and philosophical. Parts, as Aquinas says, correspond to parts, and every medieval poet or commentator anticipates Ramus in what he makes of images. Analogy and allegory both offer imagistic shorthands, particulars that stand in relation to other particulars and to universals beyond them. More important, they validate each other: the rhetorical structure reproduces the logical structure of thought, and that very correspondence is a further validation of both. In this system, the meaning of the thing works to support the interpretation of the word, and Bernardus's criticism comes very close to escaping the confines of purely linguistic systematizing. It appeals outside itself — through analogy — for confirmation, even though it is finally still a closed linguistic system. The analogies themselves arise from language, and the whole interpretation depends in its totality on language: this explains the prominence and importance of Bernardus's synthetic puns — puns like *gravitas-gravidus* or *anima* as wind and soul or *humor* as sea and element — that linguistically join together disparate areas of reference. In the *Tale of a Tub*, Swift's narrator, Peter and Jack, the Sartorists and the Aeolists, will all join forces to turn this mode of analysis on its head.

Bernardus applies these logical and critical categories with some care. He knows that circumstances change cases, and his allegorizing almost never falls into the wooden equations characteristic of the psychomachy as genre. His remarks about the meaning of Aeneas and what these give rise to indicate clearly the self-consciousness of his interpretation.

Aeneas is called the son of Anchises and Venus. Anchises Bernardus interprets as *celsa inhabitans* (loosely, the high-dweller), which we understand to be the father of all presiding over all. We understand that there are two Venuses, the lawful goddess and the goddess of wantonness. We say that the lawful Venus is

> mundanam musicam i.e. aequalem mundanorum proportionem, quam alii Astraeam, alii naturalem iustitiam vocant. Haec enim est in elementis, in sideribus, in temporibus, in animantibus [the harmony of the created world, that is, the even symmetry of wordly things, which some call Astrea and

others call natural justice. This Venus subsists in the elements, in the stars, in time, in living things]. (p. 9.16–18)

However, we call the shameless Venus, the goddess of wantonness, concupiscence of the flesh because she is the mother of all fornications.

Note here that in this as in other mystical volumes equivocations and multivocations and diverse applications of the integument are found. According to Martianus' book, you take Jove sometimes for the superior fire, sometimes the star, sometimes even the creator himself, Saturn now for time and now for the planet, Mercury here for eloquence and there for a star. This multiplex signification with respect to the diverse meanings of the integument should be observed in all mystical works, since truth is not static [*sin vero stare veritas non poterit*]. Therefore in this work these things are discovered because the same name indicates diverse natures and on the other hand different names indicate the same; as when Apollo sometimes designates divine wisdom, sometimes human, Jupiter sometimes fire, sometimes God [*summum deum*], Venus sometimes concupiscence of the flesh, sometimes the harmony of the world [*mundi concordiam*]; or when Jupiter and Anchises designate the creator. Therefore when you find Venus, the wife of Vulcan, the mother of Iocus and Cupido, understand the pleasure of the flesh, because she is joined to natural heat and produces levity and sexual desire. Whenever you read that Venus and Anchises had a son Aeneas, understand through Venus the harmony of the world, through Aeneas the human spirit. For Aeneas is so called because *ennos demas* is the inhabitant of the body [*habitator corporis*]. . . . *Demas,* the chain, is identified with the body because it is the prison of the soul. Therefore Aeneas is the son of Venus and Anchises because the human spirit, from God, through concord begins to enter and live in the body. We say these things about Anchises, Aeneas, and Venus because in many places in this book we see they are necessary. (pp. 9.21–10.19)

In this manner, Bernardus continues to explain the first book of the *Aeneid* in terms of the tribulations of infancy. The second book he interprets briefly as describing boyhood and the acquisition of speech. The third book displays the weaknesses and passions of adolescence. After various misadventures, Aeneas arrives at Delos, where he is warned by Apollo "to seek his ancient mother."

> Two ancient mothers, two regions, Crete and Italy, are the two beginnings of Aeneas, the nature of the body and the nature of the soul. For by Crete we understand bodily nature, which is the beginning of the temporal life of Aeneas. And Crete is called by antiphrasis *crasis theos*, that is, divine judgment. For carnal nature judges badly about divine things when it places them after temporal. Through Italy, which is interpreted "increase," we understand the nature of the soul, which is rationality and immortality, virtue, knowledge. He is ordered to seek these things by Apollo, that is, wisdom. For wisdom warns him to love that divinity he possesses. But because Aeneas mistakes the oracle, he seeks Crete when ordered to go to Italy. He mistook the oracle of Apollo in this manner: he sought wisdom from man as you read in Boethius [Bernardus here quotes from the *Consolation of Philosophy*, 2.4.72 ff.]. . . . (p. 20.3–18)

Thus misdirected, Aeneas continues wandering and encountering various vices until his father dies.

> He buries his father in Drepanum. Drepanum (*drimos pes*) is interpreted puerile acerbity, which is wrath which customarily infests boys with excessive fervor. In wrath his father is buried, that is, God is given to oblivion. For the wrathful are almost apostates. Burial is forgetfulness. (p. 23.16–21)

Bernardus's treatment of book 4 provides a good example of both the subtlety and implications of his method. The whole interpretation holds together by virtue of an elaborate series of physical, emotional, and

intellectual analogies that are expressed simultaneously and inter-
changeably by the linguistic relations of the *coct*-word forms Bernardus
ubiquitously employs.

In this fourth book the nature of youth is mystically expressed. But first we give the narrative summation, then the
exposition.

Having buried his father he goes hunting. Driven by storms
into a cave, he diverts himself with Dido and then commits
adultery. Which shameful habit he abandons by the counsel
of Mercury. Dido, having been left behind, withdraws and
dies, cooked to ashes [*Dido vero deserta in cineres excocta
et demigrat*].

By manifest and mystic narration the nature of youth is
described. Burial of the father designates forgetfulness of the
creator; he assiduously occupies himself in hunting and other
occupations which pertain to youth. . . . By storm and rain
he is forced to the cave, that is, by the commotions of the flesh
and profusion of *humor* arising from the superfluity of food
and drink he is led to the impurity of flesh and *libido*. Which
carnal impurity is called cave, because it obscures serenity of
mind and discretion. The profusion of *humor* from food and
drink leads to impurity in this manner: *in decoctione* there
are four humors: *liquor, fumus, spuma et faex*. After the
humors of food and drink have been cooked [*Decoctis . . .
humoribus*] in the cauldron of the stomach, the *fumus* thence
resulting and ascending as the nature of lightness demands
and by ascending and by purification through the arteries
made rarer, comes to the brain and produces animal powers
[*animales virtutes*]. By *liquor* the members grow strong.
Faex is sent out into departure through the lower passages,
spuma partly through perspiration, partly through the caves
of the senses [*foramina sensuum*]. When however there is an
excessive superfluity of *spuma*, which occurs in drunken
feasts and drinking sessions, it is emitted through the male
organ, which is nearest and subject to the stomach, converted
into sperm, that is, male seed. Whence you read that Venus is

born from the *spuma* of the sea and so is called *"frodon."*

Therefore the rains lead Aeneas to the cave. He is joined to Dido and delays a long while with her. The shameful crying of rumor does not recall him because youth ensnared in *libido* seeks neither what is lovely, or useful, or shameful, or not. At length, after a long deviation, he is warned by Mercury to leave. . . . .

He warns and rebukes Aeneas because he finds him not regarding any useful task. . . . Aeneas departs from Dido and puts aside *libido*. Dido, abandoned, perishes and parts from this life burned into ashes [*in cineres excocta*]. For disused *libido* fails, and consumed by the fervor of manhood falls into ashes, that is, into solitary cogitations. (pp. 23.23–25.27)

Superfluity of *humor* in nature produces rain, in man, physiologically, sperm, emotionally, lust, intellectually, sin. All of these result from some form of decoction, and the ultimate fate of the libido produced is to be consumed in yet another — different and better — decoction.

Book 5, according to Bernardus, describes the nature of manhood. Having abandoned the indulgence of youth, Aeneas now offers four exercises in virtue to God (the funeral games in Anchises' honor). The games illustrate the virtues of temperance, fortitude, prudence, and justice. At the conclusion of this book, Aeneas is warned by the image of his father that he will have to descend to hell to see him there. This means, says Bernardus, that Aeneas will have to descend to mundane things through cogitation, and thus he will see the creator (his father) because although the creator is not in creatures, he may be known by the cogitation of creatures. At this point in the narrative, the helmsman Palinurus (whom Bernardus etymologically interprets as "wandering vision") dies. Until now, wandering vision steered the will (ship) of Aeneas; but when Aeneas guides it, Palinurus perishes.

As prologue to his explanation of the sixth book, Bernardus discusses the possible meanings of the *descensus ad inferos,* drawing heavily on Macrobius's notions in his commentary on the *Somnium Scipionis.* Essentially, he understands four different kinds of *descensus:* the way of nature, the way of virtue, the way of vice, and the way of artifice. The natural way is birth, the descent of the soul into the body that, he explains at length, is properly called *infernum*. The virtuous way is that of the wise man who descends to creatures through contemplation in order to better know the creator; such were Hercules and Orpheus. The vicious way is to serve *temporalia* with the whole mind; such was Eurydice. The artificial way is, simply, magic. The integument of the sixth book describes the fourth way (Bernardus sees the death and cremation of Misenus as a magical rite, a sacrifice to demons), while the substrate of the book describes the second. Bernardus also links Aeneas's activities at this point to the process of formal education: the grove of Trivia is the study of eloquence; the three ways equal the three arts — grammar, dialectic, and rhetoric. The golden roofs of the temple are the four mathematical arts in which the gold of philosophy is contained. The faithful Achates is the habit of study. Like Servius, Bernardus links the golden bough with the study of philosophy in its two branches, theoretic and practical; and like Fulgentius, he sees Aeneas's journey through hell as some sort of educational tour.

Bernardus glosses almost every word of the text in a detailed expansion and explanation of Aeneas's descent as the contemplative descent of the wise man to an examination of creatures. It is not possible to reproduce this in any great detail; his incomplete commentary on the sixth book is more than three times as long as his commentaries on the first five books combined. Essentially — and this is perhaps the most important aspect of his *Commentum* — he sees Aeneas's descent with the Sybil and his progress through the lower world up to his entrance into the Elysian fields as a recapitulation of what has preceded in the poem. Just as the spirit descended into matter at birth (a descent to hell in itself: the natural way), the mind now descends to a contemplation of creatures and reviews the paths it has taken and the errors it has committed: thus the meetings with Trojan heroes, thus the encounter with Dido. The Sybil herself functions as, and is to be understood in a way similar to, Boethius's Lady Philosophy, guiding Aeneas to an understanding of his past mistakes. The purpose of this journey is to free Aeneas from his bondage to creatures by a thorough knowledge of them, so that he may pass on to see the creator (i.e., Anchises). This is the circular motion of thought as conceived by medieval speculation: the mind descends from God into creatures and proceeds through a contemplation of creatures to return to God again.[22] This circular pattern forms the core of Bernardus's understanding of the *Aeneid*: it is for him a poem about the acquisition of wisdom that re-creates in itself the form of the process it describes. This notion provides the basis for his explanation of the first half of the poem, and he recapitulates it in his interpretation of the first half of book 6 and again, more briefly, in his allegorizations of the myths of Orpheus and Eurydice and of Castor and Pollux, both of which he understands as expressing the relations of soul and body, divine mind and infernal matter. Bernardus's *Commentum* breaks off before Aeneas enters the fields of the blessed and sees Anchises, but from its similarities to Fulgentius and from the exegetical patterns he has already set up, we can readily see the probable outlines of his allegory: having acquired knowledge of terrestrial matters, Aeneas will obtain from Anchises the requisite celestial lore to return to his earthly life and, in yet another recapitulation, triumph over those vices and material forces to which he had earlier fallen victim so that, after the conclusion of Virgil's poem, he will be ready to ascend once again to God as the reward of his achieved virtues (so at least Maphius Vegius understood the poem in the fifteenth century when he wrote a thirteenth book, explicitly giving Aeneas the apotheosis he seems to have earned). Aeneas will choose as his wife Lavinia, the way of labors, rather than Dido, the way of pleasure. The pattern seems quite simple, quite clear. Aeneas accomplishes his first *descensus ad inferos* by birth, as all men must, and he continues it throughout his minority by succumbing to a series of vices: these are Bernardus's first and third ways. In the sixth book, he once again descends to hell, this time according to Bernardus's second and fourth ways, by contemplation and by magic. This time of course a conversion takes place, and Aeneas comes to a recognition of his failings and begins to mend them. Consequently, in the same book he begins an ascent to God — contemplatively here — that will be later continued and confirmed when he returns to active life and triumphs over the vices and trials that previously defeated him. The Sybil makes this aspect of things explicit when she warns

Aeneas that he shall again have to fight Greeks, again encounter an Achilles, see another Simois and Xanthus and Doric camp, again because of a foreign bride, another Helen (*Aeneid* 6.83–94). So the second half of the *Aeneid* is in effect a repetition of the first half, with the important difference that the direction of the narrative and of Aeneas's fortunes is upward rather than downward, ascent toward God rather than descent to creatures. This sixth book functions as the nexus, the conversion point, that terminates one journey and transforms it into its mirror image — all of which, by the way, is not in any structural particular untrue to Virgil's text. However much our understanding of the events of the Aeneid may differ from Bernardus's, we can hardly quarrel with his perception of its structure.

Cristoforo Landino's immensely important *Disputationes Camaldulenses* continues and refines this kind of reading of the *Aeneid*.[23] Like Fulgentius and Bernardus, Landino begins his allegorization *ab ovo*, with "the first age of man." Unlike the earlier commentators, Landino does not start with book one of the poem, but rather with the chronologically earliest events in the poem, Aeneas's recollections of Troy. From that point, he proceeds through the sequence of events contained in books 1–6, following the loose pattern of the maturation of the hero. Landino's hero, however, is not the Everyman of Fulgentius and Bernardus; he is a particularly gifted man working toward a full achievement of his traditional epithet, *pius* — a word that in Landino's reading comes to embrace the whole range of relations of fathers and sons, king and subject, mind and body, individual intelligence and eternal wisdom (this emphasis, by the way, bears very directly on *Absalom and Achitophel*, which Dryden carefully locates "in *pious* times"). Aeneas's goal is Italy, which Landino flatly equates with contemplation, and he struggles to free himself from the attractions of corporeal existence and to achieve the stability of the contemplative life. Although Landino differs slightly from his predecessors in his more careful attention to details of the text (he occasionally understands as the allegory of a passage what Bernardus would identify as only the overt moral) and in his interpretation of some of those details (Anchises, for example, he understands as sensuality because he is Aeneas's mortal parent, the father of his body), and although his platonizing of the text is distinctly Renaissance and much marked by the thought of his friend Marsilio Ficino (he identifies Aeneas's mother Venus with the angelic intelligence discussed in the *Symposium*), the broad outlines of his interpretation still follow those of Fulgentius and Bernardus. Aeneas's descent into hell is still the descent of the mind *in sensualitatem* that it may gain knowledge of what ought to be sought and what to be avoided. Misenus still remains, etymologically, false glory, and must be buried before the mind can free itself to pursue true knowledge. And however much he ignores the last six books, Landino still implicitly preserves Bernardus's mirroring structure in his explanation of the Sybil's warning to Aeneas of the graver dangers yet before him: having passed through the storms of the active life, he must yet face the resurgence of memory and desire for those things that the life devoted to contemplation must put aside.

Since Landino's reading of the *Aeneid* is discussed in rather great detail by Don Cameron Allen in his *Mysteriously Meant,* and since the major points of Landino's exegesis are not that radically different from those of his predecessors, it would be just as well here to examine his departures from them. Landino makes three really important changes in the interpretative tradition: first, he raises his hero to the status of exceptional man, destined for glory; second, he focuses attention almost exclusively on Aeneas's journey and makes that central to his reading; and third, he explains the Dido episode, in accordance with his active-contemplative dialectic, not as the attraction of carnality but as the lure of the active, civic life that distracts man from his progress toward the true *summum bonum,* the contemplation and possession of wisdom. This last is completely consistent with Landino's overall view of the *Aeneid* and with the positions taken by the participants in the discussions that form the first two books of the *Disputationes Camaldulenses:* the contemplative life is superior to, and provides the norms for, the active life. But consistent or not, these changes put the formal verse epic on an unswervable path toward extinction. They set up a crucial disjunction between tenor and vehicle, between the almost mutually exclusive demands of an "executive" story — the journey — and a "deliberative" meaning — the growth of a superior mind in contemplative virtue.[24]

Landino's reading of the *Aeneid* completes a process that began with Macrobius by completely externalizing the epic plot and internalizing the real action. Faced with this bifurcation, would-be writers of epic had two choices: to perpetuate the split but utilize it through allegory, as Spenser did (who, incidentally, also disposes of contemplation as an ultimate goal in his first book when he has the holy hermit point out to Red Crosse Knight that he is not called to contemplation, that he must return to the world and the active life); or to jettison the external action and redefine human heroism in purely internal terms, as Milton did.[25] In any event, after Landino the breach must have been apparent. Epic was inextricably tied up with notions of education, of knowledge, of wisdom. That did not change, but the meanings of those words most emphatically did. If in the Middle Ages the words *knowledge* and *wisdom* could encompass the whole range of human consciousness, from what we would consider basic common sense through to the theological entity Wisdom, by the Renaissance those meanings had flown apart, and contemplative wisdom grew steadily more remote from life. The aesthetics of the sublime, tied onto epic in the course of the revival of Longinus, perhaps only raised two notes higher what had become an "O Altitudo" already beyond the range of human hearing.

So too with the epic hero. Following Landino's lead, later commentators and critics increased his stature from exceptional man to impossible man; they made a paragon of him. At the logical conclusion of this process, neoclassical epic theory demanded a perfect hero whose character is a constant, who is the absolutely devoted and aware servant of a cause that is really the subject of the poem. The hero became personalityless, identified with and desiring only the cause. He became the commander-in-chief, the leader of the cause. His supremacy of rank was the prerequisite of his being the chosen hero. His nobility now meant the end of his freedom of action, the subordination of his high qualities to the will of the cause. As a character symbolizing the beliefs and endeavors of a whole people or culture, he had to concern himself with the government of a state in its religious, political, and cultural aspects.[26] For illustration of the literal truth of all this, one need only read Fénelon. His *Télémaque* is totally personalityless — indeed, comes at last to the explicit realization that the ideal ruler must be totally selfless, having no desires whatever that spring from himself. *Télémaque* is a good illustration of the absolute irrelevance of neoclassical conceptions of epic: it could only possibly apply to one man, or a very few men, in a whole society; and what it demands of them, or would teach them, is simply beyond the reach of human nature.

Most of these notions are simply exaggerations or literalizations of traditional, and in many cases quite sound, insights into epic. They result, it seems to me, from a confusion of the interpretation and the poem, or — at worst — from a substitution of the interpretation for the poem. Epic, at the close of the Renaissance, had to bear the burden of its own hermeneutics. What I want to explore in the rest of this book is the process by which epicists first exploited that burden and then freed themselves of it, the process by which they restored epic to itself.

IV

Absalom and Achitophel provides a small-scale, straightforward adaptation of epic materials and a synopsis of the state of traditional epic poetry in the late seventeenth century. Central to it is the hero's recognition of his identity and goal, just as the revelations of book 6 are crucial to Aeneas's knowledge of himself and his goal, both in the fable and in the allegory. Dryden depicts this twice: parodically, as Achitophel tempts Absalom to assume a false messianic role,[27] and straightforwardly, as David abandons the indulgence of the doting father and accepts his proper role as divinely appointed ruler. The hero's self-knowledge — the kind of wisdom he is to attain and consequently the kind of person he is to be — determines the direction and shape of epic. David, as "godlike" ruler, must abandon his fatherly feelings and human compassion for his divine role. He must raise himself above human vicissitude to divine immutability. In the poem, David does not change, he only repeats; his mortal paternity is reiterated in his implicit divine paternity at the end of the poem and "Once more the Godlike *David* was Restor'd" (1030).

The poem takes its shape from this static conception of David. For one thing, in *Absalom and Achitophel* — even the title is revealing in this respect — only the villains act. David and his party literally do nothing. Dryden identifies David so closely with the God whose image he bears that he seems to share in the divine immutability: he is so tightly linked to the cause he personifies, the reflection in the good order of human society of God's providential governing of the universe, that Dryden is forced in the poem to present him as essentially inhuman — personalityless, actionless, almost passionless, a mere exponent of the office he occupies. Everything about the fable assumes a necessity, an immutability, that is at once historical and ontological: given such and such evil men, given such and such a hero with such virtues, given a just and watchful God, given such historical precedent, then such a conclusion follows of necessity.

Even with Dryden's skillful handling, the static nature of the narrative stands out sorely and perhaps explains the many critical complaints about the incompleteness of the poem and the unrelatedness of its conclusion. Dryden has made of the allegorical epic fable and the exemplary hero that prescriptive criticism required of him an extended metaphysical conceit, in which the important factors are not what the human characters do but the changes that can be rung on the ideas they embody. He has structured the poem out of a series of antinomies that are finally resolved into oxymoric unities — the rebels and the royalists, motion and stability, time and eternity, flesh and spirit, idol and God, nature and grace, lie and truth. The Davids of the beginning and the end of the poem remain the same person: what changes is only our perspective on him, which of the king's two bodies Dryden directs our attention to. This process wrenches the epic out of the area of even ritualized human drama or even the formalized interactions of personalities and wills and moves it closer to the domain of psychomachy where ideas and virtues act directly upon each other with the essentially passive human soul as prize rather than protagonist: the ultimate hero of such an epic must become one of Swift's Houyhnhnms.

But Dryden also exploits several facets of the traditional epic that continue after him to play a large and important role, principally in the development of the novel. His shifting of perspective from time to eternity, from the here-and-now to the over-arching providential plan and its consequent escape from motion into rest — these, for instance, become of increasing importance to Fielding, until they find their natural scope in *Amelia,* the last important attempt to write a "regular" epic in English. More important, Dryden clearly preserves and transmits the same sort of symmetrical structural pattern the commentators saw in the *Aeneid:* across the central nexus of the disquisition on government, parts correspond to parts — David's human paternity and divine, Absalom's false messianic role and David's true one, a catalogue of villains and a catalogue of heroes, the descending action of the conspiracy and near-rebellion and the ascending action of the loyalists and the king's stand.[28] Neither do I think it farfetched to see in Dryden's detailed analogy between particular bodies and the body politic, between what boils in Absalom and what ferments in the mob, a strong similarity to the Virgilian commentators' concern with the "physiology" of intellectual and emotional processes: Swift's *Tale of a Tub* will exploit this aspect of epic. In addition, Dryden preserves the self-consciousness of epic about its own limitations: his implicit appeal outside the poem to the divine Word for verification is of a piece with the commentators' attempts to break through fiction into reality — an eruption that Pope will render chillingly in Dulness's "uncreating word." The emphasis Dryden consequently puts upon the central position of verbal truth, the right use of words, also looms large in mock epics and novels, from his own *MacFlecknoe* through *A Tale of A Tub* and *The Dunciad* and into *Joseph Andrews* and *Tom Jones.* But Dryden's poetic revitalization of the conservative ideas of a patriarchal, patrilinear society forms his greatest contribution to the tradition that will culminate in Fielding's novels. In *Absalom and Achitophel,* the structural pivot point is the disquisition on government, which is couched in terms of the relations of fathers and sons, and David's paternity is the source of the poem's major problem. Virgil never let his reader forget the importance of Aeneas's paternity or of the race that will succeed him, from Iulus down to Julius and Augustus Caesar; and Homer drew a concise picture of the restoration of proper patriarchal order and government when he showed, at the end of the *Odyssey,* Odysseus standing between his father Laertes and his son Telemachus, preparing to assert their hegemony over the island kingdom of Ithaca — a picture not greatly different, ideologically, from the scene at the end of *Absalom and Achitophel* where David stands between his God and his ultimate progeny to assert hegemony over his island kingdom. Neither does that scene differ greatly from the conclusion of another allegorical epic, *Tom Jones,* where Tom, at last restored to his proper relation with the paternal Squire Allworthy, is last seen founding his own family on his newly acquired private Hesperia, Squire Western's estate. The image of paternity and its associated ideas of fertility and birth lend themselves readily to parody, too, as Dryden shows in *MacFlecknoe,* where misuse of language leads to miscreation of all sorts. Such ideas crop up with an insistence that demonstrates their importance in *A Tale of A Tub, Gulliver's Travels, The Dunciad,* and *Tristram Shandy,* in all cases owing greater or lesser debts to the pattern established by Dryden. At any rate, all of this provides the final context in which it is necessary to see Dryden's poem: if we can see in David's stand against the rebels the same definitive stand against the forces of social disorder that Virgil portrayed in Aeneas's struggle with Turnus or Homer in Odysseus's battle with the suitors; if we can see in David's verbal assertion of the order of law and grace the same imposition of physical and metaphysical order that the divine fiat fixed upon chaos, then we are that much closer to a true understanding of Dryden's fiction and the resonances it held for its seventeenth-century audience.

V

Although chronologically prior, *MacFlecknoe* logically succeeds *Absalom and Achitophel.* It is full-blown mock epic: its protagonists, Flecknoe and Shadwell, stand in the same debased parodic relation to the conventional epic hero — to Aeneas, say — as Satan does to God. *MacFlecknoe,* moreover, bites the tail of epic and turns it upon itself. Its obsessive concern with literature, with language, with words, perverts the closed linquistic system of epic and transforms the container of the highest wisdom into a sterile bag of wind — literally and figuratively.

It begins the demonstration, which *The Dunciad* will complete, of the manner in which bad art and dullness debase life.

London appears in *MacFlecknoe* as Augusta — "The fair *Augusta* much to fears inclin'd" of lines 64–65. Dryden's few descriptive details pertinently link the city with Flecknoe and Shadwell and transform it from a place, the mere *locus* of their empire, to an actual extension of them and an embodiment of their art. The name Augusta itself connects the city with Flecknoe, whom the opening of the poem compared to Augustus (3). The Barbican and its surroundings (66–84) share, in their collapse, in the general decay to which all human things are subject and which, in Flecknoe's particular case, provides the occasion of the poem. It, too, like Flecknoe, is "now flouishing in Peace, / And blest with issue of a large increase" (7–8; cf. 72–78); and its mother-strumpets, infant punks, future heroes, and little Maximins provide a handy gloss on the nature of Flecknoe's progeny and confuse artistic and sexual production in exactly the same way that he and Shadwell do. Augusta's inclination to political fears parallels Shadwell's inclination to artistic dullness (65; cf. 189–90), and the line describing the Barbican — "An ancient fabrick, rais'd t'inform the sight" (66) — significantly reproduces the language and thought of one of Flecknoe's tributes to Shadwell: "his goodly Fabrick fills the eye" (25). Dryden metamorphoses Augusta into a body of which Flecknoe and Shadwell are the mind and soul.

Flecknoe chooses the city as the site of Shadwell's throne because it is receptive to the kind of empire he seeks to found there: city taste is ready for Shadwell. The genealogy Dryden has Flecknoe so carefully provide for his successor — Dekker, Heywood, Shirley, Ogilby — forces us to see Shadwell as the culmination of a long line of vulgar, inept poets who stand as representative of, and spokesmen for, the tastes of the city audience.[29] That taste preferred masque, music, and spectacle to poetry, pageantry and opera to heroic drama;[30] and this, I think, explains the appropriateness of the moldering "fabrick, rais'd t'inform the *sight*" as the location of Shadwell's throne: it physically recreates Shadwell's and the city's aesthetic. For this same reason, Shadwell is described in identical terms: the style *is* the man (and that, I may say prematurely, is the secret of *MacFlecknoe*.)

Shadwell's city genealogy reflects more than bad taste, however: it also possesses a political aspect that illuminates another facet of London's role in the poem. By placing Shadwell in succession from a string of city poets and from Ogilby, who had managed the city's ceremonies at the coronation of Charles II, Dryden identifies him with the fluctuations of London's political allegiance — a trick that Shadwell himself made easier by his fawning dedication of *Psyche* (to which *MacFlecknoe* frequently alludes) to the Duke of Monmouth.[31] The political aspects of Flecknoe's and Shadwell's roles have been present fairly explicitly from the beginning of the poem, of course, in the overt analogy of Flecknoe's kingdom of nonsense. More particularly, the comparison of him to Augustus would serve to call to mind the contemporary comparisons of the restoration of the Stuarts to the accession of Augustus and thus link Flecknoe in some strained way with Charles II. More explicitly, of course, Flecknoe's confrontation of the problem of succession aligns him with Charles and the Exclusion Crisis and makes the whole situation of *MacFlecknoe* roughly — very roughly — analogous to the contemporary political situation.

Neither Flecknoe nor Shadwell is Charles, however, and there are in Dryden's presentation of his case some significant differences that enable us to see them as the opposite in art of what Charles is in politics. Flecknoe's succession problem, for instance, involves not the fact that he has no legitimate son but that he has too many. And again unlike Charles, although Flecknoe rules "Through all the Realms of *Non-sense,* absolute" (6), his is also paradoxically an elective monarchy, as is shown by his choice of successor (rather than succession on the basis of primogeniture) and by his people's ratification of that choice: "He paus'd, and all the people cry'd *Amen*" (144). All this tends to make him a figure more like Cromwell than like Charles and to tighten the bonds among Flecknoe, Shadwell, and the city.

This identification of the protagonists with their scene appears to be part of the overall strategy of the poem. Dryden on the one hand makes of Flecknoe, Shadwell, and Augusta (the use of the literary name rather than its common one has value too) interchangeable counters, signs of and for each other: in the most literal sense, Augusta embodies what Flecknoe and Shadwell stand for. On the other hand, this identification

enables Dryden to blur distinctions, to force the various theoretically
("in real life") distinct characters of the satire actually ("in art") to merge
together: that is, Dryden erases the border line between art and reality,
between person and thing, mind and matter, just as Flecknoe's empire
ignores it. One bad poet, in such a world, can be the equivalent of a
Whiggish city just as easily as he can be an example of simple dullness; it
is, after all, just a matter of words. For example: the queens and future
heroes, unfledged actors and infant punks of the Nursery (74–78) mingle
promiscuity and rant just as Shadwell, "Swell'd with the Pride of thy
Celestial charge; / And big with Hymn" (40–41), graphically merges
two kinds of miscreation. The distinction between sexual and artistic
creativity (and/or sterility) has been completely lost.

Against this background, the central action of *MacFlecknoe,* the
coronation, acquires new depth of meaning. Dryden leads us to see in it
not just the passing on of empire but the founding of a city, a *polis,* with
all that that implies about the building of a civilization and a culture. His
allusions to the *Aeneid* draw almost exclusively on the Virgilian preoc-
cupation with the founding of Rome: his references to Shadwell as "our
young *Ascanius"* (108) and *"Rome's* other hope" (109) recall precisely
this emphasis of the *Aeneid.* Dryden draws the analogy quite overtly
when Shadwell, at his coronation, sees "twelve reverend *Owls"* (129):

> So *Romulus,* 'tis sung, by *Tyber's Brook,*
> Presage of Sway from twice six Vultures took.
>
> (130–31)

The vultures, as Plutarch reports, indicated not only that Romulus
should rule but also where the city should be built.[32] This is the main
action that *MacFlecknoe* imitates, the founding of Rome, the city of
Augustus, the new Troy: Shadwell is founding Augusta, the English
Troynovant.[33]

If the similarity I earlier suggested between Shadwell and the city is at
all true, their likenesses should extend beyond their mutual "thoughtless
majesty" to more substantial flaws. This, I think, is the case. Dryden
presents both Flecknoe and Shadwell on one hand and Augusta on the

other as essentially self-contradictory: he embodies in them opposing characteristics that reflect their mutual confusions of value and role. Augusta is Rome, but it is also Carthage; Dryden calls Shadwell Ascanius, but he casts him as Hannibal.

> At his right hand our young *Ascanius* sate,
> *Rome*'s other hope, and pillar of the State.
> His Brows thick fogs, instead of glories, grace,
> And lambent dullness plaid around his face.
> As *Hannibal* did to the Altars come,
> Sworn by his *Syre* a mortal Foe to *Rome*;
> So *Sh---* swore, nor should his Vow bee vain,
> That he till Death true dullness would maintain;
> And in his father's Right, and Realms defence,
> Ne'er to have peace with Wit, nor truce with Sense.
>   (108–17)

The "lambent dullness" recalls the lambent flames that played around Ascanius's brow and convinced Anchises of Aeneas's mission, thus initiating the journey that brought them to Italy (*Aeneid* 3.166–68). Immediately after this in *MacFlecknoe* follows the vow that brought Hannibal to Rome for very opposite reasons: Silius Italicus's description of the scene has Hannibal explicitly swearing to once again destroy Troy —"*Rhoeteaque fata revolvam*" (*Punica* 1.115). All of these contradictions, however, are absorbed into the overriding reversal of the idea of Rome: the eternal city becomes the site of temporal decay; the Rome of law and culture dwindles to an Augusta of disorder and dullness. In the Flecknoe-Shadwell version of nature and art, there is nothing else. As Shadwell bears Flecknoe's "perfect image" (15), and as Shadwell's characters are "All full of [him], and differing but in name" (162), so, too, Dryden makes their city in their own image, and renders the act of crowning Shadwell identical to the act of founding Augusta: they are in fact tautological.

　　Image — both the word and the conception — brings us closer to the center of *MacFlecknoe*. Flecknoe's quandary about the succession and the basis of his resolution of that problem provide the first major use of the word in the poem and invoke most of the ideas about it which the rest of the poem will reverberate.

> 'tis resolv'd; for Nature pleads that He
> Should onely rule, who most resembles me:
> *Sh*--- alone my perfect image bears,
> Mature in dullness from his tender years.
> *Sh*--- alone, of all my Sons, is he
> Who stands confirm'd in full stupidity.
>
> (13–18)

Although nature may plead for Shadwell ("What share have we in Nature or in Art?" Flecknoe will later ask), Flecknoe's argument is ultimately drawn from supernature. His language rather obviously echoes the scriptural description of God's creation of man: "So God created man in his own image, in the image of God created he him" (Genesis 1:27). If this is the case, of course, then Flecknoe becomes a figure of God the Father — a preposterous enough idea, even if we accept it metaphorically as referring to him in his capacities as playwright and king: that then makes of Shadwell a creature with the same level of existence as Flecknoe's plays (most of which, appropriately, have not survived). This confusion of Shadwell's status is, I think, deliberate on Dryden's part and useful for his purposes, but discussion of this aspect of the passage will have to wait until other elements in the poem are clarified.

More important than the reminiscence of the language of Genesis is Dryden's appropriation of ideas drawn from the theology of the Logos, the second person of the Trinity, who bears the "perfect image" of the Father. The situation at this point most resembles Milton's descriptions of the Father's promulgation of the regency of his Son (*Paradise Lost*, book 5), but it also draws upon the same sort of conceptions that Milton utilizes in Book 3, the dialogue in heaven between the Father and Son about the fate of man. There the second person is presented in his capacity as the Logos, the perfect expression of the Father: "in him all his Father shone, / Substantially express'd . . . " (*Paradise Lost*, 3.139–40). This particular *locus* makes more than this clear, however, since the dialogue between the two persons necessarily dramatizes explicitly the implicit relationship between them. That relationship is, in human terms, tautological. What the Father speaks, the Son embodies and repeats. For example, after announcing that man will fall and be punished, God concludes, "But Mercy first and last shall brightest shine" (3.134). Here is what follows that statement:

> Beyond compare the Son of God was seen
> Most glorious, in him all his Father shone
> Substantially express'd, and in his face
> Divine compassion visibly appear'd,
> Love without end, and without measure Grace,
> Which uttering thus he to his Father spake.
>   O Father, gracious was that word which clos'd
> Thy sovran sentence, that Man should find grace
>   (*Paradise Lost,* 3.138–45)

To make the relationship even more clear, Milton has built Christ's speech out of almost every device of repetition known to Renaissance rhetoric — again, for example:

> For should Man finally be lost, should Man
> Thy creature late so lov'd, thy youngest Son
> Fall circumvented thus by fraud, though join'd
> With his own folly? that be from thee far,
> That far be from thee, Father, who art Judge
> Of all things made, and judgest only right.
> Or shall the Adversary thus obtain
> His end, and frustrate thine, shall he fulfil
> His malice, and thy goodness bring to naught. . .?
>   (*Paridise Lost,* 3.150–58)

The whole dialogue is formed from just such dramatization of the basic theological relationship, and I suggest that Dryden here draws upon this same relationship for his own ends. A few lines further on in this passage, Dryden makes this explicit when he has Flecknoe refer to Shadwell as a Christic anti-type of his "Old Testament" precursors:

> *Heywood* and *Shirley* were but Types of thee,
> Thou last great Prophet of Tautology:
>
> (29–30)

To finish the parallel, Dryden reverts to it once more at the crucial point
of the anointing of Shadwell, the climax of the coronation ceremony:

> The *Syre* then shook the honours of his head,
> And from his brows damps of oblivion shed
> Full on the filial dullness . . .
>
> (134–36)

He here alludes to a specific text in *Paradise Lost:*[34]

> He said, and on his Son with Rays direct
> Shone full; hee all his Father full exprest
> Ineffably into his face receiv'd,
> And thus the filial Godhead answering spake.
>
> (*Paradise Lost,* 6.719–22)

Immediately before this, God has transferred to Christ power to defeat
Satan and to teach him and his followers what it means "to despise / God
and *Messiah* his annointed King" (6.717–18).

The logical question to ask at this point is, of course, what all this
means. It means, on one very simple level, the obvious charge that
Flecknoe and Shadwell are tautological writers, that their plays are filled
with repetitions both of themselves and of other writers — hack work and
plagiarism. And it means, equally obviously, that the relation between
Flecknoe and Shadwell is tautological, that they are repetitions of each
other, mirror images of dullness. But the text says that explicitly, and we
certainly do not need an elaborate theological framework for the com-
monplaces of a literary quarrel. What all this really implies is that the
relationship among Flecknoe, Shadwell, and their respective plays is
totally tautological, not just literarily, but ontologically as well: the
"issue of a large increase" with which Flecknoe is blessed (8) — and this
includes Shadwell as well as Flecknoe's plays — *is* (not "is like") a

repetition of himself, just as Shadwell's plays are "Not Copies drawn, but Issue of thy own" (160) and so repeat him — "All full of thee, and differing but in name" (162). Flecknoe explicitly counsels Shadwell about his foolish characters:

> Let 'em be all by thy own model made
> Of dullness, and desire no foreign aid
>
> (157–58)

This creation in Shadwell's own image returns us to our starting point in Genesis and completely rounds out the tautology by now casting Shadwell as God the Father.

The fundamental point of this elaborate analogy rests on the role of the Logos in creation. God creates by and through the Word: the Word is the agent and model of creation. What Flecknoe and Shadwell produce amounts to a travesty of the divine creativity. Their version of it reduces it to the all-too-human level of simple foolishness. If tautology is meaningful in God — and in orthodox Christianity it is the one meaningful act that provides the ground for all other acts — in man it is boring. God *is* tautological: his existence and essence are identical, as Aquinas and many others point out. He expresses himself in tautologies: in the Logos, who mirrors him; in his tautological declaration to Moses, "I am that I am"; in his creation of man in his own image. But God is tautological because there is nothing outside of himself to which he can refer; he encompasses all being and provides its ground and source. In this sense, God is a closed ontological system, just as epic is a closed linguistic system: in both, tautology is the ground of being and meaning. God creates out of this fullness of being; Flecknoe and Shadwell create out of their vacuity. Shadwell, bearing Flecknoe's "perfect image," "never deviates into sense" (20). His fools "stand in [his] defence, / And justifie their Author's want of sense" (155–56); that last pentameter beautifully and pointedly parodies Milton's "And justify the ways of God to men." There is no distinction between them and their creations, just as there can be no distinction between them as persons. Here, of course, lies the total difference between their creativity and God's: his creation is really distinct from him, just as the Son is really distinct from the Father. The divine tautology results in infinite variety, the human one in mere repetition. God unites three in one, but Flecknoe and Shadwell repeat one in two.

Theologically and literarily, in Genesis and in epic, the word bridges the gap between human and divine, between material and spiritual, and herein lies the enormity of what Flecknoe and Shadwell do. They reverse that process and use the word to divide, to subtract soul from body. Their creations are marked not by life but by corporeality; sheer physical bulk is their distinguishing characteristic, inertness their chief glory: Flecknoe calls Shadwell "A Tun of Man" (195); "his goodly Fabrick fills the eye" (25); "loads of *Sh*--- almost choakt the way" (103). Appropriately, Dryden depicts this by means of an essentially blighted sexuality and ubiquitous scatology. Shadwell's throne is erected on the scene "of lewd loves, and of polluted joys" (71); he early practiced the lore of *Love's Kingdom* (124); *Psyche* sprung from his loins (125) — surely an unlikely source for Psyche.[35] Even "his Sceptre and his rule of Sway" (123) priapically and perhaps autoerotically comments on the sterile bawdry of his plays. Flecknoe offers to teach him "Pangs without birth, and fruitless Industry" (148), a lesson he seems not to need, since he begins the poem "big with Hymn" (41) and ends it still flatulent and swollen, a "mountain belly" with "a tympany of sense" (193–94) — certainly the longest false pregnancy in literature.[36] I presume it is only academic squeamishness that has prevented someone from pointing out that Dryden's consistent use of "*Sh*---" frequently demands, despite the meter, a monosyllabic reading. I doubt that when the echoes call from "*Pissing-Ally*" (47) it is "Shadwell" they are saying. Surely, after we have been told that "neglected Authors" are "Martyrs of Pies, and Reliques of the Bum" (100–101), we must read "Loads of *Sh*---" (103) scatologically. And it seems to me equally clear that the "double portion of his Father's Art" (217) that Shadwell inherits shares this same taint. At any rate, all of this exactly defines the nature of Flecknoe's and Shadwell's art. Quintessentially material, it represents the overflow of life and energy only in the most grossly parodic sense; it is formed from the remnants of life rather than from life itself. The metaphor is precise, and quite unanswerable.

Imagery of this sort enables Dryden to make maximum use of bodies as a debasing device, as he did in *Absalom and Achitophel*, since all flesh becomes tainted by association with its least reputable uses. This results in the poem in the pronounced emphasis upon the physical representation of what is not necessarily perceived as physical. The dwelling on Shadwell's enormous size is straightforward and obvious enough, but Dryden continues to employ the language of physical properties when talking about what should be intellectual or artistic matters. Flecknoe warns Shadwell not to let "alien *S-dl-y* interpose, / To lard with wit thy hungry *Epsom* prose" (163–64). Sir Formal fills his dedications (169–70) just as his characters — once more tautologically — are full of him (162). Shadwell "whole *Eth'ridg* dost transfuse" (184) to his plays. His "writings lean on one side still" (191); he himself is "A Tun of Man" and "a Kilderkin of wit" (195–96). In the same way too the kingdom of letters is reified. Dryden accomplishes this in part by localizing it for the moment in London and suggesting thereby that it actually possesses physical extension. Flecknoe, with his insistent materialization of all metaphor, finishes the task:

> Heavens bless my Son, from *Ireland* let him reign
> To farr *Barbadoes* on the Western main:
> Of his Dominion may no end be known,
> And greater than his Father's be his Throne.
> Beyond loves Kingdom let him stretch his Pen.
>
> (139–43)

Such a process as this inevitably leads to a blurring of distinctions between fictions and facts and among people, places, and plays. Flecknoe consistently fails to differentiate between his artistic and his actual (if any) progeny; and Shadwell, as we have already seen, falls somewhere in a shadowy area between the two. In this same manner, at the coronation the path of the procession is strewn with "scatter'd Limbs of mangled Poets" (99), an image that drastically reifies Horace's already metaphorically concrete *"disjecta membra poetae."*[37] In the same passage, the neglected authors who come from dusty shops, "Martyrs of Pies, and Reliques of the Bum" (100–101) are equally ambiguous: they could just as easily be books or people. The same confusion holds true when Flecknoe speaks of Shadwell's characters, who are his ambiguous issue:

> Yet still thy fools shall stand in thy defence,
> And justifie their Author's want of sense.
> Let 'em be all by thy own model made
> Of dullness, and desire no foreign aid:
> That they to future ages may be known,
> Not Copies drawn, but Issue of thy own.
> Nay let thy men of wit too be the same,
> All full of thee, and differing but in name.
>
> (155–62)

In another instance of this, Sir Formal attends his pen (169–70) just as earlier in the poem Dekker foretold that his pen would bring forth "*Humorists* and *Hypocrites* . . . / Whole *Raymond* families, and Tribes of *Bruce*" (92–93). This whole process culminates, of course, in the mad science-fiction moment when the creatures slip from the creator's control, assume autonomy, and turn on their inventor:

> He said, but his last words were scarcely heard,
> For *Bruce* and *Longvil* had a Trap prepar'd,
> And down they sent the yet declaiming Bard.
>
> (211–13)

Here the artifact has achieved the same level of existence as the artist — or vice versa — and the artist pays the price for his own hack work. His inability to make clear distinctions in the realm of art produces, in the realm of being, a world that is all *Love's Kingdom,* populated only by *Humorists, Hypocrites,* and *Virtuosos*. Sloppy art, Dryden is arguing, effects a confusion in reality; or, put another way, since our art embodies the reality we live in, confusion in art and reality are necessary corollaries of each other. This relation between art and reality goes far beyond a simplistic mirror-to-nature conception: it is *essentially* the relationship of the first and second persons of the Trinity, tautological, two versions of the same thing. Thus the incoherence of Flecknoe's and Shadwell's minds *is* the incoherence of the world they create around them, and they themselves are no more or less real than their characters Bruce or Longvil.[38] From this point of view, *MacFlecknoe* is a poem as much about ontology as about literature — as indeed epic has always been.

Once again the hapless Shadwell bears the burden of this unreality. Flecknoe presents him to us as the incarnation of this tautology, as what Pope will later call the anti-Christ of wit:

> *Heywood* and *Shirley* were but Types of thee,
> Thou last great Prophet of Tautology:
> Even I, a dunce of more renown than they,
> Was sent before but to prepare thy way;
> And coursly clad in *Norwich* Drugget came
> To teach the Nations in thy greater name.
> My warbling Lute, the Lute I whilom strung
> When to King *John* of *Portugal* I sung,
> Was but the prelude to that glorious day,
> When thou on silver *Thames* did'st cut thy way,
> With well tim'd Oars before the Royal Barge,
> Swell'd with the Pride of thy Celestial charge;
> And big with Hymn, Commander of an Host,
> The like was ne'er in *Epsom* Blankets tost.
>
> (29–42)

Dryden conglomerates a good many traditional motifs here, all of them pointing with greater or lesser precision to Shadwell as poet, prophet, and messiah. The reference to Heywood and Shirley as types of Shadwell, Flecknoe's description of himself as John the Baptist and his parody of the inspired harpist and poet David (another type of Christ), all force us to see Shadwell as a travesty of Christ, a *reductio ad absurdum* of the divine tautology. The divine Word was made flesh, and this was paradox enough for seventeen centuries of Christianity; but Dryden provides us in *MacFlecknoe* with paradoxes on top of that: the satire makes Shadwell's flesh, his mode of existence, exclusively verbal, while at the same time demonstrating how he converts all words to flesh, reduces them to inert matter. Shadwell, tautological in every respect, becomes the vehicle for his own very literal incarnation of the word: he is "Swell'd with the Pride of [his] Celestial charge"; he bears the word within him, "big with Hymn." Another aspect of this confusion of literature and reality, spirit and matter, can be seen in Flecknoe's later description of Shadwell, "A Tun of Man in thy Large bulk is writ" (195), where the word once again merges into the flesh. Here, of course, we are dealing explicitly with a parody, a debasement, of the central moment of Christian history. If the Incarnation of Christ actualizes the nexus of human and divine, Shadwell's false pregnancy shatters that connection. What he produces is the complete reification, the total corporealization, of word and spirit. His flatulence parodies inspiration, and his verbal and physical constipation for the duration of the poem (Shadwell never speaks in *MacFlecknoe*) again quite literally embody Dryden's final judgment on the man and his works.

All of this elaborate theological paraphernalia provides the basis for the poem's mode of procedure: the playing with the theology of the Logos subverts the framework of reality and brings into being an exclusively verbal world — but a verbal world that is paradoxically trapped in matter. If God, creating through the Word, made a material world capable of rising to spirit, Shadwell through the degradation of the word creates an immaterial, verbal world that is quickly sinking into matter. In an ambivalent sense, this world possesses no reality outside the printed page. It exists as literature exists and draws its sustenance from — and only from — literature; this explains the superabundant allusions that punctuate the poem. On the other hand, literature exists in this world as only the physical reality of the printed page — "loads of *Sh*--- almost choakt the way" (103). Such a world closes upon itself. It cannot have reference to any reality outside itself and so must be tautological. Neither can it transcend in any way the limitations of finite, physical existence: "All humane things are subject to decay" (1).

Dryden knows that to carry a joke too far is to make it very serious indeed, and he consciously carries *MacFlecknoe* to extremes. He makes of tautology one of the governing structural principles of the poem, thereby illustrating in the world of *MacFlecknoe* the world of Flecknoe and Shadwell and at the same time creating the poem (and cosmos) they are incapable of. For example: Flecknoe's second speech repeats and amplifies the characteristics of Shadwell and the motifs presented in his first speech and in the coronation episode. The two speeches in themselves constitute variations on the same theme: both consider the facts that prove that Shadwell was destined for "annointed dullness" (63). The imagery of prophets and of Flecknoe's drugget robe (29–33) reappears at the end of the poem; Flecknoe's lute and Shadwell's music of lines 35–56 recur in lines 209–10. The emphasis on mere words, which first occurs in. lines 53–59 and surfaces again in lines 83–84, the garrulous Flecknoe expands upon in lines 197–208. Characters from several of Shadwell's plays pop up frequently throughout the poem (56–59, 75–78, 151–70, 211–13), and mention of related or rival playwrights occurs even more ubiquitously (29, 79–93, 142, 151–52, 163–64, 171–85), all within the framework of a simple dichotomy: abhor Jonson, Etherege, Sedley; follow Dekker, Heywood, Shirley, and Ogilby. Dryden packs the poem even more frequently and repetitiously with references or allusions to plays, almost all of them Shadwell's (42, 53, 58, 62, 81, 84, 90–93, 122–25, 143, 148, 164, 179–80, 187–90, 198, 211–13). In addition to all this, Dryden amply increases the tautology and the sense of a closed, purely verbal world by a wealth of allusions, frequently repeated, to Genesis, Deuteronomy, Nehemiah, the Book of Kings, the New Testament accounts of John the Baptist, Cowley's *Davideis,* Davenant's *Gondibert,* Milton's *Paradise Lost,* Shakespeare's *Antony and Cleopatra,* Virgil's *Aeneid,* Horace's *Satire I.iv* and *Ars Poetica,* Plutarch's and Livy's account of the founding of Rome, and Shadwell's own Epilogue to *The Humorists.*

But Dryden has managed this material more artfully than merely by heaping up repetitions. He has carefully arranged these parts into an integral, if redundant, whole that bears a parodic relation to the symmetries of epic. The second half of the poem mirrors exactly the first. The nature that pleaded for Shadwell at the beginning reappears as the nature to which he is to trust at the end; Shadwell himself is described in exactly the same way at beginning and end — massive, swollen, obese. His initial false pregnancy is further mirrored in the "Pangs without birth, and fruitless Industry" (148) that Flecknoe offers to teach him. The long section on Shadwell's "want of sense" (156) simply magnifies Flecknoe's opening remarks about Shadwell's "full stupidity" (18). The very "action" of the poem also reflects this pattern of repetition: the first third (roughly) of the satire contains Flecknoe's monologue about the succession to the throne and the reasons why Shadwell should inherit; the next part dramatizes, in a symbolic landscape that links Flecknoe's two speeches and Shadwell's virtues with their political environment, the fact of that succession and some of Shadwell's qualifications; the final third of the poem is once again Flecknoe's speech, this time in the genre of instructions to the prince, advising Shadwell how to do the things he has already done well enough to earn the crown. In such a framework, Shadwell logically inherits Flecknoe's drugget robe; he is, after all, a repetition of Flecknoe. And equally logically, his last acquisition is a "double portion of his Father's Art" (217); since that art is nothing if not tautology, a double portion is only appropriate.

   MacFlecknoe superimposes a variety of structures upon each other. One of the most obvious, of course, is the tautological structure we have just been discussing, the repetitious correspondence of parts to parts, which can only be described as static — a parody of the sort of structure Dryden used in *Absalom and Achitophel.* In terms of this structure, the poem goes nowhere: the beginning contains the end, and nothing is changed. In other terms, the poem *does* progress, from the deliberations about the problem of succession through the act of succession to the young king's assumption of his powers. This essentially linear, straightforward structure involves simply the handing on of power from one generation to another — the *translatio imperii* or, more exactly here, a parody of the *translatio studii.* But the poem's opening aphorism sets in motion another and this time circular structure — the recurrent cycle of human mutability and decay. The process of decay is illustrated repeatedly throughout *MacFlecknoe:* in Flecknoe himself, who, when fate summons, must obey (2); in the ruin of the Barbican (66–69); in the quality of the plays, players, and playwrights spawned there (74–92). The repeated contrasts between the founding of Aeneas's city and Shadwell's evidence once again the consistent cycle of degeneration. Even Flecknoe's final speech, which begins by praying,

> Heavens bless my Son, from *Ireland* let him reign
> To farr *Barbadoes* on the Western main;
> Of his Dominion may no end be known,
> And greater than his Father's be his Throne,
>
> (139–42)

ends by pathetically urging him to

> Leave writing Plays, and chuse for thy command
> Some peacefull Province in Acrostick Land.
>
> (205–6)

In fact, Flecknoe's final speech details an extended process of diminishment as Shadwell receives advice that ranges downward from

> Let *Virtuouso's* in five years be Writ;
> Yet not one thought accuse thy toyl of wit,
>
> (149–50)

to the creation of individual characters, to the rhetoric of his dedications, to his use of bawdry. It pauses briefly to sum up his artistic practice as promising a play and dwindling to a farce (181–82), but from that point on enumerates the steps of an even more drastic decline. Shadwell's province shrinks to "New Humours to invent for each new Play" (187–88), and Flecknoe quickly proceeds to disqualify him from tragedy, comedy, and satire (197–202), urging him now to "chuse for thy command / Some peacefull Province in Acrostick Land" (205–6). But even this is not the end, and Flecknoe's last suggestion, which is scarcely heard, exhorts Shadwell to become completely like him and "Set thy own Songs, and sing them to thy lute" (210). The rest, of course, is silence, the logical conclusion to that rapid declension through genres, words, and mere sounds. Fittingly, Flecknoe's final action — if it can be called that — brings the poem full circle: the fall that leaves Shadwell "Through all the Realms of *Non-sense,* absolute" (6) is a literal realization of the poem's opening sentiment, "All humane things are subject to decay" — decay, of course, being derived from *decadere,* to fall down. This combination of literalism and vulgar slapstick functions, to my mind, as the ultimate symbol of the cosmos of Flecknoe and Shadwell: it sums them up in the act of putting them down. Debased word realizes itself in debased thing.

From one final perspective, nothing in the poem progresses: once we have seen Flecknoe as Shadwell's precursor, the poem freezes. All else becomes a repetition of that relationship. The situation remains the same; only our point of view, shifted by allusions and references, changes and returns. Shadwell, the obscene bearer of his own travesty incarnation, remains exactly so until the end of the poem, and Flecknoe, now as Aeneas, now Melchisedek, now God the Father, goes on precursing, preparing Shadwell's way, until the end of the poem. And even there nothing changes: Shadwell is not delivered, and the precursing goes on. Shadwell assumes Flecknoe's lute and the drugget robe that Flecknoe-as-John-the-Baptist wore. He receives as well the double portion of his master's art that Elias biblically bequeathed to his successor, and since the New Testament identifies Elias with John the Baptist,[39] all this can only mean that Shadwell has now taken over the role of precursor for some one — or something — that will never come. He merely repeats Flecknoe — thus his name, MacFlecknoe — repeats the precursing, which is, in the most succinct paradox of the poem, all that can be expected of the "last great Prophet of Tautology."

VI

Dryden's two epics embrace both ranges of allegorical reading, public and private, political and philosophical. But — as their similarities of image and theme (fertility, paternity, sonship, succession, bodies, language and its contents) should already have hinted — there is no division in epic between politics and philosophy or between public and private life. They are all encompassed by varying conceptions of wisdom; they are all included in epic's concern for right order in every sphere. *MacFlecknoe*'s parodic versions of the external epic action — the founding of a kingdom — and the internal — the hero's recognition of the full dimensions of his calling and attainment of the requisite knowledge — unite them all the more firmly in order to undo them. The epic tradition as Dryden received it already included within its spacious confines a concern for philosophic truths about human life as well as for the fate of kingdoms. It embraced a private aspect that elaborated the difficulties of attaining personal tranquillity — whether that was construed as philosophic calm or Christian salvation — as well as its more obvious public interests in good order in government and the working-out of the (or a) providential design in history. That archetypal epic wanderer, Odysseus, already illustrated many of these concerns at the very beginnings of the tradition. His devotion to Athena, his long series of trials, his sustaining desire for return to his domestic comforts and for reunion with his wife, son, and father, all readily lent themselves to the most patent of interpretations as a moral journey toward personal salvation. At the same time, his reestablishment of the proper order of succession on Ithaca equally easily defined his journey as a political allegory, a *Bildungsroman* for princes. In the *Aeneid,* Anchises' various discourses in the underworld and Aeneas's adventures in the upper just as readily served as exempla for a whole battery of moral, metaphysical, and political truisms. And, in any event, an English poet writing after Spenser and Milton would have needed very little prompting to see that the epic form was most properly concerned with physics and metaphysics, politics and morality. If all these come, literature, as the conservator of them all, cannot be far behind. In fact a concern for literature, for the arts in general, already held a place in formal epic explicitly, as we have already seen in the Virgilian commentators, and implicitly through the analogous ideas of the transference of empire and the transference of studies. Arts followed arms, and the course of both was, along with the epic journey, ever westward. Dryden's conception of all these concerns as not only simultaneous but as intimately and essentially related derived from the simple realization that the epic, a literary form, was the vehicle for them. Epic, in simple fact, occupied an absolutely central cultural position as the formulator and preserver of civilization's highest knowledge and belief; it and the Bible shaped the reality men lived.

From this logically flowed the fusion of ontology and aesthetics that *MacFlecknoe* illustrates. To tamper with language, to abuse the word, must, in such a view, produce ontological consequences — consequences that are symbolically illustrated in *MacFlecknoe* when Shadwell's creatures take control. That action embodies the Renaissance's version of the results of the mad scientist's labors, the reign of the monsters. Renaissance culture differed from ours in being still basically a literary culture, and the results of world-tampering presented themselves to it *sub specie verbi,* but the vision that *MacFlecknoe* sardonically presents remains the vision of cultural annihilation we still share and in our own terms fear. At any rate, Dryden's vision of the creatures run mad, of man assimilated to, and controlled by, the forces of his own unreason, established the pattern for this type of writing from that time forward. It informed Swift's *Tale of a Tub,* which collapses into the morass of its own metaphorics, leaving its mad author to write out the contents of his own brain, nothing. It can be seen behind Gulliver's submission to the superiority of the horses, a surrender to the autonomy of a definition — *animal rationale* — that man originally made for, not against, himself. And it most assuredly inspired the fiction of the fourth book of *The Dunciad;* it is clearly visible in the apocalyptic closing scene, when Dulness reestablishes her power over the no longer animate world. This same fear of the consequences of the literary imagination misused, of art and consequently of life deformed, provided the impulse for Fielding's responding to *Pamela* first with *Shamela* and then with *Joseph Andrews.* It explains why Parson Adams must, at a crucial moment in "real" life, throw his Aeschylus into the fire, why, in *Tom Jones,* Sophia drops her sentimental romance at the entrance of Lord Fellamar, and why, in Fielding's last attempt to make epic an ontological force in human life, a pamphlet converts Captain Booth to true belief. It all ends in the futility of Walter Shandy's hopelessly irrelevant Tristrapaedia, which cannot even keep up with the life it was meant to control. *Tristram Shandy* realizes the world Dryden feared, though it decks it with a brilliance he would never have guessed it capable of. The disjunctive punning, the bawdry held in check only by the pervasive impotence of the characters, the dissolution of knowledge into mere words in Walter's theory of the auxiliary verb, the collapse of the whole world of the novel into a cock-and-bull story — "and one of the best of its kind, I ever heard" — all these demonstrate the radical dissociation of literature from the framework of ideas in which Dryden conceived *MacFlecknoe*. Sterne accepts as goods — or at least as facts — the things that Dryden rejected in advance. Neoclassical literature polarizes neatly around these two points — at one, concern for the establishment of a cosmos, for order, for society; at the other, an attempt to write a knowing self into existence. Somewhere between these two points, Shadwell, with Colley Cibber as midwife, had given birth to the "modern sensibility." The continuity that epic sought between art and reality had been established, but the price of the establishment was the death of the world that spawned epic, the world that made clear distinctions between matter and spirit while it saw clear connections between them.[40] Just as epic's allegory tended to replace epic's action, the success of epic's linkings destroyed the reality of its distinctions.

•

1. *Monsieur Bossu's Treatise of the Epick Poem . . . Made English,* by W.J., 2 vols. (London, 1719), 1:11.

2. See Barbara Lewalski's "The Scope and Function of Biblical Allusion in *Absalom and Achitophel*," *ELN* 3 (1965–66): 30. Various points in my discussion of Dryden's poem have been influenced by this article and by Morris Freedman's "Dryden's Miniature Epic," *JEGP* 57 (1958): 211–19, and by A. B. Chambers's "Absalom and Achitophel: Christ and Satan," *MLN* 74 (1959): 592–96.

3. The implicit image of the scattering of seed the rest of the poem capitalizes upon by linking it with the parable (Matthew 13:1–12) as in lines 194–95.

4. See the Epistle to the Romans, 5:12–21.

5. See Ernst Kantorowicz, *The King's Two Bodies* (Princeton, N.J., 1957). Kantorowicz's contention that the doctrine of the king's two bodies developed out of the theology of the mystical body of Christ seems to me to have genuine relevance to Dryden's poem.

6. See especially Sir Robert Filmer's *Patriarcha*, ed. Peter Laslett (Oxford, 1949), pp. 57–60 and 74–78. *Patriarcha* was published in 1680 after circulating in manuscript for many years; obviously it was brought out as a document in support of the royalist cause.

7. See Filmer, *Patriarcha,* pp. 81–82. It is also worth pointing out, as Filmer does, that the seventeenth century believed that the duty of obedience to magistrates and kings was biblically enjoined by the fourth commandment, "Honor thy father and thy mother."

8. *The Works of Joseph Hall, D.D.,* 12 vols. (Oxford, 1837), 1:41. Some reference to Jacob and Esau may also appear in lines 405–6, "His Right, for Sums of necessary Gold, / Shall first be Pawn'd, and afterwards be Sold." In general, Dryden seems to have drawn many ideas and some phrases from Hall's various *Contemplations on the Old Testament:* compare *Absalom and Achitophel,* 1030–31, and Hall, 1:106, for instance.

9. Dryden's reference to Corah's obscure birth parallels Horace's own mention in the ode of the obscurity of his birth.

10. See for instance the commentary of Simon Patrick on the passage: *A Commentary upon the Historical Books of the Old Testament,* 2 vols. (5th ed., London, 1694).

11. See Ernst Robert Curtius's treatment of Macrobius, to which my discussion is heavily indebted, in *European Literature and the Latin Middle Ages,* trans. Willard R. Trask (New York, 1953), pp. 443–45.

12. Macrobius, *The Saturnalia,* 5.1.18–20, trans. P. V. Davies (New York and London, 1969), p. 285.

13. "Discourses on the Heroic Poem," in A. H. Gilbert, *Literary Criticism: Plato to Dryden* (Detroit, 1962), pp. 500–501.

14. The phrase is Curtius's, p. 443.

15. The phrase is Terence McVeigh's. I have throughout my discussion of Fulgentius's commentary availed myself of the language of his translation in "The Allegory of the Poets: A Study of Classical Tradition in Medieval Interpretation of Virgil" (Ph.D. diss., Fordham University, 1964).

16. Fulgentius 25, McVeigh, p. 220.

17. Fulgentius 12, McVeigh, p. 209.

18. McVeigh's discussion of Fulgentius's allegoresis makes this point also.

19. Fulgentius 10, McVeigh, p. 207.

20. McVeigh, pp. 142 ff., discusses some of the similarities between Fulgentius and Bernardus.

21. The text used is *Commentum Bernardi Silvestris super sex libros Eneidos Virgilii.* Nunc primum edidit Guilielmes Reidel. Gryphiswaldae, typis Julli Abel, MDCCCCXXIV. Since the completion of this study, two important works dealing with Bernardus have appeared whose findings I was unfortunately unable to incorporate into this book; they are Brian Stock's *Myth and Science in the Twelfth Century* (Princeton, N.J., 1972) and Winthrop Wetherbee's *Platonism and Poetry in the Twelfth Century* (Princeton, N.J., 1972).

22. Compare, for example, *The Sphere of Sacrobosco,* ed. and trans. Lynn Thorndike (Chicago, 1949), p. 123: "Be it understood that the 'first movement' means the movement of the *primum mobile,* that is, of the ninth sphere or last heaven, which movement is from east through west back to east again, which is also called 'rational motion' from resemblance to the rational motion in the microcosm, that is, in man, when thought goes from the Creator through creatures to the Creator and there rests."

23. The only modern edition of Landino's allegorization is the edition and translation of the second two books of the *Disputationes Camaldulenses* by Thomas H. Stahel,

"Cristoforo Landino's Allegorization of the *Aeneid:* Books III and IV of the Camaldolese Disputations" (Ph.D. diss., Johns Hopkins University, 1968). Some of my discussion of Landino draws on the introduction to this edition. A very full discussion of the nature of Renaissance allegoresis of Virgil can be found in the chapter "Undermeanings in Virgil's *Aeneid*" in Don Cameron Allen's *Mysteriously Meant* (Baltimore, 1970), pp. 136–62. See especially his remarks on Filelfo as a transition from Bernardus to Landino, p. 155.

An Italian edition of Virgil's works, first printed in 1576 and republished many times thereafter up until at least 1710, served as an important means of disseminating, with elaborations, Landino's allegorization of the *Aeneid*. See *L'opere di Virgilio Mantoano, commentate . . . da Fabrini, Malatesta, e Venuti.*

24. The terms *executive* and *deliberative* are borrowed (and slightly altered) from Thomas M. Greene's important work *The Descent from Heaven: A Study in Epic Continuity* (New Haven, Conn., and London, 1963).

25. Ibid., p. 407. This process of internalization has also to do, of course, with the identification of beatitude (variously defined) as the end of epic poetry: see John M. Steadman's important and illuminating "Felicity and End in Renaissance Epic and Ethics," *JHI* 23 (1962): 117–32.

26. I have here been badly condensing Peter Hägin's excellent argument in *The Epic Hero and the Decline of Heroic Poetry,* The Cooper Monographs, No. 8 (Bern, 1964). See especially pp. 39 ff.

27. See Chambers. "Absalom and Achitophel."

28. The persistence of this structure will be discussed more fully below, in connection with *The Rape of the Lock.*

29. Rachel Trickett, reviewing Aubrey Williams's *Pope's Dunciad: A Study of Its Meaning* in *RES,* n.s., 8 (1957): 318, succinctly establishes the Puritan, Whiggish nature of the city background Dryden assigns Shadwell.

30. Tom H. Towers, in "The Lineage of Shadwell: An Approach to *MacFlecknoe,*" *SEL* 3 (1963): 323–34, convincingly argues that in linking Shadwell with Flecknoe, Heywood, Dekker, Shirley, and Ogilby, Dryden is associating him with practitioners of vulgar theatrical spectacle.

31. See Michael W. Alssid, "Shadwell's *MacFlecknoe,*" *SEL* 7 (1967): 387–402, for a full appraisal of this aspect of the poem.

32. See Plutarch's *Life of Romulus* for the full account (cap. 9–10) and Livy, 1.7.

33. Aubrey L. Williams, in his important book *Pope's Dunciad: A Study of Its Meaning* (New Haven, Conn., and London, 1955), has established the importance to epic and mock epic of the action of founding (or refounding) an empire and the related concepts of *translatio imperii* and *translatio studii:* see especially pp. 44–48.

34. Earl Miner, in *Dryden's Poetry* (Bloomington, Ind., and London, 1967), has already pointed out this similarity. I want to acknowledge here that my argument about *MacFlecknoe* resembles and draws upon Miner's in several particulars, though we are ultimately working in different directions.

35. This seems designed as an obscene parody of the emergence of Athena, goddess of wisdom, from the head of Zeus.

36. Johnson's dictionary, as Kinsley's note on this line relates, defines *tympany* as "A kind of obstructed flatulence that swells the body like a drum." In this context, Shadwell's mountain belly may well recall Horace's line about inept poets from the *Ars Poetica,* "parturiunt montes, nascetur ridiculus mus" (139).

37. Satire 1.4.62. The general context of this poem, a defense of satire and particular satiric examples, is relevant to *MacFlecknoe;* it may relate to Dryden's allusion to Shadwell's Epilogue to *The Humorists,* which is, among other things, a defense of general, as opposed to particular, satire. Here, of course, the allusion points out the manglings that true poets suffer in the hacks' plagiarisms.

38. It should be pointed out that Dryden has Flecknoe very carefully differentiate properly ordered art from the work of Shadwell by precisely the principle of distinction that the royal dunce violates. Etherege makes "*Dorimant* betray, and *Loveit* rage" (152); he controls them rather than they him. His fools "in their folly shew the Writers wit" (154); they do not reproduce his fatuity.

39. Matthew 17:12–13. J. E. Tanner, in "The Messianic Image in *MacFlecknoe,*" *MLN* 76 (1961): 220–23, makes this connection and argues very coherently for the importance of messianic imagery in the poem.

40. I have discussed the changing relations of matter and spirit and words in "Language and Body in Augustan Poetic," *ELH* 37 (1970): 374–88.

*HE RAPE OF THE LOCK* plays with epic in a much different way than *MacFlecknoe*. Traditional wisdom calls them both mock epic; the name is accurate enough as long as we realize that the mock can attach itself in many fashions to the epic. *The Rape of the Lock* is not the same kind of mock epic as *Mac-Flecknoe,* no more than it is the same kind of mock epic as *The Dunciad.* If we have been dealing, in *MacFlecknoe* and *Abasalom* (and, I plan to argue, in *The Dunciad*), with poems that appropriate to themselves a whole chunk of what we can legitimately describe as epic *matter,* the *Rape* aligns itself with epic essentially through its *manner*: its content is the "trivial things" from which "mighty contests rise."

I

The poem announces its separation of form and content from the outset. If the first line's generality of reference prods us to think momentarily of Troy and Helen and that "dire Offence" that "from am'rous Causes springs" (1), the second line quickly deflates that. The verse of *The Rape* characteristically proceeds in this manner, both in style and in substance. It jostles the reader back and forth between the contrary motions of epic expansion and mock-epic contraction. Ariel threatens his fellow sylphs with pseudo-Miltonic punishments if they fail their charge, concluding with an image that splendidly reconciles epic grandeur with the sylph's fragility:

> Or as *Ixion* fix'd, the Wretch shall feel
> The giddy Motion of the whirling Mill,
> In Fumes of burning Chocolate shall glow,
> And tremble at the Sea that froaths below!
>
> (2.133–36)

The rhetoric leaves no resting place, no firm ground from which to see and judge, but rather hurls us from one extreme viewpoint to another, from Ixion's hellish torment to the aroma of the tea table. This rhetoric provides the stylistic equivalent of what Pope's use of zeugma accomplishes grammatically and what Belinda's toilet, or the card game, or the battle of the belles and beaux, offers narratively. This manipulation of perspectives provides a sense of continuous flux, of constant becoming, in which the potentialities for grandeur and for absurdity exist simultaneously and can be realized at the same instant in the same act. It makes a world neither tragic nor comic, neither heroic nor silly — merely confused by its own capacity for all four. *The Rape* differs from almost all other mock epics in this way: even *MacFlecknoe,* for all of the multiplicities of possible vantage points it offers, never wavers in the value judgments it makes of its protagonists. *The Rape* does: *The Rape* insists on its own ambivalence.

The Rape remains ambivalent toward its protagonists and its subject matter for a clear and explicable reason, because it treats in an epic manner things that are not epic matter. "Slight is the Subject" (5) it says overtly and covertly — overtly in its honest dismissal of importance, covertly in its allusive claim for a particular kind of importance.

> Slight is the Subject, but not so the Praise,
> If She inspire, and He approve my Lays.
>
> (1.5–6)

Pope draws these lines (by way of Dryden's translation) from Virgil's fourth Georgic:

> Slight is the Subject, but the Praise not small,
> If Heav'n assist, and *Phoebus* hear my Call.
>
> (4.8–9)

> In tenui labor; at tenius non gloria, si quem
> numina laeva sinunt auditque vocatus Apollo.
>
> (4.6–7)

Pope reinforces the importance of the allusion to the fourth Georgic by using another in lines 11 and 12:

> In Tasks so bold, can Little Men engage,
> And in soft Bosoms dwells such mighty Rage?

This seems to pick up Virgil's "ingentis animos angusto in pectore versant" (Georgic 4.83). The fourth is the apiary georgic, and Virgil's description of the colorful fragility of the bees and the ferocity of their quarrels — the last quoted Virgilian line describes the tiny warriors on the eve of battle — has a lovely ironic propriety as a framework for Pope's equally colorful, fragile, and fierce cast. There are other allusions to the *Georgics* in *The Rape*, notably during the game of Ombre (usually to Georgic 4, and frequently by way of Dryden's translation), but the position and prominence of these two make them the most important.

What they both do, of course, is focus the poem and us on the disparity between — ignoring the pun — tenors and vehicles, forms and contents — slight subjects, great praise; bold tasks, little men; soft bosoms, mighty rage. They focus us as well on Virgil's precedent in using epic language, epic style, to describe the mundane activities of the farm. Virgil used the *Georgics* as a dry run for his epic, as a chance to test his skills; Pope certainly knew of the precedent and his own georgic reflects it.[1] I view Pope's use of these allusions here as a direct announcement that the poem that follows will use the epic manner to talk about things that are *not* epic matter, and that the central point of the poem is precisely the kind of disjunction that this initial separation of form and content accomplishes — the disjunction of artistic form from artistic content, of social form from social content, of sexual form from sexual content, of cosmological form from cosmological content. That is why he employs this sort of mock epic and invokes the *Georgics* — not because he is describing the perversion of an epic ideal or of anything that has any real connection with epic, but because he is delineating the shattering of connections, the separation of ideas from the vehicles that should embody them. Like Swift's tub, *The Rape* is a container that contains nothing, a form deliberately inappropriate to its content. This is not to say that the poem is a failure. I hope to argue eventually that this inappropriateness is the highest form of propriety for Pope's purposes.

Technically speaking, this sort of impropriety constitutes a formal breach of decorum, and the poem seems to devote a good deal of itself to the three related conceptions of inappropriateness, impropriety, and indecorousness and their positive opposites. That is to say, Pope makes an indecorous poem reflect an improper world, a world whose citizens behave according to inappropriate codes of conduct. When Belinda, triumphing at Ombre, lets out her war whoop, she — it needs no subtlety to see — is being unladylike; when the Baron compares the scissors that snipped Belinda's lock to the swords that leveled "th' Imperial Tow'rs of *Troy*" (3.174), he is appealing to an inappropriate standard; when the poem describes a queen who "Dost sometimes Counsel take — and sometimes *Tea*" (3.8), either the poem or the queen is guilty of impropriety in distributing emphases. *The Rape* forms out of such disparities as these its own essential mode: it proceeds by exploring them, revealing their built-in tensions and showing their inevitable breakdown, and reassembling their shattered materials into a more decorous, more appropriate world that turns out to be, by Popean sleight-of-hand, itself.

In Pope's view — at least Pope's view of 1714 — order always defeats chaos, and art triumphs over artifice. The problems presented by *The Rape* are, whose order and whose art? Belinda and her attendants, both physical and metaphysical, offer an order and a corollary aesthetic; these amount, in the poem, to an alternative cosmology, a Belindacentric universe competing with, and almost eclipsing, the heliocentric world of "reality." Belinda unquestionably replaces the sun in her world: she is "the Rival of his Beams" (2.3):

> Bright as the Sun, her Eyes the Gazers strike,
> And, like the Sun, they shine on all alike.
>
> (2.13–14)

All through the poem, Pope associates Belinda's actions with the motions of the sun:

> Sol thro' white Curtains shot a tim'rous Ray,
> And op'd those Eyes that must eclipse the Day.
>
> (1.13–14)

The sun "declining from the Noon of Day / . . . obliquely shoots his burning Ray" (3.19–20) while Belinda triumphs at the card table; and when she loses at the coffee table, at "that sad moment . . . / Umbriel, a dusky melancholy Spright, / As ever sully'd the fair face of Light" (4.11–14) does as his name implies and clouds Belinda's radiance.

All that, of course, is no more than the extension into interesting detail of one of the most hackneyed metaphors of love poetry — but is it? Is the sun metaphor for Belinda? Or Belinda metaphor for the sun? Or both for something else? All the old analogies hover around this poem — man: woman::sun: earth:: reason: passion::head: body::king: state::god: universe — and Belinda dominates the puny males of the poem (she wins at cards and becomes the *Ombre,* the man) and is in turn dominated by the vicissitudes of her emotions; a queen rules England and strangely mixes matters of state and trivia, while statesmen divide their attention between foreign affairs and sexual affairs (3.1–8). Belinda momentarily becomes the god of this confused universe — *"Let Spades be Trumps!* she said, and Trumps they were" (3.46) — and creates an order she can almost perfectly dominate, in which she can almost literally become "the man," exulting over her fallen foe (3.99–100). But this is all false, and because it is false, Belinda cannot sustain it. She may win at cards, but the "real world" defeats her — the Baron cuts her lock; Umbriel uses her; her looks, as Clarissa warns, will fade; and she, too, as Pope warns, will die. *Soles occidere et redire possunt,* but for her, *nox est perpetua una dormienda.*[2] The sun can set and rise again, but not Belinda, and therefore Belinda's eyes — and Belinda herself — are nothing like the sun.

•

> For, after all the Murders of your Eye,
> When, after Millions slàin, your self shall die;
> When those fair Suns shall sett, as sett they must,
> And all those Tresses shall be laid in Dust;
> *This Lock,* the Muse shall consecrate to Fame,
> And mid'st the Stars inscribe *Belinda's* name!
>
> (5.145–50)

Belinda's immortality and her importance are peripheral, not central, and her place is as one star among many rather than as the single sun of the world. Pope's Muse, a woman with a better sense of order than Belinda, puts her in her place most firmly: we must "trust the Muse" (5.123) for the truth of the lock's metamorphosis, just as Belinda must trust the Muse's inscription of her name "mid'st the Stars" for the eminence she so woefully fails to attain for herself.

The Muse and her "quick Poetic Eyes" (5.124) form the precise counterpoint to Belinda. Belinda, knowingly or not, espouses, defends, embodies an order and an aesthetic that Pope and his Muse connive at, display in this poem, only to transform as the lock is transformed. When Belinda takes her place before the mirror, she begins a creative act — an artistic act — that reaches its logical conclusion in the game of Ombre.

> And now, unveil'd the *Toilet* stands display'd,
> Each Silver Vase in mystic Order laid.
> First, rob'd in White, the Nymph intent adores
> With Head uncover'd, the *Cosmetic* Pow'rs.
> A heav'nly Image in the Glass appears,
> To that she bends, to that her Eyes she rears;
> Th' inferior Priestess, at her Altar's side,
> Trembling, begins the sacred Rites of Pride.
> Unnumber'd Treasures ope at once, and here
> The various Off'rings of the World appear;
> From each she nicely culls with curious Toil,
> And decks the Goddess with the glitt'ring Spoil.
> This Casket *India's* glowing Gems unlocks,
> And all *Arabia* breaths from Yonder Box.
> The Tortoise here and Elephant unite,

Transform'd to *Combs,* the speckled and the white.
Here Files of Pins extend their shining Rows,
Puffs, Powders, Patches, Bibles, Billet-doux.
Now awful Beauty puts on all its Arms;
The Fair each moment rises in her Charms,
Repairs her Smiles, awakens ev'ry Grace,
And calls forth all the Wonders of her Face;
Sees by Degrees a purer Blush arise,
And keener Lightnings quicken in her Eyes.
The busy *Sylphs* surround their darling Care:
These set the Head, and those divide the Hair,
Some fold the sleeve, whilst others plait the Gown;
And *Betty's* prais'd for Labours not her own.

(1.121–48)

This scene of Belinda's toilet furnishes an elaborate and important use of the mirror image. Here Belinda engages in a complex artifice that parodies the process of true art and produces a very corporeal version of the golden world of art as she "sees by Degrees a purer Blush arise, / And keener Lightnings quicken in her Eyes" (143–44). The "heav'nly Image" (125) she sees in the glass imitates and debases the idea seen in the mirror of the mind and reproduced in the mirror of art — a conception that forms the basis of most Neoplatonic aesthetics. The whole situation simply literalizes the metaphor of the mirror of art and reifies the art work. Significantly, the art work in this case is not the mirror itself, nor is it in the mirror, but is rather Belinda herself. She performs a completely tautological, reflexive act, beginning and ending in herself; she is both priestess and goddess of her own cult, worshiper and worshiped, artist and artifact. Such an artifact not only distorts Sidney's Neoplatonic version of the art work but re-creates quite exactly the kind of art that Plato banned from his republic. Belinda explictly imitates an imitation, the ironically "heav'nly Image" she sees in the mirror. We cannot forget at this point that Plato pejoratively linked art and the mirror as both illusory, both representers of a falsely seeming reality, so that Belinda's adornment of the mirror image removes her yet further from the ideally conceived real. Let me quote the concluding remarks of this section of Plato's argument:

> We may conclude, then, that all poetry, from Homer on-
> wards, consists in representing a semblance of its subject,
> whatever it may be, including any kind of human excellence,
> with no grasp of the reality. . . . Strip what the poet has to
> say of its poetical coloring, and I think you must have seen
> what it comes to in plain prose. It is like a face which was
> never really handsome, when it has lost the fresh bloom of
> youth.[3]

Plato's judgment is far too harsh to be applied literally to the fragile
Belinda, but it does force another perspective on Pope's ambiguous use
of comparatives in "keener Lightnings" and "purer Blush."

Taken in its widest implication, this passage parodies the whole late
Renaissance notion of the poet and his relation to the corporeal and the
ideal worlds. Belinda is explicitly a creator god whose fiat "calls forth all
the Wonders of her Face" (42), and she engages in the same kind of
world-building that Renaissance poets saw as the highest reach of their
craft.[4] This lies behind her invoking "the Cosmetic" — rather than
cosmic — "Pow'rs" (124) and her selecting from "The various Off'rings
of the World" (130). It accounts, too, for the presence here of the united
tortoise and elephant, miniaturized into combs: although they are only
superficial artifacts here, they bring with them echoes of their famous
appearance in Locke's discussion of false notions of substance as an
illusory explanation of the structure of the universe.[5] Here their union
forms a step in the formation of a false world of false art that extends from
the general disorder of "Unnumbered Treasures" (129) and "The various
Off'rings of the World" (130) to the fully realized but still disordered
plenitude of "Here Files of Pins extend their shining Rows, / Puffs,
Powders, Patches, Bibles, Billet-doux" (137–38). Belinda creates a
Whiggish world, a highly ornamented, unpatterned plenitude of which
she is center and exemplar — which is precisely, in small, her role in the
whole of *The Rape*.[6]

The same confusion of artist and artifact that we saw in *MacFlecknoe*
lies at the core of Pope's passage: Belinda paints, and what she paints is
herself. The mirror only returns a surface appearance: what is affected is
not the intellectual vision, but only the corporeal surface, of Belinda's

face. Pope's lines make prominent also another aspect of this web of ideas: the reflexive nature of bad art. It is always, in the language of *MacFlecknoe,* tautological. It begins and ends in itself. I cannot emphasize this point too much, because it is so antithetical to what we have all been taught to recognize as a virtue in poetry. By these standards of judgment, poetry fails when it does not go outside itself, when it is self-contained, when it is the subjective expression of a subjective world — like Belinda's — even when that world is internally consistent and self-supporting — like Belinda's. (Perhaps this is why epic tries so often to exceed its purely linguistic bounds: it is attempting to validate itself by contact and correspondence with reality.) Pope elegantly insists on this insufficiency at the end of *The Rape* when the Muse, with "quick Poetic Eyes," sees Belinda's lock metamorphosed into a star. Belinda, who has been the sun in her own miscreated universe, is moved by proper poetry, by Pope's own Muse, from center to circumference, from false divinity to true poetic immortality. The poem opens with "those Eyes that must eclipse the Day" (1.14) and Belinda's vision of the "heav'nly Image in the Glass" (1.125); it closes with the setting of "those fair Suns" (5.147) and the inscription of Belinda's name "midst the Stars" (5.150) by the Muse.

The game of Ombre shows the full extent of Belinda's ability to miscreate. Here she acts completely the part of the creator-god, calling into being an ordered and hierarchical cosmos, ludicrously miniaturized, by means of a parodically deflated version of the divine fiat: "*Let Spades be Trumps!* she said, and Trumps they were" (3.46). The card game that follows is a model of order, as all such rigidly ruled games must be: card triumphs over card in proper hierarchical succession, and Belinda's paradoxical victory, the victory that makes her "the Man," is achieved by the king of hearts who "mourn'd his captive Queen" (3.96) and "springs to Vengeance with an eager pace" (3.97). In effect, the lesson is there for Belinda to learn in the world she has created: the cards act their parts properly — the queen's "hands sustain a flow'r, / Th' expressive Emblem of their softer Pow'r" (3.39–40); the kings are their consorts, protectors, and superiors. In the center of the pseudo-mock-epic *Rape* lies a real mock epic, a heroic combat played out by

pasteboard kings and queens, that counterpoints and criticizes the later
and disturbingly non-heroic combat Belinda will provoke. It offers us, in
a single moment, a miniaturized remembrance of heroic grandeur, a
glimpse of sensible, natural, and possible order, and the age's sad and
funny insensitivity to these.

> An *Ace* of Hearts steps forth: The *King* unseen
> Lurk'd in her Hand, and mourn'd his captive *Queen*.
> He springs to Vengeance with an eager pace,
> And falls like Thunder on the prostrate *Ace*.
> The Nymph exulting fills with Shouts the Sky,
> The Walls, the Woods, and long Canals reply.
>
> (3.95–100)

If the content, which is Belinda, is inappropriate to the form of epic
heroism, this central point of the poem returns us to Pope's opening
pronouncements of the disjunction of the tenor and the vehicle he intends
to employ. Belinda herself is the trivial thing from which mighty contests
rise, and the mighty contest that does in fact take place in the fifth canto
enacts, in a fine Popean paradox, this radical separation of style and
meaning. Its sustained doubleness of vision also beautifully typifies
Belinda's "immortal longings"—

> No common Weapons in their Hands are found,
> Like Gods they fight, nor dread a mortal Wound.
>
> (5.43–44)

Belinda's world reduces the battles of the *Iliad* to explicitly literary
contests of cliché. She ignores Sarpedon's heroic rhetoric, transmitted
and transmuted through the commonsensical Clarissa, and chooses the
tired metaphors of shopworn love poetry — doubly ironic, of course, in
the light of her reaction to her lover's advances.

> While thro' the Press enrag'd *Thalestris* flies,
> And scatters Deaths around from both her Eyes,
> A *Beau* and *Witling* perish'd in the Throng.

One dy'd in *Metaphor,* and one in *Song.*
O cruel Nymph! a living Death I bear,
Cry'd *Dapperwit,* and sunk beside his Chair.
A mournful Glance Sir *Fopling* upwards cast,
Those Eyes are made so Killing — was his last:
Thus on *Meander*'s flow'ry Margin lies
Th'expiring Swan, and as he sings he dies.
    When bold Sir *Plume* had drawn *Clarissa* down,
Chloe stept in, and kill'd him with a Frown;
She smil'd to see the doughty Hero slain,
But at her Smile, the Beau reviv'd again

  .   .   .   .

    See fierce *Belinda* on the *Baron* flies,
With more than usual Lightning in her Eyes;
Nor fear'd the Chief th'unequal Fight to try,
Who sought no more than on his Foe to die.
But this bold Lord, with manly Strength indu'd,
She with one Finger and a Thumb subdu'd:
Just where the Breath of Life his Nostrils drew,
A Charge of *Snuff* the wily Virgin threw;
The *Gnomes* direct, to ev'ry Atome just,
The Pungent Gains of titillating Dust.
Sudden, with starting Tears each Eye o'erflows,
And the high Dome re-echoes to his Nose

  .   .   .   .

    Boast not my Fall (he cry'd) insulting Foe!
Thou by some other shalt be laid as low.
Nor think, to die dejects my lofty Mind;
All that I dread, is leaving you behind!
Rather than so, ah let me still survive,
And burn in *Cupid*'s Flames, — but burn alive.

(5.57–102)

Double entendre is omnipresent, because the sexuality of Belinda's
world is just as real as its heroism — and both are, in the most pejorative
sense, literary. Epic is epic, and sex is sex, and rape is simple enough,
except when artifice is substituted for art, sneezes for orgasms, and the

rape of a lock for "Hairs less in sight, or any Hairs but these" (4.176).
What has come into being, in the course of *The Rape,* is a totally
self-contained, totally artificial world, a literal reflection in large of
Belinda at the mirror. "To die" is metaphor — death the vehicle, climax
the tenor — but in this battle the metaphor "to die" is used reflexively:
climax is the vehicle, death the tenor. The beaux and belles turn
language upon itself as Belinda turned painting upon herself. Pope's
awareness of the ironies he here heaps up runs deep, just as his own
notion of the disjunction between artifice and art holds firm. He laconi-
cally annotates Sir Fopling's time-worn *"Those Eyes are made so
killing"* (5.64) with *"The Words in a Song in the Opera of* Camilla.*"*
The Virgilian Camilla was a "fierce Virago" (5.37) not unlike Thalestris,
which is quite appropriate since Fopling's line is addressed to her. But
here are the lyrics of the song:

> Those eyes are made so killing,
> That all who look must dye;
> To art I'm nothing owing,
> From art I nothing want;
> These graces genuin flowing
> Despise the help of paint.
> 'Tis Musick but to hear me,
> 'Tis fatal to come near me,
> For death is in my eyes.[7]

Irony on ironies. A tissue of artificialities dispraises art, and the art
described is the very one Belinda practiced when she "call[ed] forth all
the Wonders of her Face" and saw "keener Lightnings quicken in her
Eyes" (1.142, 144). Pope concentrates all of his awareness of what is
wrong with his society here in this use of artifice to mock artifice. He
does not damn Belinda; she is herself as much an artifact as an artificer,
as fragile and perishable as the lock she lost. The blame — if there is any
— is on something missing, an absence at the core: the failure of society
at large to preserve the dignity and decorum that can be glimpsed,
fleetingly and ironically, only in a game of cards. Belinda cannot sustain
the weight of the roles she must play — worshiper and goddess, artist and

artwork, chaste maiden and coquette — no more than the baron can play virile Paris to her Helen or triumphant Odysseus to her Troy. They are too small, too vulnerable, like the lock itself — surrogate for Belinda's chastity, surrogate for Belinda, bait, snare, and victim in one: the lock must be severed and lost, as Belinda must age and die, because the demands made upon them are disproportionate to their strength. The continuing grandeur of heroic ideals in the face of simple human inability to realize them is the final and central impropriety of *The Rape of the Lock*.

Only the Muse succeeds. The Muse can at least transform part of Belinda into what she would be, can move her out of this mutable sublunary world into "the shining Sphere" (5.142) of the fixed stars. The Muse and her poet accomplish this by the one truly heroic act in the whole poem: by telling Belinda the truth — that she is *not* the center of the world, that she is not immortal — they restore the world and value. By their final, elegiac lines, they raise Belinda beyond the need for elegy.

II

The preceding remarks about *The Rape of the Lock* have contained several implications about its structure that now need elaboration. With disorder and disproportion occupying so much of his attention, Pope seems to have devoted understandable pains to eliminating both from his poem: *The Rape* is a masterpeice of achieved symmetry, of order imposed on chaos. Indeed, as I have hinted before, the final paradox and the ultimate triumph of *The Rape* lies in the simple fact that in it, while dealing with a whole world of disparities and disjunctions of form and content, Pope manages to fuse his own form and his own content into aesthetic unity. Belinda's world was reflexive in the precise sense that it mirrored only her; everywhere she looked she saw reflections of Belinda. *The Rape* is a transitive mirror: it reflects itself to enable us to pass through itself. The reflexive act provides the building blocks of the poem.

We can see this in the way in which the poem organizes itself around the nuclear events of the third canto, which function — to continue the terms I have used above — both as mirror and transition. There, at the heart of the poem, Belinda both triumphs and falls: the card game and the rape, Belinda and the Baron, dramatize the apparently polar extremities of the poem. This bifurcation of the canto both reflects the structure of the cantos that have gone before it and predicts that of those that will follow.

To analyze the structure of *The Rape* properly, we must cast away notions of plot; it is far more useful to trace the articulation of episodes — taking that word in its broadest and most neutral sense — and their relation to each other. That is to say, rather than examining event A to determine how it gives rise to event B, we should examine the content and shape of event A to discover how it corresponds to, or differs from, events B, C, and D: that investigation will free us from the story and bring to light the *structure* of the piece. To this end, episodes — even when there are causal relationships among them — should be regarded as entities in themselves, subject to even further reductive analysis, right down to the level of stylistic and grammatical investigation. I am suggesting, in effect, that we imitate Fulgentius's and Bernardus's mode of treating the *Aeneid*. Such a notion will, I think, bring us much closer to what Augustan critics and their predecessors meant to designate by the word "episode."

The Rape makes such analysis easy by the brevity and clarity of its episodes. Putting aside for the moment the short invocational and epilogous sections spoken directly by the poet, we can break down the content of the five cantos roughly as follows:

Canto 1
Belinda (briefly) / Ariel and the dream / Belinda's toilet

Canto 2
Belinda (briefly) / the Baron's prayer / Council of Sylphs / Belinda (briefly)

Canto 3
Hampton Court Setting / Ombre / Coffee setting / the Rape

Canto 4
Belinda (briefly) / Umbriel and the Cave of Spleen / Thalestris
and Sir Plume / Belinda

Canto 5
Belinda (briefly) / Clarissa / Battle / Transformation of Lock

Mechanical though it is, such a schema helps us to consider in an
isolated fashion the content of the various episodes. Canto 1 consists of
three clearly distinct parts: the introduction of the heroine; Ariel's urging
a course of conduct upon her; and her first action in the poem. Belinda's
toilet, it must be remembered, is totally disjunct from Ariel's admoni-
tions: he tells her to "most beware of Man" (1.114),[8] but he is then
interrupted and totally forgotten as Belinda prepares herself for Man:

> He said: when *Shock,* who thought she slept too long,
> Leapt up, and wak'd his Mistress with his Tongue.
> 'Twas then *Belinda*! if Report say true,
> Thy Eyes first open'd on a *Billet-doux;*
> *Wounds, Charms,* and *Ardors,* were no sooner read,
> But all the Vision vanish'd from thy Head.
>   (1.115–20)

Belinda appears in this canto peripherally to the central action of
Ariel's exegesis of the Rosicrucian system and warning to her, although
she clearly remains the center of interest. The same state of affairs
remains roughly true of canto 2: Belinda is the cause and source of all the
actions of the canto even though, once again, her actual appearances in it
are distinctly peripheral. The two major actions relate closely to each
other: the Baron's prayer informs us of the nature of the threat to Belinda,
and the Council of the Sylphs informs of the steps taken to meet the (to
them still unknown) threat. In the first half of canto 3, Belinda acts in a
manner parallel to her performance in canto 1. There she armed herself
for battle; here she battles. There she played goddess; here she plays
god. There she prepared for Man; here she becomes Man. And just as
Belinda's careful tending of her locks in canto 1 may be said to provoke

the Baron's desire to cut them in canto 2, so here her action in the card game may legitimately be said to provoke the Baron's reaction in the second half of the canto. The actions are closely related, but are presented narratively as disjunct: Pope prefaces each, sets the scene for each, by a description of a ritualized setting (Hampton Court and the coffee table). His point, I believe, is to make us see them as separate in the way that Belinda no doubt sees them. Just as for Belinda the toilet was a self-contained reflexive act, for Belinda the game of Ombre is a completion of that act, equally reflexive and lacking meaning for anyone but herself. We, of course, who have heard the Baron's prayer, know that in this poem no act can be truly self-contained and therefore can perceive the connection between Belinda's action and the Baron's reaction. The snipping of the lock stands as direct counterpoint to the careful tending of it in the mirror episode and strips Belinda of her putative divinity. Canto 4, as can be seen even in the outline, returns to the structural pattern of canto 2. Belinda appears once more only at the periphery, although she is still the passive source and cause of the two major actions. The appearance of Umbriel and his journey to the Cave of Spleen (carefully synchronized in the text with the appearance of the earthly lover in Belinda's heart and Ariel's withdrawal [4.11–16]) may at first glance appear to correspond with Ariel's appearance to Belinda in canto 1 or to the Council of the Sylphs in canto 2, but its actual content parallels much more closely the Baron's appearance in canto 2. Both episodes involve a prayer to a god or goddess; both involve designs upon Belinda. And the consequent episodes in each case — the Council of the Sylphs and the appearances of Thalestris and Sir Plume — involve actions taken ostensibly on behalf of Belinda. That is to say, canto 4 structurally answers canto 2 with a reverse or mirror image of itself — even down to the details of Belinda's role. Her depression in 4.1–10 reverses her exaltation in 2.1–18; her lament for what has already come to pass (4.147–76) parallels the anxiety about the future at the end of canto 2 (137–42). Clarissa's speech in canto 5 tallies with Ariel's in canto 1 in that both offer Belinda advice about prudential modes of conduct — advice that is in both cases disregarded. The battle of the beaux and the belles antithesizes Belinda's toilet point for point. There she created an arbitrary order; here disorder reigns — and the disappearance of the lock shows the impossibility of reestablishing that previous, fragile order. There "awful Beauty [put] on all its Arms" (1.139); here the metaphor is ludicrously realized. There Belinda saw "keener Lightnings quicken in her Eyes" (1.144); here "Fierce *Belinda* on the *Baron* flies, / With more than usual Lightning in her Eyes" (5.75–76). Canto 1 raised its subject matter by metaphor; canto 5 reduces it by the facts that correspond to those metaphors. The metamorphosis of the lock into a comet[9] and thence into a star offers Pope's alternative — and the only viable one — to Belinda's attempt to translate herself into divinity. This final transformation answers fully the transformation Belinda attempted in canto 1 and replaces the Belindacentric order that Ariel and Belinda attempted with a new and workable order, with Belinda factually and metaphorically (star rather than sun) peripheral rather than central — as she has indeed been in the structure of the poem all along. *The Rape* has contained throughout and embodied throughout the order it finally establishes: its form and content, meaning and expression, are totally one.

The mirror expresses the nature of this sort of structure wherein, in a curious scholastic manner, parts correspond to parts across the nexus of a central rearrangement or redefinition of those parts. *The Rape* schematizes in the following fashion: i ii (i-ii) II I. The poem encloses itself, and its various components are to be understood by virtue of their relation to each other and not by virtue of anything outside the poem — e.g., the few lines about Queen Anne (3.7–8) are to be explicated not by Pope's known attitude toward Queen Anne but by her relations to Belinda and the Muse and the queens in the card game; thus in this poem the fact of a woman ruling England offers a sign of the other inversions the poem deals with. This does not mean that one cannot go outside the poem on the track of allusions; allusions are very much *in* the poem — as the ubiquity of Catullus should testify. Part of the point of the poem, after all, is made by the simultaneous presences of Homer, Virgil, and Catullus in the same poem. But the poem itself, by the kind of internal relationships it sets up, decides what is relevant, and by appeal to, and consonance with, these we can judge the relevance and importance of our notions about it. All this is simply to say that epic, like satire, is not a static thing, but exists more in a relation than as an absolute: they define themselves not *in se* but by a network of relationships *inter partes*. The final paradox remains, of course, that in the case of epic at least these relationships are internal and reflexive and that by this means the poem also defines itself *in se*. Ultimately, it mirrors itself. In a final sense, the real nature of the mock epic in *The Rape of the Lock* lies in the enclosure of everything by epic.

This reflexiveness should be by now familiar. It is exactly the same structural relationship I described in *MacFlecknoe*. It reappears in *Absalom and Achitophel,* where the central metaphors of fathers and sons define themselves first as the relation of king and subjects, pass through the nuclear realignment of the disquisition on liberty that redefines them by virtue of Adam's relation to his posterity, and finally emerge in the light of the all-encompassing divine paternity. More than this, this reflexiveness is exactly the same phenomenon that the commentators I discussed in chapter one discerned in the *Aeneid*.[10] The triad formed by *The Rape* (i ii [i–ii] II I) corresponds in more than mere outline to the circular pattern of thought as described by Medieval thinkers[11] or to what Wind calls a "Platonic emanating triad,"[12] and it just as strongly resembles the pattern of rites of initiation[13] and what Jung names "Enantiodromia."[14] None of this is accidental; I believe it presents a paradigm case of cultural conservatism, in which a pattern of psychological discovery, a way of knowing and enlightenment, was early affiliated with a mode of literature deeply concerned with the same problems. The centrality and importance of the subject matter ensured the survival of the form — ensured, in fact, that the form would be constantly reinterpreted and rearticulated in the light of each civilization's definitions of knowledge and wisdom — as long as it could continue to bear the weight put upon it and as long, of course, as the relation of the container to its contents was understood.[15] Let me be perfectly clear about what I am suggesting here: I want to say that the reflexive, triadic, and palindromatic pattern I have described above is, in effect, the skeleton key to epic. It is the basic structural form that constituted an implicit part of the notion of the genre of epic, and it appears to have been understood as such for at least 1,700 years. It is the grammar of the genre, over which a good many syntaxes and rhetorics have been laid.

The *Faerie Queene* and *Paradise Lost* display both the persistence of the structural framework and the variety of styles it will support. This is not the place for any extended analysis of either poem, so I will only try here to map out some of the broader structural relations that employ the pattern we are interested in.

In the *Faerie Queene,* certain large correspondences present themselves immediately. Whatever Spenser's encompassing plan for his projected twelve books may have been, the six we have fit easily into the triadic pattern.[16] The intertwined and interlocking events of books 3 and 4 have been frequently commented upon and need no particular mention here. These two central books treat a private virtue and a public one, chastity and friendship, and unite them thematically as well as narratively through a generous Renaissance conception of love and constancy. Spenser works these concerns out through the quests of individuals for individuals; he symmetrically arranges on either side of them quests involving the fate of cities or kingdoms. Both books 2 and 5 culminate in parallel and simultaneous actions carried out by the titular hero of the book and Arthur. In book 2, this involves Arthur's slaying of Maleger and raising the siege on Alma's castle while Guyon sails to Acrasia's island, destroys the Bower of Bliss, and restores her thralls to their proper forms. In book 5, Arthur defeats Geryoneo and frees Belge from virtual imprisonment in her castle while Artegal sails to Irena's land, defeats Grantorto, and restores justice. Discordant events close both books: Grill berates the successful Guyon, and Envy, Detraction, and the Blatant Beast set upon the triumphant Artegal. In both cases, the heroes accomplish the purgation of a kingdom and the restoration of what had been distorted (human souls and justice) to its proper form. In both books, too, Spenser invokes the figure of Hercules. Arthur's battle with Maleger parallels very closely Hercules' battle with Anteus, and Guyon's conquest of Acrasia and destruction of her power over men

seems a clear ideological reversal of Hercules' subservience to Om-
phale, an episode that forms the basis of Artegal's capture by Radigund
in book 5.[17]

The action pattern of book 6 practically repeats that of book 1, but the
men and women of the poem have somewhat exchanged roles. In book 1,
Red Crosse Knight is imprisoned by the giant Orgoglio and rescued
through the efforts of Una, who brings Arthur to his aid. In book 6,
Pastorella is imprisoned by the brigands and rescued by Calidore.
Spenser attaches to Pastorella a modified version of Red Crosse Knight's
personal history: both are foundlings; both are left in a field, and both
bear names derived from the circumstances of their abandonment and
adoption (George and Pastorella); both in the course of the poem discover their true identities. Spenser utilizes some direct correspondences
as well. The Salvage Man answers to Satyrane, Defetto, Decetto, and
Despetto to the Sans Brothers. The remedies the holy Hermit applies
correspond to those Red Crosse Knight received at the House of Holiness. Both Calidore and Red Crosse Knight temporarily forget their
quests, and both receive visions, on the Mount of Contemplation and on
Mount Acidale, respectively (both visions take place in the tenth canto,
by the way). Both reunite a daughter and her parents, both engage a great
beast, and — most important of all — both nearly achieve the reestablishment of a pastoral, prelapsarian existence — Red Crosse Knight by
the liberation of Eden and the freeing of Una's parents, Calidore by the
restitution of Pastorella to her parents, the defeat of the brigands, and the
capture of the Blatant Beast. Both accomplishments are similarly marred
by the predicted escapes of Archimago and the Blatant Beast (and, in
the case of book 1, by the continued freedom of Duessa). There are also
important parallels between the ideological conceptions and functions of
Archimago-Duessa and the Blatant Beast, but this discussion should
already be long enough to show the presence of the kind of symmetrical
structure we are interested in. Put briefly, the action pattern of book 1 of
the *Faerie Queene* parallels the action of 6, that of 2 parallels 5, and 3
and 4 are completely intertwined and function as the narrative and
ideological nexus of the whole poem. I think — though this is not the
place to demonstrate it — that the same sort of palindromatic, triadic
structure informs each of the individual books of *The Faerie Queene,* so

that the relationship between whole and part in the poem is a shifting relationship of metonomy and synechdoche: whole and parts are simultaneously container and contained.

The same relationship holds true for *Paradise Lost,* where the circularity of the structure reinforces the simultaneity of the events of the poem.[18] Books 6 and 7 provide the crossover point for all of *Paradise Lost,* moving the action of the poem irrevocably out of the divine sphere and into the human. These books mirror each other exactly: the same characters — Adam, Eve, and Raphael — figure in the same situation — Raphael is instructing Adam and Eve about events in heaven before their creation. In book 6, he describes the war in heaven, the Son's entrance into the fight, the defeat and expulsion of Satan's legions, the Son's triumphal return, and the heavenly jubilation. Book 7 parallels and antithesizes that by presenting the work of creation rather than destruction. Raphael describes God's intention to repopulate the heavens with a new race, the Son's entrance into chaos, its replacement by the newly created universe, and, once again, the Son's triumphal return and the heavenly jubilation. The other books arrange themselves symmetrically like types and antitypes around these two. Some examples are in order. Book 5 opens with Raphael's arrival in Paradise; 8 closes with his departure. Both books contain his crucial warnings to Adam about Satan's plans. Book 5 also recounts the beginnings of Satan's rebellion against the dominion of God and the kingship of the Son; 8 nicely counterpoints that with Adam's account of his own creation and his immediate recognition of the necessity of "some great Maker" (8.278; cf. particularly 5.852 ff.). Books 4 and 9: in 4, Satan adopts the form of a toad, in 9, that of a serpent. In the earlier book, he discovers the prohibition placed upon the fruit of the tree; in the latter he utilizes that knowledge. Book 4 contains the first temptation of Eve, in her dream; 9 contains the successful temptation in actuality. Both books close with a quarrel: 4, between Satan and Gabriel; 9, between Adam and Eve. More examples:

Book 3	*Book 10*
Prediction that man will sin	Announcement that man has sinned
The Son offers to satisfy divine justice	The Son judges the sinners

| Sin and Death proceed toward earth | Satan proceeds toward earth |
| A hellish triumphal council, ending in hisses | A heavenly council, ending triumphantly in hosannahs |

Book 11	*Book 2*
Heavenly council	Council of Demons
Sentence of death pronounced on Adam and Eve; Adam sees consequences of his sin in his son Abel's death	Satan meets Sin and Death; sees consequences of his own sin in his son
Adam's first glimpse of new world he has made	Satan's first glimpse of newly created world

Books 1 and 12 complete the process and round the poem: book 1 begins with the expulsion of Satan and 12 ends with the expulsion of Adam and Eve. Babel, Nimrod, and the blasphemous city dwellers of 12 correspond to Pandemonium and its inhabitants. The catalog of patriarchs and prophets in the last book answers the catalog of devils and false gods in the first. The demonic speculation about Adam and Eve in book 1 is confuted by the announcement of advent of the second Adam in 12. Earth is "but the shadow of Heav'n" (5.575), and the poem ends as it began with the near-total defeat of Satan.

Within this overall structure, the two halves of the poem also break down into repetitions of this pattern, books 1 through 6 and 7 through 12 constituting smaller repetitions of the original structure. I will list the parallels briefly (and not exhaustively, as the preceding view of the entirety of the poem has also been only partial). Book 1 opens, as 6 climaxes, with the fall of Satan. Somewhat informal satanic councils take place in each book, and the demonic artifacts, associated in both cases with wind, match each other — Pandemonium in 1 and cannon in 6. The Son's triumphal entry into the heavenly court at the end of the sixth book counterpoints the entry of Satan into council at Pandemonium. Both books 2 and 5 contain formal demonic councils, but beyond this the correspondences exist more as antitheses than parallels: Satan leaves hell to attack Adam and Eve, and this is counterpointed in

book 5 both by Raphael's departure for earth to warn them and by
Abdiel's leaving the rebel camp to warn God. Raphael's flight through
creation to earth answers Satan's journey through chaos to earth in the
same manner that Adam's and Eve's prayers and tasks in book 5
correspond to the diversions of the demons in book 2. At the center of
this, in 3 and 4, we have the same sort of mirroring that we saw more
grandly in 6 and 7, and the same sort of crossover from heaven to earth,
also less grandly. Satan seen approaching the earth in 3 is counterbal-
anced by Satan captured in Paradise in 4; the revelation of the second
Adam in 3 anticipates the appearance of the first Adam in 4; Satan's use
of the form of a lesser angel in 3 prepares for his diminishment into the
shapes of cormorant and toad in 4 — even his dialogue with Uriel about
the wonders of God's new creation anticipates his monologue of self-
doubt and wonderment at his first sight of Adam and Eve in 4.

So also in the unit formed by books 7–12 — but by this point, it
would probably be best only to list the parallels:

Book 7	*Book 12*
Creation of new world to replace loss of Satan and his followers	New beginning of the human race from Noah
Sabbath of Creation	The Second Coming
Opening of Paradise	Closing of Paradise

Book 8	*Book 11*
Adam denied knowledge of physical heavens	Adam gains knowledge of life on earth
Creation of Adam and Eve; their dominion in Paradise	Announcement of the expulsion of Adam and Eve from Paradise
Departure of Raphael from earth	Arrival of Michael in Earth

Book 9	*Book 10*
Adam and Eve discuss their labors	Adam and Eve discuss penitence
Satan tempts Eve in form of serpent	Satan forced into form of serpent
The fall and the sympathetic fall of earth	Sin and Death start toward earth
Adam and Eve clothe themselves	The Son clothes Adam and Eve

In addition to all these uses of the epic pattern, *Paradise Lost* falls into a triad of four-book units. Each has its own protagonist and its own pervasive locale: in the first four books, Satan initiates all of the major actions, and Hell — which Satan carries with him — provides the setting; in the second four, the Son performs the crucial acts and Heaven furnishes the stage; in the last four books Man — particularly Adam, but also the idea of Man — dominates events and earth serves as landscape. Particular episodic correspondences will probably stand out from what has already been said, but there are important correspondences of large actions as well. In each unit of the triad, the first two books deal in a paradoxical manner with the work of destruction. In books 1 and 2, the devils build Pandemonium and hold their Grand Conference, which results in the plans for the fall of Adam and Eve; under the guise of physical (Pandemonium) and political (Satanic empire) creation, the demons begin the task of undoing God's creation. Conversely, books 5 and 6 apparently describe destruction — the defeat and expulsion of Satan and his legions from Heaven — but what is destroyed is the principle of destruction itself, which the Son negates and exiles. Books 9 and 10 return to the original paradox with the fall of Adam and Eve and the creation of the empire of Sin and Death. Correspondingly, the second two books of each unit deal with the workings of Providence: 3 and 4 describe God's foreknowledge and concern for Man and the steps he takes to safeguard Adam and Eve; 7 and 8 describe his creative activity in restoring the heavenly balance Satan sought to disrupt; 11 and 12 present this latter activity functioning in exactly the same way in time rather than in space.

Milton's subject matter and theme also create a paradox in the relation of the units of the triad. As we have discussed it so far, the pattern consists of a processional series of events leading up to a point of conversion, a nexus, that capsulizes and alters them and leads in turn to a recessional series of events that mirror the first — the Red Crosse Knight fights the dragon Error badly, is enlightened at the House of Contemplation, and fights the great dragon well. This still remains true in *Paradise Lost:* God's Providence in capturing Satan at Eve's ear is matched by God's Providence working itself out in the historical process of redemption, and both relate to God's bringing good out of evil by his creation of the world. But it is much more proper and more accurate, in the case of *Paradise Lost,* to see events i and I not as mirroring each other but as both mirroring the events encapsulated in (i–ii). The central unit of *Paradise Lost* is God and God's works, which can be adequately mirrored only by his Son, the Logos, and not by the human word. He is the source and end of all the reality that art is supposed to mirror, and as such cannot reflect anything himself: all other things reflect him. So the real mirrors in *Paradise Lost* are the first and last units of the poem, and what they mirror is the center. Satan, of course, is a distorting mirror. What he does in his attempts to emulate God is a travesty of him: darkness visible is not the equivalent of light invisible. In that sense, Satan and Hell are high burlesque; they are the possibility of mock epic — and perhaps the direction of it — already contained within the epic. Adam and Earth are the legitimate mirrors of the poem; created in God's image and bearing his impress, they are the high art our "erected wits" still let us reach to, though our "infected wills" will not let us attain them. This is why, I believe, the poem ends at a point that corresponds to book 6 of the *Aeneid:* Adam has been illuminated, his goal has been explained, and his real epic works — and ours — are about to begin. Everything before has been prologue; what follows is "the better fortitude / of Patience and Heroic Martyrdom" (9.31–32) and the "argument / Not less but more Heroic than the wrath / Of stern *Achilles*" (9. 13–15). What it offered was a viable direction for epic, if only epicists had known it.[19] None but Fielding seems to.

This is a long way about to *The Rape of the Lock,* but it returns us to it with sharper insight. The structure of *The Rape,* not the subject of it, is what indissolubly links it to epic, and the self-enclosure and symmetry of that structure should now be apparent and meaningful. The parallelisms of the structure naturally lend themselves to the expression of allegorical and analogical ideas, and its repetitions and reflexiveness make it a natural vehicle for the depiction of simultaneous events. The notion of synchronicity seems tied up very closely with it. The marshaling of villains and heroes in *Absalom and Achitophel* occurs simultaneously.

MacFlecknoe transpires in a no-time of tautological prophecy. At the center of *The Rape,* Ariel's abandonment of Belinda, the cutting of the lock, and the mission of Umbriel to the Cave of Spleen happen at the same moment. The various quests of the *Faerie Queene* are simultaneous. In *Paradise Lost,* the falls of Satan and of Man take place in eternity that contains in the same instant and forever the triumph of the Son and the triumph of Christ: the poem ends a few minutes after it began, for time only starts with the Fall and the expulsion from the garden. The palindromatic pattern makes possible the solution of Milton's central problem in *Paradise Lost:* the expression in sequential terms of what occurred instantaneously and simultaneously.[20] This perhaps explains somewhat the phrase *ut pictura poesis:* poetry is only able to articulate the simultaneous, which painting *can* present simultaneously through spatial organization, by a sequential verbal construct that rounds upon itself, provides its own borders and frame, and by parallelism and repetition of incident links events that painting would group by line and form. Painting is metaphor for the linguistic conversion of extension into sequence, of space into time; conversely, space, in poetry, is the nexus that converts eternity into time and time into eternity. In *Paradise Lost,* God first creates a paradise in space and then re-creates it in time. Human history is the palette with which he sequentially rebuilds what he originally made instantaneously and plastically. Indeed, human history is in *Paradise Lost* conceived of as a verbal construct, an exposition of the promise made to Adam and renewed to Abraham, redeemed by the Word and fulfilled in the second coming of the Word. Human time is divine space, and poetry that breaks through the merely phenomenal into the realm of plan and pattern reproduces, in human, sequential terms (the terms Raphael had to use to tell Adam of the war in Heaven) a picture of the divine, of eternity, of infinite correspondence — of an infinity of mirrors reflecting an inexhaustible oneness. In exactly that sense, poetry is a speaking picture. And in exactly that sense, *The Rape of the Lock* locates Belinda spatially at the end of the poem and by doing so deifies her: by making her peripheral, the Muse makes her eternal. The shift in human space reveals the true pattern of divine time and frees Belinda and the poem itself from the traps of sequence, succession, and change. It reconstitutes a meaningful order, which, it seems, it is the formal and thematic goal of epic to posit. Achilles guarantees the fall of Troy. Odysseus restores the proper succession of dominion on Ithaca. The many heroes of the *Faerie Queene* strive against the continuing effects of the Fall. Providential history will culminate in the reestablishment of Paradise. David restores proper rule to Israel. And Belinda finds her humbler but proper place in the great pattern. That pattern was left awry by Adam's fall, and its restitution is the heroic task of all men and all poets since, as Milton realized. That restitution *is* the form and meaning of epic.

III

Aubrey Williams has explained the basic relation of *The Dunciad* to classical epic and has particularly elucidated its adaptation of the *Aeneid* to its own poetic uses.[21] My own study of *The Dunciad* is in many particulars indebted to Williams's seminal work. Pope's use of the notion of the *translatio imperii* and its analogue the *translatio studii* to shadow the spread of Dulness's empire fulfills the idea of restitution we discussed before: in his model, the transference of power involved the restitution of the Trojan empire through Rome; in his own poem, Dulness moves outward from the English Troynovant to reestablish the ancient hegemony of her parents, Chaos and Night. That comprehends the essential action of the poem. The precise means by which Dulness and her dunces accomplish that action are not so easily pinned down.

That Dulness employs Cibber as the spearhead of her campaign is clear. He is the mortal manifestation of Dulness; she sees "her Image full exprest, / . . . chief in Bays's monster-breeding breast" (1.107–8). The precise relationship between Dulness and Cibber is quite crucial to an understanding of the poem, because it is conceived in exact and consistent terms, terms comparable to those Dryden used to conceptualize Flecknoe and Shadwell. Cibber is the Messiah; Dulness is a direct parody of Sapientia, who is most commonly identified with Christ as the Son, the Logos.[22] Thus they are the mortal and immortal forms of the same entity. Evidences of the theological basis of the relationship abound in the poem, from the lines quoted above to Cibber's coronation as "the Antichrist of wit" (2.16) and beyond. This relationship bears relevantly on the action of the poem in that Cibber's status, at the outset, resembles Christ's at the beginning of *Paradise Regained* or Aeneas's before his descent to hell: all these heroes stand at turning points of their lives, aware that in some way they are called, but unclear and unsure to what or for what, and most uncertain about their own identities and roles. None knows he is a hero; none knows what his task will be. Like *Paradise Regained* and the first half of the *Aeneid, The Dunciad* centers its interest on the gradual revelation of its hero's identity and mission.

Cibber's first — and almost his only — action in *The Dunciad* consists of his praying to Dulness to illumine him about his course of action.

> What can I now? my Fletcher cast aside,
> Take up the Bible, once my better guide?
> Or tread the path by venturous Heroes trod,
> This Box my Thunder, this right hand my God?
> Or chaired at White's amidst the Doctors sit,
> Teach Oaths to Gamesters, and to Nobles Wit?
>
> (1. 199–204)

The poem has before this identified Cibber as an incarnation of Dulness (1. 107–8, quoted above); this passage ironically adds to that identification by forcing us to see Cibber, "chair'd . . . amidst the Doctors," as the young Christ in the temple "sitting in the midst of the doctors" (Luke 2:46).[23] The irony does not lie so much in the simple juxtaposition of Christ and Cibber and the inversion of values that represents as it does in Cibber's unawareness of what he has said. The biblical episode includes Christ's direct acknowledgment of his messianic role: "Know ye not that I must be about my father's business?" (Luke 2:49). The whole was traditionally regarded as a foreshadowing of Christ's public life. Cibber, as a true son of Dulness, remains sublimely unaware of the significance of what he is saying. He remains indomitably the private individual, the self-contained and reflexive:

What then remains? Ourself. Still, still remain
Cibberian forehead, and Cibberian brain.
This brazen Brightness, to the Squire so dear;
This polished Hardness, that reflects the Peer:
This arch Absurd, that wit and fool delights;
This Mess, tossed up of Hockley Hole and White's;
Where Dukes and Butchers join to wreathe my crown,
At once the Bear and Fiddle of the town.

(1.217–24)

This privateness and reflexiveness are the very qualities that make him the perfect *public* exponent of Dulness. There follows this prayer a series of recognitions or expositions of Cibber's identity and role. First Dulness responds to his prayer by transporting him to "her sacred Dome" (1.265) where "she plann'd th' Imperial seat of Fools" (1.272). Cibber responds to this by recognizing a correspondence between himself and the place:

Well pleased he entered, and confessed his home.
So Spirits ending their terrestrial race,
Ascend, and recognize their Native Place.

(1.266–68)

The book ends with further adumbration of his role. Dulness anoints and crowns him in a ceremony that simultaneously parodies royal coronations (and should remind us of the corresponding scene in *MacFlecknoe* and the linking there between the protagonists and their locus) and the baptism of Christ.

The Goddess then, o'er his annointed head,
With mystic words, the sacred Opium shed.
And lo! her bird, (a monster of a fowl,
Something betwixt a Heideggre and owl,)
Perch'd on his crown. 'All hail! and hail again,
My son! the promis'd land expects thy reign.'

(1.288–92)

The baptism of Christ signaled the beginning of his public career; Dulness develops the broadest implications of this aspect of the event in her half-question, half-exhortation —

> 'O! when shall rise a Monarch all our own,
> And I, a Nursing-mother, rock the throne,
> 'Twixt Prince and People close the Curtain draw,
> Shade him from Light, and cover him from Law;
> Fatten the Courtier, starve the learned band,
> And suckle Armies, and dry-nurse the land:
> 'Till Senates nod to Lullabies divine,
> And all be sleep, as at an Ode of thine.'
>
> (1.311–18)

Book 2 offers at least a partial realization of Dulness's hope as "the soft gifts of Sleep conclude the day" (2.419) of heroic exercises. The book as a whole functions as a kind of confirmation and beginning of Cibber's public mission. He opens the book enthroned in ludicrous parallel to Satan's "bad eminence":

> High on a gorgeous seat, that far out-shone
> Henley's gilt tub, or Fleckno's Irish throne,
> Or that where on her Curls the Public pours,
> All-bounteous, fragrant Grains and Golden show'rs,
> Great Cibber sate . . .
>
> (2.1–5)

An extended simile makes quite explicit what is implicit above:

> Not with more glee, by hands Pontific crown'd,
> With scarlet hats wide-waving circled round,
> Rome in her Capitol saw Querno sit,
> Thron'd on sev'n hills, the Antichrist of wit.
>
> (2.13–16)

The games that follow this stand in the same relation to Dulness's real purposes that the games in the *Aeneid* do to the tasks of epic heroes: they were rehearsals, exercises in heroic virtue in small — here, almost symbolic adumbrations of the real work of the dunces. The vacuity, the obscenity, the scatology are only signs of what is to come, just as the slumber that closes the book is only a foreshadowing, a miniature, of the great darkness that will close the fourth book. The events of book 2 contain the seeds of this later growth in the form of their presentation. The outward spread of sleep, seemingly confined here to the dunces themselves and only to those under the explicit sway of Dulness, grows in implicit importance when juxtaposed with the passage it parodies:

> Who sate the nearest, by the words o'ercome,
> Slept first; the distant nodded to the hum.
> Then down are rolled the books; stretched o'er 'em lies
> Each gentle clerk, and muttering seals his eyes.
> As what a Dutchman plumps into the lakes,
> One circle first, and then a second makes;
> What Dulness dropped among her sons imprest
> Like motion from one circle to the rest;
> So from the midmost the nutation spreads
> Round and more round, o'er all the sea of Heads.
>
> (2.401–10)

> God loves from Whole to Parts: But human soul
> Must rise from Individual to the Whole.
> Self-love but serves the virtuous mind to wake,
> As the small pebble stirs the peaceful lake;
> The centre moved, a circle straight succeeds,
> Another still, and still another spreads;
> Friend, parent, neighbour, first it will embrace;
> His country next; and next all human race;
> Wide and more wide, th' o'erflowings of the mind
> Take every creature in, of every kind;
> Earth smiles around, with boundless bounty blest,
> And Heav'n beholds its image in his breast.
>
> (*Essay on Man,* 4.361–72)

Dulness converts the expansive flow of love into an expanding tide of inertia, and the circular images in both passages unite in making both acts cosmic or cosmogonic. *The Dunciad* anticipates and supports this in advance by casting Cibber as the sun of his world and by linking that image to a part of Raphael's description of creation in *Paradise Lost*. Here is Pope's image, followed by the passage from Milton:

> All eyes direct their rays
> On him, and crowds turn Coxcombs as they gaze.
> His Peers shine round him with reflected grace,
> New edge their dulness, and new bronze their face.
> So from the Sun's broad beam, in shallow urns
> Heav'ns twinkling Sparks draw light, and point their horns.
> (2.7–12)

> Hither as to thir Fountain other Stars
> Repairing, in thir gold'n Urns draw Light,
> And hence the Morning Planet gilds her horns
> (*Paradise Lost,* 7.364–66)

Cibber's role is a public one, and his coronation here only forms a small part of the function he is to perform. That coronation stands as the first foreshadowing of his real task and eminence, just as the games contain implicitly the real nature of the heroic tasks the dunces are called to.

Book 3 reproduces the conditions of the sixth book of the *Aeneid* and so offers the final and fullest explanation of the hero's goal. Cibber, sound asleep and "refin'd from Reason" (3.6), "on Fancy's easy wing" (3.13) tours the underworld and hears his Anchises, Elkanah Settle, explain the coming wonders of his reign. Like Michael and Adam, they ascend a hill from which they view in space what will transpire in time. They see an ever increasing barbarism spreading out from Cibber ("All nonsense thus, of old or modern date, / Shall in thee centre, from thee circulate" (3.59–60)) to engulf nations, arts, and culture. Goths and Huns enact in kingdoms what modern dunces do in genres, and just as they poured from the frozen north into civilized Europe, so the dunces, with Cibber at their head, erupt from the world of the stage into the stage of the world.

> His never-blushing head he turn'd aside,
> (Not half so pleas'd when Goodman prophesy'd)
> And look'd, and saw a sable Sorc'rer rise,
> Swift to whose hand a winged volume flies:
> All sudden, Gorgons hiss, and Dragons glare,
> And ten-horn'd fiends and Giants rush to war.
> Hell rises, Heav'n descends, and dance on Earth:
> Gods, imps, and monsters, music, rage, and mirth,
> A fire, a jig, a battle, and a ball,
> Till one wide conflagration swallows all.
>   Thence a new world to Nature's laws unknown,
> Breaks out refulgent, with a heav'n of its own:
> Another Cynthia her new journey runs,
> And other planets circle other suns.
> The forests dance, the rivers upward rise,
> Whales sport in woods, and dolphins in the skies;
> And last, to give the whole creation grace,
> Lo! one vast Egg produces human race.
>
> (3.231–48)

These lines describe the creation of an anti-nature, a parody of the apocalyptical new heavens and new earth, conceived of in the terms Horace uses in the *Ars Poetica* to describe the artistic misbegotten. But the process does not stop with art; its spills over into life, into what we call reality. The relationship between the two here is the same as it was in *MacFlecknoe:* bad art distorts fact, remakes reality in its own image. Pope first depicted the process early in book 1 when, in describing Dulness's cave, he also traced the growth of miscreation step by step from hints to sounds, to words, to images, to genres and out beyond these to the world itself.

> Here she beholds the Chaos dark and deep,
> Where nameless Somethings in their causes sleep,
> Till genial Jacob, or a warm Third day,

Call forth each mass, a Poem, or a Play:
How hints, like spawn, scarce quick in embryo lie,
How newborn nonsense first is taught to cry,
Maggots half-form'd in rhyme exactly meet,
And learn to crawl upon poetic feet.
Here one poor word an hundred clenches makes,
And ductile dulness new meanders takes;
There motley Images her fancy strike,
Figures ill pair'd, and Similies unlike.
She sees a Mob of Metaphors advance,
Pleas'd with the madness of the mazy dance;
How Tragedy and Comedy embrace;
How Farce and Epic get a jumbled race
How Time himself stands still at her command,
Realms shift their place, and Ocean turns to land.
Here gay Description Egypt glads with show'rs,
Or gives to Zembla fruits, to Barca flow'rs;
Glitt'ring with ice here hoary hills are seen,
There painted vallies of eternal green,
In cold December fragrant chaplets blow,
And heavy harvests nod beneath the snow.

(1.55–78)

This is the ultimate aim of Dulness — the submission of the universe, the enunciation of the uncreating word. For this task, Cibber is esential: he is the wonder child, the messiah of Dulness who will introduce the "new Saturnian age of Lead" (1.28) — or as Settle phrases it, in a gross inversion of Virgil's messianic eclogue,

This, this is he, foretold by ancient rhymes:
Th'Augustus born to bring Saturnian times.
Signs following signs lead on the mighty year!
See! the dull stars roll round and re-appear.
See, see, our own true Phoebus wears the bays!

(3.319–23)

This explains fully what it means to be the anti-Christ of wit: Cibber must undo Christ's work both as spiritual redeemer and agent of creation. He must reduce the human mind and the universe to inertia by the destruction of form and the subtraction of meaning — no more, no less.

Book 3 leaves us at the same point as book 6 of the *Aeneid:* the hero at last knows the full dimensions of his task, and it now remains for him to fulfill it. Both books 1 and 3 have focused on Cibber's growing awareness of what he must do. Book 2 shadowed some of his works. Book 4 describes the body that cast that shadow and completes the realization of Dulness's kingdom. It is the totally false world created by the false vision that passes through the Ivory Gate of the first three books.

Book 4 presents its vision of chaos within the framework of a perfect symmetry. Pope's opening plea to Dulness to "Suspend a while your Force inertly strong" (4.7) parallels his final futile plea to the Muse to "Relate, who first, who last resign'd to rest" (4.621), after which Dulness "Then take[s] at once the Poet and the Song" (4.8) as "Universal Darkness buries All" (4.656). Inside that outermost frame, matching enumerations of various arts, all extinguished or about to be extinguished, confine and define the action of the poem (4.17–44 and 4. 626–56). The center of the poem opens with the appearance of the "Harlot form" (4.45) of Opera; she pleads with Dulness to banish Handel, to separate sound from sense, to reduce all music, all harmony, to "One Trill" (4.57) so that "To the same notes thy sons shall hum, or snore, / And all thy yawning daughters cry, *encore*" (4.59–60). The central action of the poem ends when Dulness accomplishes exactly that by her yawn (4.605 ff.). Between these two points, *The Dunciad* maps the point-by-point spread of Dulness from the private life to the public, from theory to practice, from personal aberration to cultural derangement.

The action begins with Opera's plea because of the metaphoric value of the notions of music and harmony. The universe is God's poem, God's song, and in desiring to silence the Muses and "let Division reign" (4.53), Opera is seeking to banish the aesthetic and intellectual dimensions of the created universe. She wants to reduce the world to mere physical phenomena — sound without sense, noises of no meaning. The blast of "Fame's posterior Trumpet" (4.71) appropriately follows her speech and summons the dunces to their goddess. Dulness has in them already accomplished part of Opera's prayer: the dunces respond mechanically to physical laws; their motions are governed by physical phenomena.

> None need a guide, by sure Attraction led,
> And strong impulsive gravity of Head:
> None want a place, for all their Centre found,
> Hung to the Goddess, and coher'd around.
> Not closer, orb in orb, conglob'd are seen
> The buzzing Bees about their dusky Queen.
> The gath'ring number, as it moves along,
> Involves a vast involuntary throng,
> Who gently drawn, and struggling less and less,
> Roll in her Vortex, and her pow'r confess.
>
> (4.75–84)

Pope puns insistently on words like "Attraction," "gravity," "Centre," and "Vortex" to demonstrate the process by which Dulness succeeds. The puns move ambiguously between a semi-metaphorical and intellectual meaning and one that is "scientific" and physical. The dunces themselves are tracing exactly the same movement, behaving less and less like rational beings and more and more like simple bodies in motion. They enact the substitution of mechanics for metaphysics, of Descartes's and Newton's world for Aquinas's and Hooker's.[24] The language of Pope's note to the lines makes this process and its implications very clear:

> It ought to be observed that here are three classes in this assembly. The first of men absolutely and avowedly dull, who naturally adhere to the Goddess, and are imaged in the simile of the Bees about their Queen. The second involuntarily drawn to her, tho' not caring to own her influence, from ver. 81 to 90. The third of such, as, tho' not members of her state, yet advance her service by flattering Dulness, cultivating mistaken talents, patronizing vile scriblers, discouraging living merit, or setting up for wits, and Men of taste in arts

they understand not; from ver. 91 to 101. In this new world of Dulness each of these three classes hath its appointed station, as best suits its nature, and concurs to the harmony of the System. The first drawn only by the strong and simple impulse of Attraction, are represented as falling directly down into her; as conglobed into her substance, and resting in her centre.

> *---All their centre found,*
> *Hung to the Goddess, and coher'd around.*

The second, tho' within the sphere of her attraction, yet having at the same time a different motion, they are carried, by the composition of these two, in planetary revolutions round her centre, some nearer to it, some further off:

> *Who gently drawn, and struggling less and less,*
> *Roll in her Vortex, and her pow'r confess.*

The third are properly excentrical, and no constant members of her state or system: sometimes at an immense distance from her influence, and sometimes again almost on the surface of her broad effulgence. Their use in their Perihelion, or nearest approach to Dulness, is the same in the moral World, as that of Comets in the natural, namely to refresh and recreate the Dryness and decays of the system; in the manner marked out from ver. 91 to 98.

The interplay of the poem and its note make explicit here the cosmogonic implications of the allusion at the beginning of book 2. Dulness is genuinely engaged in world-building, in the substitution of her own cosmos for God's. What startles me about this (and I suspect it startled eighteenth century readers as well) is that she undertakes this task as a perfectly orthodox Cartesian. The kinds of planetary motion described, and particularly the presence of the concept of the vortex, are quite sufficient to identify the source of the system described as Descartes's.[25] The question to be answered, of course, is, Why Descartes? To what end? The answer seems to lie in the de facto Cartesian separation of mind from matter and in Descartes's resolutely materialistic explanation of the origin of the universe — the same process that Pope here attributes to Dulness. Descartes provides the theoretical base for Dulness's practice by positing the radical disjunction of mind and matter, thought and thing.[26] For this reason, the dunces' bodies obey the laws of Cartesian physics while their minds — as we shall see — share the essential solipsism of Cartesian philosophy.

The address of the specter-schoolmaster illuminates the process by which comprehension is narrowed and imagination stifled through a further disjunction. His method of education separates words from the substantial meanings they ought to convey; it separates, that is, rhetoric from dialectic and logic.

> Then thus. "Since Man from beast by Words is known,
> Words are Man's province, Words we teach alone.
> When Reason doubtful, like the Samian letter,
> Points him two ways, the narrower is the better.
> Plac'd at the door of Learning, youth to guide,
> We never suffer it to stand too wide.
> To ask, to guess, to know, as they commence,
> As Fancy opens the quick springs of Sense,
> We ply the Memory, we load the brain,
> Bind rebel Wit, and double chain on chain;
> Confine the thought, to exercise the breath;
> And keep them in the pale of Words till death.
> Whate'er the talents, or howe'er designed,
> We hang one jingling padlock on the mind:
> A Poet the first day, he dips his quill;
> And what the last? A very Poet still.
> Pity! the charm works only in our wall,
> Lost, lost too soon in yonder House or Hall.
> There truant WYNDHAM ev'ry Muse gave o'er,
> There TALBOT sunk, and was a Wit no more!
> How sweet an Ovid, MURRAY was our boast!
> How many Martials were in PULT'NEY lost!
> Else sure some Bard, to our eternal praise,
> In twice ten thousand rhyming nights and days,

Had reach'd the Work, the All that mortal can;
And South beheld that Master-piece of Man."

(4.149–74)

The attributes Pope gives to the speaker of these lines help define his role. He is a specter (4.149), Moloch-like ("Dropping with Infant's Blood, and Mother's tears" [4.142]), and he bears Mercury's caduceus (4.140 and Pope's note) — the first of several figures in the poem who shall do so (see 4.347 and 4.637). He is a specter because, literally, he represents the ghost of learning, the disembodiment of education; he is Moloch-like because to his whims children are sacrificed; he bears the caduceus because, like Mercury, with it he guides the souls of the dead, because, like Mercury, he is the mediator, the messenger, between gods and men, and finally because, like Mercury, he is a god both of eloquence and of lies, of, in effect, false wit.[27] His position as schoolmaster enables him to warp the mind right at the outset of education and provide a bias toward words in themselves that will prevent his students from ever reaching behind them to ideas — so his fitness as mediator between Dulness and men. More than this, his function, although primarily to corrupt the private life and destroy the processes of individual thinking, also spills over to corrupt the public life, as his effect upon "The pale Boy-Senator" (4.147) shows. Dulness recognizes this aspect of his work in her reply to him by exclaiming happily about the blessings of "some pedant Reign" (4.175) and the doctrine "which my Priests, and mine alone, maintain . . . The RIGHT DIVINE of Kings to govern wrong" (4.185–88). At this point in the poem, Pope does not stress this matter, but one of the poem's tacit assumptions remains that corruption of education and the private life will inescapably culminate in corruption of the public life, of government, and of human society in general.

   Bentley-Aristarchus carries the undermining of education yet further. Speaking for the critics and simultaneously for the colleges, he describes the reduction of learning from the level of the word to the level of the letter:

Roman and Greek Grammarians! know your Better:

> Author of something yet more great than Letter;
> While tow'ring o'er your Alphabet, like Saul,
> Stands our Digamma, and o'ertops them all.
> 'Tis true, on Words is still our whole debate,
> Disputes of *Me* or *Te*, or *aut* or *at*,
> To sound or sink in *cano*, O or A,
> Or give up Cicero to C or K.
>
> (4.215–22)

What the master critic accomplishes is the total diversion of the human mind from entities to fragments, from language as a conveyor of meaning to language as — literally — *thing* in itself. This results in the production — in a physical sense — of words for their own sakes, words on a page, books conceived as material body rather than repository of ideas.

> For thee we dim the eyes, and stuff the head
> With all such reading as was never read:
> For thee explain a thing till all men doubt it,
> And write about it, Goddess, and about it:
> So spins the silkworm small its slender store,
> And labours till it clouds itself all o'er.
>
> (4.249–54)

Aristarchus appropriately delivers as the final proof of the efficacy of his system the thing itself:

> With the same Cement, ever sure to bind,
> We bring to one dead level ev'ry mind.
> Then take him to develop, if you can,
> And hew the Block off, and get out the Man.
> But wherefore waste I words? I see advance
> Whore, Pupil, and lac'd Governor from France.
>
> (4.267–72)

The pupil has just completed the last step in the educational process, the grand tour. He represents the finished product of Dulness's educational innovations, a paragon of her *vertu,* whom she accepts as a hero (4.335). He has nothing to say.

His tutor does all the talking, and describes a grand tour that schools
the pupil in sensuality and frivolity and erases any last traces of thought
from his head. He

> Dropt the dull lumber of the Latin store,
> Spoil'd his own language, and acquir'd no more;
> All Classic learning lost on Classic ground;
> And last turn'd *Air*, the Echo of a Sound!
> See now, half-cur'd, and perfectly well-bred,
> With nothing but a Solo in his head.
>
> (4.319-24)

He embodies the fulfillment of Opera's prayer and the total evacuation of
intelligibility; he is a form without a content, a body without a mind, and
a hero of Dulness's kingdom. Within the complex mock epic of *The
Dunciad,* the tutor's description of his pupil's tour presents another,
miniature mock epic: the pupil, "the young Aeneas" (4.290),

> The Stews and Palace equally explor'd,
> Intrigu'd with glory, and with spirit whor'd;
> Try'd all *hors d'oeuvres,* all *liqueurs* defin'd,
> Judicious drank, and greatly daring din'd
>
> (4.315–18)

and returned at last to the court of Dulness to insure the restitution and
continuance of her reign (4.330–34). Pope invokes the *Aeneid* here
precisely because of the values that allegorists and commentators like
Landino had seen in it: because it depicted a process of education that
culminated in an individual's attainment of philosophical beatitude,
because it rejected sensuality and worldly dominion for the calm of
contemplation and intellectual self-mastery. This Aeneas reverses that.
He represents the total corruption of the private life, the impossibility of
thought. His journey offered him a series of tests that he progressively
failed and brought him back to his starting point, totally vacuous, to
enlist himself as another minion of Dulness. This episode marks the
completion of the first half of Dulness's undertaking. Words have been

totally separated from meaning; the private life has been completely
devalued. What now remains is the corresponding destruction of the
public life and the undoing of things themselves.

The dunces have now completed their miseducation, and like Cibber
at the end of book 1 are on the point of beginning their public lives. The
poem signals this shift of focus by the presentation of another character
bearing Mercury's wand ("Annius, crafty Seer, with ebon wand" [4.346])
and explicitly linked with that deity ("taught by Hermes, and divinely
bold" [4.381]). This episode apparently centers on a quarrel between
Annius and Mummius about the possession of *things* — specifically
coins — but they speak of the things as deities, matter raised to the level
of divinity. Pope has his characters appropriately convey this by means
of an extended image of a parodic incarnation:

> Then taught by Hermes, and divinely bold,
> Down his own throat he risqu'd the Grecian gold;
> Receiv'd each Demi-God, with pious care,
> Deep in his Entrails — I rever'd them there,
> I bought them, shrouded in that living shrine,
> And, at their second birth, they issue mine.
>
> (4.381–86)

Particular phrases, like "Demi-God," "pious care," "rever'd," charge
the passage with its special significance; "living shrine" establishes the
final field of reference, since it is a formal title and salutation of Christ's
earthly mother and is used as such in the Roman Catholic litany of the
Virgin.[28] Annius's reply to this ratifies these notions:

> "Witness great Ammon! by whose horns I swore,"
> (Reply'd soft Annius) "this our paunch before
> Still bears them, faithful; and that thus I eat,
> Is to refund the Medals with the meat.
> To prove me, Goddess! clear of all design,
> Bid me with Pollio sup, as well as dine:
> There all the Learn'd shall at the labour stand,
> And Douglas lend his soft, obstetric hand."
>
> (4.387–94)

They return to Pollio because he provides the conjunction of the classical and Christian traditions they are perverting: the most notable Pollio of classical literature is the Pollio of Virgil's fourth eclogue, the messianic eclogue, in whose consulship will be born the wonder child who will reintroduce the Saturnian age. Douglas's "soft, obstetric hand" completes the travesty: "(God's) obstetric hand brought forth the winding serpent" (Job 26:13, Douai and Vulgate). Biblical commentators take the serpent for many things, among them Satan himself.[29]

The appearance of this episode at this point in *The Dunciad* signifies many things. By its very nature, it indicates a shift of Dulness's activities from the private realm she has by this time totally pervaded to the public world of human activity and social intercourse. The coins themselves hint of the money obsession of that world; the emphasis on collection and acquisition demonstrates its absorption in things for themselves as separate from any meaning the things might possess. The theological and classical framework against which these are played indicates the extent to which all this opposes the spirit of Christian culture and the extent to which it is simultaneously blasphemous and inhuman. Beyond this, the allusions show in very precise detail the process Dulness is now initiating. The incarnation provides the nexus of spiritual and material: the word is made flesh. In the most literal sense, that is what the episode tokens in *The Dunciad*. Dulness has already thoroughly corrupted language and she is now turning her attention to the degradation of material objects. This involves the contrary but simultaneous motions of exaltation and debasement. The coins become the demigods whose images they bear and usurp a spiritual dimension to which they have no claim. At the same time, their ascension is contradicted by their incarnation, and they become excrement. Rather than bearers of life, they are the by-products of life — waste, inert matter reduced to its lowest common denominator. Exaltation of matter provides Dulness's method; the reduction of it to lifeless extension and mass explains her goal. She seeks to parallel publicly and in matter what she has accomplished privately and in mind. All this, of course, works out in greater detail exactly the same web of ideas we have already encountered in *MacFlecknoe*.

Dulness forms her attack on two fronts, one the kind of specialization and fragmentariness of vision exemplified by Annius and Mummius and later by the botanist and butterfly-collector, and the other the kind of generalization that substitutes fragments for system, as does the "gloomy Clerk" (4.459). Both of these end in a corrupted conception of Nature as atomistic. Both substitute parts for wholeness — a point that Dulness herself stresses:

> "O! would the Sons of Men once think their Eyes
> And Reason giv'n them but to study *Flies*!
> See Nature in some partial narrow shape,
> And let the Author of the Whole escape:
> Learn but to trifle; or, who most observe,
> To wonder at their Maker, not to serve!"
>
> (4.452–58)

The "gloomy Clerk" offers the theoretical basis for this in Lucretius's indifferent deity or, alternatively, in the pervasive but amorphous object of Shaftesbury's soft-headed enthusiasm.

> Oh hide the God still more! and make us see
> Such as Lucretius drew, a God like Thee:
> Wrapt up in Self, a God without a Thought,
> Regardless of our merit or default.
> Or that bright Image to our fancy draw,
> Which Theocles in raptur'd vision saw,
> While thro' Poetic scenes the Genius roves,
> Or wanders wild in Academic Groves;
> That NATURE our Society adores,
> Where Tindal dictates, and Silenus snores.
>
> (4.483–92)

Both are projections of the human ego, extrapolations of finite conceptions that make God in man's image rather than man in God's.

> All-seeing in thy mists, we want no guide,
> Mother of Arrogance, and Source of Pride!

> We nobly take the high Priori Road,
> And reason downward, till we doubt of God:
> Make Nature still encroach upon his plan,
> And shove him off as far as e'er we can:
> Thrust some Mechanic Cause into his place;
> Or bind in Matter, or diffuse in Space.
> Or, at one bound o'erleaping all his laws,
> Make God Man's Image, Man the final Cause,
> Find Virtue local, all Relation scorn,
> See all in *Self,* and but for self be born:
> Of naught so certain as our *Reason* still,
> Of naught so doubtful as of *Soul* and *Will.*
>
> (4.469–82)

These passages extend the process of materialization further into creation, constantly reducing the role of spirit and mind. The "Mechanic Cause" thrust into God's place links up intelligibly with the Cartesian creation that opened book 4 and marks the process by which matter usurps the function of mind. Pope parallels this in the passages in question by a simultaneous allusive retracing of the path of history, moving steadily backward toward the point of creation. From the incarnation presented in the Annius and Mummius episode, the poem jumps back to Eve's account of her creation and the first object that interested her, herself:

> As I bent down to look, just opposite,
> A Shape within the wat'ry gleam appear'd
> Bending to look on me, I started back,
> It started back, but pleas'd I soon return'd,
> Pleas'd it return'd as soon with answering looks
> Of sympathy and love . . . .
>
> *(Paradise Lost,* 4.461–65)

Pope recreates this situation in his butterfly-collector's account of the pursuit of his quarry:

> I saw, and started from its vernal bow'r
> The rising game, and chac'd from flow'r to flow'r.
> It fled, I follow'd; now in hope, now pain;
> It stopt, I stopt; it mov'd, I mov'd again.
>
> (4.425–28)[30]

A line in the Clerk's speech — "Or at one bound o'er-leaping all his laws" (4.477) — invokes Milton's description of Satan's entrance into Eden — "At one slight bound high overleap'd all bound" (4.181). The poem reaches the creation point with Silenus, who "shook from out his Pipe the seeds of fire" (4.494). Pope's own notes to the poem insist on Silenus's identification as the Epicurean teacher of Virgil's sixth eclogue, where he gives an Epicurean account of the creation of the world from the seeds of fire, earth, air, and water. He has a twofold function in *The Dunciad:* to unite in one figure and one hypothesis — atomism — all of the various theories — Cartesian, Hobbesian, Lucretian — offering "Mechanic Causes" instead of spiritual principles, and to extend the power of those causes to the work of creation itself, thus banishing mind and spirit retroactively from the origin of the universe. He brings Dulness one step closer to the total removal of God, one step closer to the state of chaos that existed *before* creation, before the informing word of divine wisdom imposed form on matter. To this point in the poem, Dulness has succeeded in separating thought and thing, in enmeshing thought further in the trap of language conceived of as thing, and in reducing language from expression of thought to random conglomeration of letters and sounds; she has made matter the principal component of the universe and further reduced that matter to a random conglomeration of atoms, hostile to the impress of mind and obedient only to mechanical laws. Silenus describes the same process of reduction at work in the human sphere, contracting human beings from their intellectual potentiality to a servitude to the basest forms of matter.

> Then thus. "From Priest-craft happily set free,
> Lo! ev'ry finish'd Son returns to thee:
> First slave to Words, then vassal to a Name,

Then dupe to Party; child and man the same;
Bounded by Nature, narrow'd still by Art,
A trifling head, and a contracted heart.
Thus bred, thus taught, how many have I seen,
Smiling on all, and smil'd on by a Queen.
Mark'd out for Honours, honour'd for their Birth,
To thee the most rebellious things on earth:
Now to thy gentle shadow all are shrunk,
All melted down, in Pension, or in Punk!
So K* so B** sneak'd into the grave,
A Monarch's half, and half a Harlot's slave.
Poor W** nipt in Folly's broadest bloom,
Who praises now? his Chaplain on his Tomb.
Then take them all, oh take them to thy breast!
Thy *Magus,* Goddess! shall perform the rest."
                                            (4.499–516)

The Magus competes the task by means of his potion, which banishes consciousness totally and leaves only a human form existing in and for matter.

With that, a WIZARD OLD his *Cup* extends;
Which whoso tastes, forgets his former friends,
Sire, Ancestors, Himself. One casts his eyes
Up to a *Star*, and like Endymion dies:
A *Feather*, shooting from another's head,
Extracts his brain; and Principle is fled;
Lost is his God, his Country, ev'rything;
And nothing left but Homage to a King!
The vulgar herd turn off to roll with Hogs,
To run with Horses, or to hunt with Dogs;
But, sad example! never to escape
Their Infamy, still keep the human shape.
                                            (4.517–28)

The cup, of course, is Circe's cup, and the human shapes rolling with hogs an ironic reversal of Circe's ability to transform the body while the mind remained untouched. In this same section, Pope quickly invokes two other episodes from Odysseus's journey — the Cimmerians and the Sirens (4.532, 541). The whole section, from the introduction of Silenus forward, corresponds to the episode of the tutor and pupil returned from the Great Tour earlier in the poem. Silenus, too, is a tutor who introduces a band of youths to the goddess and addresses her on their behalf. Pope makes the situations parallel and reintroduces the imagery of the epic journey because this later scene presents the final corruption of the public life as an exact analogue to the earlier scene's presentation of the corruption of the private. He invokes the figure of Odysseus rather than Aeneas because (in addition to the fact that he has already used Aeneas as exemplar of the private virtues) Odysseus is the one epic figure explicitly and unwaveringly loyal to country, family, and self, and the one epic figure whose final actions clearly result in the reassumption of his rightful identity and the reunification of his family and kingdom, all presided over and blessed by Wisdom herself in the form of Athene. The dunces here precisely reverse this set of values: the Magus's cup brings forgetfulness of friends, sire, ancestors, self, brain, principle, god, country, everything — "And nothing left but Homage to a King" (4.524). These lines eradicate every possibility of public virtue, of sensible government, of honorable society.

The Magus passage also marks the beginning of what Pope calls "the celebration of the *greater Mysteries* of the Goddess" (note to 4.517), which involve initiation and consequent transformation. The transformations involve increasingly great reductions in activity, both of mind and body, reaching toward an ultimate point of total inertia, from

> The vulgar herd turn off to roll with Hogs,
> To run with Horses, or to hunt with Dogs
> (4.525–26)

down to

> Others the Syren Sisters warble round,
> And empty heads console with empty sound.

No more, alas! the voice of Fame they hear,
The balm of Dulness trickling in their ear.
(4.541–44)

After this, "a Priest succinct in amice white" (4.549) celebrates the ultimate mystery, the transformation and reduction of matter itself.

On some, a Priest succinct in amice white
Attends; all flesh is nothing in his sight!
Beeves, at his touch, at once to jelly turn,
And the huge Boar is shrunk into an Urn:
The board with specious miracles he loads,
Turns Hares to Larks, and Pigeons into Toads.
Another (for in all what one can shine?)
Explains the *Seve* and *Verdeur* of the Vine.
What cannot copious sacrifice atone?
Thy Treuffles, Perigord! thy Hams, Bayonne!
With French Libation, and Italian Strain,
Wash Bladen white, and expiate Hays's stain.
Knight lifts the head, for what are crowds undone
To three essential Partriges in one?
(4.549–62)

The form of the mystery draws upon the mass, principally the consecration and transubstantiation of the Host as celebrated in the Roman rite. "Three essential partriges in one" parodies the relationship of the persons of the Trinity, Father, Son, and Holy Spirit, each separate and distinct, yet all forming one being. This element is present here because in transubstantiation the Host is converted into the Body and Blood of Christ, and since Christ is both man and god, second person of the Trinity, the whole Trinity is present in the form of the Host. The appearance of the Host is unchanged, but its actuality is radically altered. The celebrant here in effect reverses the process and reaches upward through matter to alter the nature and substance of divinity. The mystery is not that he "Turns Hares to Larks, and Piegons into Toads" but that he reduces God to matter; the central mystery is the transubstantiation of spirit into "three essential Partriges in one." Dulness materializes spirit, while at the same time subtracting from matter all properties save extension and mass. Everything else, everything mutable, she eliminates — a thorough Cartesian to the last. After this, there is nothing else for her to do except welcome her initiates and send them off to their final task, to extend this mystery to all creation, to find or to make the leader who "shall three Estates command, / And MAKE ONE MIGHTY DUNCIAD OF THE LAND" (4.603–4).

Dulness has reached the moment of uncreation, signaled once again in the poem by Hermes' wand, this time cosmically extinguishing the stars (IV.637–38). She yawns the uncreating word that will restore the empire of Chaos, and the yawn *is* the uncreating word. It antithesizes the divine fiat by which the world was created; it is unarticulated vocal breath, sound without substance or form, that subtracts form from the universe. It restores Chaos because it *is* chaos; yawn and gulf (*chaos*) share in Greek a common root, and the yawning gulf of Chaos that Pope here describes darkly translates them both. This is the way the world ends, not with a bang but a pun.

IV

The poem ends with Chaos because chaos is material and what Pope has described is a world increasingly immersed in matter.[31] By and large, he has employed Cartesian conceptions to convey his vision of the disjunction of mind from matter and the gradual triumph of mindless matter. For this reason, the poem concludes with fully realized inertia: for Descartes, the only true property of matter is extension. Even motion is alien to it, and is consequently eliminated at the end of *The Dunciad*. The few brief mentions of Lucretius and Epicurus serve primarily to locate Cartesian physics within the general framework of an atheistic atomism, with its consequent implications of fragmentary and chaotic materialism, a cosmos without form or plan. But the Cartesian system offered Pope the sustaining myth or metaphor he needed to depict in orthodox epic form the complete inversion of orthodox epic subject matter. If Wisdom is the patron deity of epic heroes, Dulness is certainly her appropriate perversion, and materialism, broadly and philosophically considered, her sustaining creed. In that sense, *The Dunciad* is not mock epic but epic — and its final, apocalyptic lines, the requiem for a culture, are epic in any sense. Pope was not unique either in seeing materialism as the Damoclean sword of his civilization or in perceiving the connection between the tenets of contemporary physics and the wisdom of traditional epic. Swift anticipated him in both and dealt with both even more elaborately, and it is to Swift that we must now turn our attention.

1. Pope links his *Windsor Forest* with *Paradise Lost* through his comparison of the forest with "The Groves of *Eden*," which still "look green in Song" (7–8) and most explicitly through his concluding plea to Granville to write the great English national epic (423–34). *Windsor Forest* is, of course, itself a georgic, and is linked to Virgil's Georgics by numerous allusions and imitations.

2. For the importance of Catullus to *The Rape of the Lock*, see Earl R. Wasserman's fine "The Limits of Allusion in *The Rape of the Lock*," *JEGP* 65 (1966): 425–44.

3. *The Republic of Plato*, trans. F. M. Cornford (New York, 1963), 10.600, p. 331.

4. See, for example, Sidney's *Defence of Poesie*, or Tasso's remarks quoted in chapter 1.

5. *Essay on Human Understanding*, 2.23.2.

6. Ralph Cohen, in "The Augustan Mode in English Poetry," *Eighteenth-Century Studies* 1 (1967): 3–32, argues that these lines present "an inverted prospect" (p. 12). It seems to me that the "prospect" is not inverted at all, culminating as it does in a fully realized microcosm. Rather, the serious flaw would appear to be the prospect itself, "implying a world locatable in Newtonian space and time, leading (though not necessarily) to an infinity beyond man's comprehension" (p. 31): these are the very aspects of the prospect that Pope apparently regards with horror and that made it a natural vehicle for Belinda's perversion of art into material, time-bound artificiality. Thus I would have to argue that in Pope's view — and implicitly in Dryden's and Swift's — the prospect is not one of the major modes of Augustan poetry, but one of the threats to it.

7. Reprinted in the Twickenham Edition, 2:205.

8. The irony of this is not simply the "Earthly lover lurking at her Heart" (3.144), but also that Belinda becomes, by winning the card game, "the Man."

9. That the metamorphosis has a linguistically sound base is, I think, part of Pope's point. Greek *komes*, hair = English comet.

10. Classical scholars have discerned similar structural patterns (which they refer to as "ring composition") in Homer, and Cedric H. Whitman, in his chapter "Geometric Structure of The Iliad" (*Homer and the Heroic Tradition* [Cambridge, Mass., 1958] pp. 249–84), describes a pattern very similar to the one I am positing here.

11. Compare the passage from *The Sphere of Sacrobosco* quoted in chapter 1, note 22.

12. Edgar Wind, *Pagan Mysteries in the Renaissance* (New Haven, Conn., 1958),

pp. 39 ff. An example: "To expound the system in all of its ramifications, Pico required several hundred *Conclusiones*. . . . All we must remember is that the bounty bestowed by the gods upon lower beings was conceived by the Neoplationists as a kind of overflowing (*emanatio*), which produced a vivifying rapture or conversion (called by Ficino *conversio, raptio,* or *vivificatio*) whereby the lower beings were drawn back to heaven and rejoined the gods (*remeatio*). The munificence of the gods having thus been unfolded in the triple rhythm of *emanatio, raptio* and *remeatio,* it was possible to recognize in this sequence the divine model of what Seneca had defined as the circle of grace: giving, accepting, and returning" (p.40).

13. The readiest comparison is with the process Joseph Campbell and many others describe as departure, initiation, and return: see, for example, *The Hero with a Thousand Faces,* chapters 1 through 3.

14. "Every psychological extreme secretly contains its own opposite or stands in some sort of intimate and essential relation to it. Indeed, it is from this tension that it derives its peculiar dynamism. There is no hallowed custom that cannot on occasion turn into its opposite, and the more extreme a position is, the more easily we may expect an enantiodromia, a conversion of something into its opposite" (C. G. Jung, *Symbols of Transformation* [New York, 1962], vol. 2, chap. 7.581, p. 375).

15. The misunderstanding of the container starts taking place when Landino gives priority to the journey and is compounded when the aesthetics of the sublime are tacked onto epic.

16. *Paradise Lost* may provide a parallel: there the twelve books are palindromatic, and smaller units within the whole are also, in themselves, palindromatic.

17. For the importance of the Hercules myth to book 5, see the extended discussion by Thomas K. Dunseath in *Spenser's Allegory of Justice in Book Five of the Faerie Queene* (Princeton, N.J., 1968).

18. For an exposition of the synchronicity of events in *Paradise Lost,* see A. R. Cirillo's "Noon-Midnight and the Temporal Structure of *Paradise Lost," ELH* 29 (1962): 372–95.

19. See Hägin, *The Epic Hero and the Decline of Heroic Poetry.*

20. See Cirillo, "Noon-Midnight and the Temporal Structure of *Paradise Lost."*

21. *Pope's Dunciad: A Study of its Meaning* (New Haven, Conn., and London, 1955).

22. The most readily available sources of information about Wisdom as theological entity are the introduction and commentary in *John Donne: The Anniversaries,* ed. Frank Manley (Baltimore, 1963) and Charles S. Singleton's *Dante Studies 2: Journey to Beatrice* (Cambridge, Mass., 1958).

23. For a full exposition of this allusion, see David M. Vieth's "Pope's *Dunciad,* I, 203–4, and Christ among the Elders," *PLL* 2 (1966): 71–73. I have here and in the following few pages made use of several of Vieth's suggestions.

24. On this point see Robert Hugh Kargon's *Atomism in England from Hariot to Newton* (Oxford, 1966), E. J. Dijksterhuis' *The Mechanization of the World Picture,* trans. C. Dikshoorn (Oxford, 1961), and S. L. Bethell's *The Cultural Revolution of the Seventeenth Century* (London, 1951).

25. The passage draws particularly heavily on chapter 8 of the *Traité de la Monde* and on Descartes's subsequent description of the origins of planets and comets.

26. That this is an oversimplification of Descartes's thought I am fully aware; but it is

also quite true to the implications of his ideas.

27. See David R. Hauser's "Medea's Strain and Hermes' Wand: Pope's Use of Mythology," *MLN* 76 (1961): 224–29, for more information about Pope's use of the figure. It is important to remember in this connection that Hermes' wand appears as one of the world-extinguishing forces at the end of the poem.

28. I have borrowed several ideas here from Jessie Rhodes Chambers, "The Episode of Annius and Mummius: *Dunciad* IV. 347–96," *PQ* 43 (1964): 185–92.

29. See, for instance, Cornelius à Lapide, Commentary on Job.

30. Pope's own note to these lines calls attention to the Miltonic allusion.

31. For more information about the material nature of Chaos, see A. B. Chambers's "Chaos in *Paradise Lost*," *JHI* 24 (1963): 55–84.

*TALE OF A TUB* is among the most extraordinary works in any literature, and it is something of a standing wonder to me that any of our clichés about Augustanism have survived the simple fact of its existence. The period bracketed by *A Tale of a Tub* and *Tristram Shandy* cannot constitute a literary Age of Reason. For all that, the *Tale* is a thoroughly Augustan work, having important links with both *The Rape of the Lock* and *The Dunciad* and with the same body of materials that lies behind them. Its concerns resemble those of Pope's poems: in its radical disjunction of form and content it links intelligibly with *The Rape of the Lock;* in its employment of a pervasive materialism as a central metaphor it connects with *The Dunciad*. The same process of reification that informed *Dunciad* 4 proceeds also in the *Tale*:

> However, for this Meddly of Humor, he made a Shift to find a very plausible Name, honoring it with the Title of *Zeal*; which is, perhaps, the most significant Word that hath been ever yet produced in any Language; As, I think, I have fully proved in my excellent *Analytical* Discourse upon that Subject; wherein I have deduced a *Histori-theo-physi-logical* Account of *Zeal*, shewing how it first proceeded from a *Notion* into a *Word*, and from thence in a hot Summer, ripned into a *tangible Substance*. (6.86)

The growth of notions into words in the *Tale* briefly summarizes the spread of Dulness from Cibber's leaden works to the great work of the achieved leaden age: ontogeny recapitulates phylogeny. That is the relation of *A Tale of a Tub* to the epic ancestors we have been studying.

I

Swift's manipulation of materialism here both resembles and differs from Pope's use of it. As in *The Dunciad,* it provides a control and a touchstone for the central concerns of the book. Such plot as there is depends entirely upon the "thingness" of the will and the coats — the will as a collection of words, syllables, and letters to be sorted and arranged to produce the desired meanings, the coats as a surface to be filled up to produce the desired appearance. Peter's search through the will *totidem literis* reduces it and its contents effectively to manipulable objects; Jack's use of it as an umbrella merely ratifies this. At the extremes, the opposites meet: Peter's total disregard for the literal meaning of the will evacuates it of meaning and makes of it only a piece of paper; Jack's exaggerated respect for its literal meaning makes it no more or no less than that. The real will, like the Scriptures it represents, is a *tertium quid* that responds neither to literalizing nor to allegorizing but provides the nexus of both, just as the coats, for the reader, are transparently coats and Christian faith at one and the same time.

Metaphor — human language — causes all the difficulty. In one sense bread is the staff of life that Peter claims it is; in another sense, it is not *"excellent good Mutton"* (4). So, too, Jack's "fair Copy of his Father's *Will"*: it both is and is not *"Meat, Drink and Cloth, . . . the Philosopher's Stone, and the Universal Medicine"* (11). Neither Peter nor Jack nor the narrator of *A Tale of a Tub* seems able to grasp this aspect of language, and as a result, language seems always to be slipping away from them, to become either a series of hieroglyphs to be arranged and interpreted according to the whim of the critic or to become a parchment to be carried, worn, consumed, and so on. Jack's attitude toward the will matches the narrator's toward the "universal System in a small portable Volume" (5), for which he gives a recipe; contradictorily, the narrator's pursuit of the allegory of the ass (3) corresponds to Peter's hunt in the will for those elusive shoulder knots (2). This failure of all three to recognize the true nature of language derives from the narrator's more fundamental failure to see the duality of human nature as a linking of corporeal and spiritual, and leads in turn to the two antithetical metaphysical systems of the *Tale*, Sartorism and Aeolism.

Sartorism offers a philosophy of outsides. It glorifies the external, the surface to be filled and adorned. Sartorism provides the compelling necessity for altering the three brothers' coats, for overlaying them with shoulder knots and filigree and silver points, just as it offers the adequate explanation of the overdecorated and fabulous nature of Grubaean art.

> In consequence of these momentous Truths, the *Grubaean* Sages have always chosen to convey their Precepts and their Arts, shut up within the Vehicles of Types and Fables, which having been perhaps more careful and curious in adorning, than was altogether necessary, it has fared with these Vehicles after the usual Fate of Coaches over-finely painted and gilt; that the transitory Gazers have so dazzled their Eyes, and fill'd their Imaginations with the outward Lustre, as neither to regard nor consider, the Person or the Parts of the Owner within. A Misfortune we undergo with somewhat less Reluctancy, because it has been common to us with *Pythagoras, Aesop, Socrates,* and other of our Predecessors. (1.40)

Moreover, Sartorism provides a refuge from reason with its "Tools for cutting, and opening, and mangling, and piercing," "which enters into the Depth of Things, and then comes gravely back with Informations and Discoveries, that in the inside they are good for nothing." Analytical thinking ends in uncovering the "many unsuspected Faults" of the beau and the sadly altered carcass of the woman flayed (9), whereas Sartorism offers to the believer a universe dressed for show, from the "fine Coat faced with Green," which is land, to the "fine Doublet of white Satin . . . worn by the *Birch*" (2).

Swift has fashioned Sartorism as a kind of parody of Hobbism: the paragraph of rhetorical questions that describes land as a green coat and sea as a "Wastcoat of Water-Tabby" (2) alludes to, and satirizes, the rhetorically and logically similar opening of *Leviathan.*[1]

Nature, the art whereby God hath made and governs the world, is by the *art* of man, as in many other things, so in this also imitated, that it can make an artificial animal. For seeing life is but a motion of limbs, the beginning whereof is in some principal part within; why may we not say, that all *automata* (engines that move themselves by springs and wheels as doth a watch) have an artificial life? For what is the *heart*, but a *spring*; and the *nerves*, but so many *strings*; and the *joints*, but so many *wheels*, giving motion to the whole body, such as was intended by the artificer? *Art* goes yet further, imitating that rational and most excellent work of nature, *man*. For by art is created that great LEVIATHAN called a COMMONWEALTH, or STATE, in Latin CIVITAS, which is but an artificial man; though of greater stature and strength than the natural, for whose protection and defence it was intended; and in which the *sovereignty* is an artificial *soul*, as giving life and motion to the whole body; the *magistrates,* and other *officers* of judicature and execution, artificial *joints; reward* and *punishment,* by which fastened to the seat of sovereignty every joint and member is moved to perform his duty, are the *nerves,* that do the same in the body natural; the *wealth* and *riches* of all the particular members, are the *strength; salus populi,* the *people's safety,* its *business, counsellors,* by whom all things needful for it to know are suggested unto it, are the *memory, equity,* and *laws,* an artificial *reason* and *will; concord, health; sedition, sickness,* and *civil war, death.* Lastly, the *pacts* and *covenants,* by which the parts of this body politic were at first made, set together, and united, resemble that *fiat,* or the *let us make man,* pronounced by God in the creation.[2]

Hobbes's argument is reductive in two ways: his mechanical metaphors (which are only half metaphors on their way to being taken literally, like the metaphors of *A Tale of a Tub*) reduce human life and human beings to purely material, physically explicable phenomena; and God's activity, for all its prominence in the first and last sentences, is very strictly paralleled with, if not equated to, man's own devices. Swift incorporates both points into his parody and makes them the basis of Sartorism. God is clearly a human artificer, and he creates artificial animals — clothes that are souls — which then possess life (if life is defined as "but a motion of limbs, the beginning whereof is in some principal part within"). Swift carries the process of materialization to its logical conclusion by a strict literalization of all metaphor:

> The Worshippers of this Deity had also a System of their Belief, which seemed to turn upon the following Fundamental. They held the Universe to be a large *Suit of Cloaths,* which *invests* every Thing: That the Earth is *invested* by the Air; The Air is *invested* by the Stars; and the Stars are *invested* by the *Primum Mobile.* Look on this Globe of Earth, you will find it to be a very compleat and fashionable *Dress.* What is that which some call *Land,* but a fine Coat faced with Green? or the Sea, but a Wastcoat of Water-Tabby? Proceed to the particular Works of the Creation, you will find how curious *Journey-man* Nature hath been, to trim up the *vegetable* Beaux: Observe how sparkish a Perewig adorns the Head of a *Beech,* and what a fine Doublet of white Satin is worn by the *Birch.* To conclude from all, what is Man himself but a *Micro-Coat,* or rather a compleat Suit of Cloaths with all its Trimmings? As to his Body, there can be no dispute; but examine even the Acquirements of his Mind, you will find them all contribute in their Order, towards furnishing out an exact Dress: To instance no more; Is not Religion a *Cloak,* Honest a *Pair of Shoes,* worn out in the Dirt, Self-love a *Surtout,* Vanity a *Shirt,* and Conscience a *Pair of Breeches,* which, tho' a Cover for Lewdness as well as Nastiness, is easily slipt down for the Service of both. (2.46)

What lies behind all this, of course, are the ancient metaphor of the body as the clothing of the soul and its somewhat younger corollary of style as the dress of thought.[3] Swift's narrator and Swift's satire materialize and mechanize both of these, so that *"Embroidery, was Sheer Wit"* (2) and art, in effect, "the Assistance of Artificial *Mediums,* false Lights, refracted Angles, Varnish, and Tinsel" (9) to cover the otherwise insipid objects of the world and to make men happy. This results in the narrator's thinking of everything in his world not only as an object, but as an object that exists primarily as a surface to be covered: the body requires clothing, books need long introductions, fables necessitate elaborate allegories.[4] Anything possessing a point, be it reason or satire, may not be allowed to pierce the surface — thus his disclaimer of having "neither a Talent nor an Inclination for Satyr" (The Preface) and his preference for general satire over particular: "Tis but a *Ball* bandied to and fro, and every Man carries a *Racket* about Him to strike it from himself among the rest of the Company" (The Preface). His own summation of the consequences of his position says it best:

> In the Proportion that Credulity is a more peaceful Posses-
> sion of the Mind, than Curiosity, so far preferable is that
> Wisdom, which converses about the Surface, to that pre-
> tended Philosophy which enters into the Depth of Things,
> and then comes gravely back with Informations and Dis-
> coveries, that in the inside they are good for nothing. The two
> Senses, to which all Objects first address themselves, are the
> Sight and the Touch; These never examine farther than the
> Colour, the Shape, the Size, and whatever other Qualities
> dwell, or are drawn by Art upon the Outward of Bodies; and
> then comes Reason officiously, with Tools for cutting, and
> opening, and mangling, and piercing, offering to demon-
> strate, that they are not of the same consistence quite thro'.
> Now, I take all this to be the last Degree of perverting Nature;
> one of whose Eternal Laws it is, to put her best Furniture
> forward. And therefore, in order to save the Charges of all
> such expensive Anatomy for the Time to come; I do here
> think fit to inform the Reader, that in such Conclusions as
> these, Reason is certainly in the Right; and that in most
> Corporeal Beings, which have fallen under my Cognizance,
> the *Outside* hath been infinitely preferable to the *In*: Whereof
> I have been farther convinced from some late Experiments.
> Last Week I saw a Woman *flay'd,* and you will hardly
> believe, how much it altered her Person for the worse. Yes-
> terday I ordered the Carcass of a *Beau* to be stript in my

Presence; when we were all amazed to find so many unsuspected Faults under one Suit of Cloaths; Then I laid open his
Brain, his *Heart*, and his *Spleen*; But, I plainly perceived at
every Operation, that the farther we proceeded, we found the
Defects encrease upon us in Number and Bulk: from all
which, I justly formed this Conclusion to my self; That
whatever Philosopher or Projector can find out an Art to
sodder and patch up the Flaws and Imperfections of Nature,
will deserve much better of Mankind, and teach us a more
useful Science, than that so much in present Esteem, of
widening and exposing them (like him who held *Anatomy* to
be the ultimate End of *Physick*.) And he, whose Fortunes and
Dispositions have placed him in a convenient Station to enjoy
the Fruits of this noble Art; He that can with *Epicurus*
content his Ideas with the *Films* and *Images* that fly off upon
his Senses from the *Superficies* of Things; Such a Man truly
wise, creams off Nature, leaving the Sower and the Dregs, for
Philosophy and Reason to lap up. This is the sublime and
refined Point of Felicity, called, *the Possession of being
well deceived;* The Serene Peaceful State of being a Fool
among Knaves. (9.109–10)

Directly contradictory to all this is the narrator's apparent fondness for
Jack and for Aeolism, for the doctrine of (somewhat loosely) the inner
light and the philosophy of insides. Aeolism depends in its very rudi-
ments upon the contents of its vessels, male and female, for its doctrine
and practice.

At other times were to be seen several Hundreds link'd
together in a circular Chain, with every Man a Pair of Bellows
applied to his Neighbour's Breech, by which they blew up
each other to the Shape and Size of a *Tun*; and for that
Reason, with great Propriety of Speech, did usually call their
Bodies, their *Vessels*. When, by these and the like Perfor-
mances, they were grown sufficiently replete, they would
immediately depart, and disembogue for the Publick Good, a
plentiful Share of their Acquirements into their Disciples

> Chaps. . . . At which Junctures, all their *Belches* were re-
> ceived for Sacred, the Sourer the better, and swallowed with
> infinite Consolation by their meager Devotes. And to render
> these yet more compleat, because the Breath of Man's Life is
> in his Nostrils, therefore, the choicest, most edifying, and
> most enlivening *Belches,* were very wisely conveyed thro'
> that Vehicle, to give them a Tincture as they passed. (8.96–
> 97)

This parodic inspiration closely resembles the narrator's own notions of
the development and flowering of that noblest of all human states,
madness, which, as he describes it, arises as well from an inward vapor.

> For great Turns are not always given by strong Hands, but by
> lucky Adaptation, and at proper Seasons; and it is of no
> import, where the Fire was kindled, if the Vapor has once got
> up into the Brain. For the *upper Region* of Man, is furnished
> like the *middle Region* of the Air; The Materials are formed
> from Causes of the widest Difference, yet produce at last the
> same Substance and Effect. Mists arise from the Earth,
> Steams from Dunghils, Exhalations from the Sea, and Smoak
> from Fire; yet all Clouds are the same in Composition, as well
> as Consequences; and the Fumes issuing from a Jakes, will
> furnish as comely and useful a Vapor, as Incense from an
> Altar. Thus far, I suppose, will easily be granted me; and then
> it will follow, that as the Face of Nature never produces Rain,
> but when it is overcast and disturbed, so Human Understand-
> ing, seated in the Brain, must be troubled and overspread by
> Vapours, ascending from the lower Faculties, to water the
> Invention, and render it fruitful. Now, altho' these Vapours
> (as it hath been already said) are of as various Original, as
> those of the Skies, yet the Crop they produce, differs both in
> Kind and Degree, merely according to the Soil. (9.102–3)

And the effects of these vapors are "those two great Blessings,
Conquests and *Systems*" (9.107) — among the latter, of course, Sartorism and Aeolism themselves.

The beliefs of Aeolism are not as distant from Sartorism as they at first sight appear: both are materialist philosophies, equally dependent upon a resolutely corporeal understanding of what is meant by soul. Aeolism literalizes metaphoric language — witness "spirit" and "inspiration" — as insistently as does Sartorism. And if we recall Sartorism's point of origin in Hobbes, the resemblance grows even stronger. The narrator explains inspiration, intuition, vision, and madness in a purely mechanical way, making of human beings comic steam engines churning out, and churned by, vapors. Hobbes claimed that "life is but a motion of limbs, the beginning whereof is in some principal part within," and went on to ask "what is the *heart* but a *spring*, and the *nerves* but so many *strings*, and the *joints* but so many *wheels* giving motion to the whole body such as was intended by the artificer?" The narrator of the *Tale* inquires similarly about a particular instance of madness:

> Now is the Reader exceeding curious to learn, from whence this *Vapour* took its Rise, which had so long set the Nations at a Gaze? What secret Wheel, what hidden Spring could put into Motion so wonderful an Engine? It was afterwards discovered, that the Movement of this whole Machine had been directed by an absent *Female*, whose Eyes had raised a Protuberancy, and before Emission, she was removed into an Enemy's Country. . . . Having to no purpose used all peaceable Endeavours, the collected part of the *Semen*, raised and enflamed, became adust, converted to Choler, turned head upon the spinal Duct, and ascended to the Brain. (9.103–4)

Aeolism provides the complement of Sartorism in offering an explanation of the "principle part within" that provides motion to the automata. Both systems work to ensure the happiness of the self-deceived, whether the focal point of the deception be the lucubrations of one's own brain or "the *Films* and *Images* . . . from the *Superficies* of Things" (9.110). As the narrator assures us, "A strong Delusion always operat[es] from *without,* as vigorously as from *within*" (9.108).

Between them, Aeolism and Sartorism generate the metaphors that control the structure and meaning of the *Tale of a Tub*. These can be found in the images and notions of insides and outsides, containers and contained, and the shifting allegiance of the narrator to one or the other. The tub itself and its antitypes, the oratorical machines, are containers to be valued for their contents. Grubaean writings, we are told, contain great arcana, and superficial readers must "be persuaded to inspect beyond the Surface and Rind of Things," for

> *Wisdom* is a *Fox*, who after long hunting, will at last cost you the Pains to dig out: 'Tis a *Cheese*, which by how much the richer, has the thicker, the homelier, and the courser Coat; and whereof to a judicious Palate, the *Maggots* are the best. 'Tis a *Sack-Posset*, wherein the deeper you go, you will find it the sweeter. *Wisdom* is a *Hen*, whose *Cackling* we must value and consider, because it is attended with an *Egg*; But then, lastly, 'tis a *Nut*, which unless you chuse with Judgment, may cost you a Tooth, and pay you with nothing but a *Worm*. (1.40)

The coats themselves are outsides, exterior souls, and the tailor-god who creates them perches emblematically upon what the narrator with uncharacteristic brevity simply calls a superficies, a surface. The critical mirror that the narrator describes (3.63) "cast[s] *Reflections* from its own *Superficies*, without any Assistance of *Mercury* from behind." Peter's feast retains the outward appearance of brown bread, but "in [this] *Bread is contained*, inclusive, *the Quintessence of Beef, Mutton, Veal, Venison, Partridge, Plum-pudding, and Custard*" (4.72). The narrator, "with a World of Pains and Art, dissected the Carcass of *Humane Nature*, and read many useful Lectures upon the several Parts, both *Containing* and *Contained*" (5.77), as a result of which "throughout this Divine Treatise," he "skilfully kneaded up both together with a *Layer* of *Utile* and a *Layer* of *Dulce*" (5.77). The Aeolists, of course, see themselves as vessels and containers of their divine winds and view these contents as of crucial importance; nevertheless, even among them outsides are held in some honor, and the size of ears were "not only lookt upon as an Ornament of the *Outward* Man, but as a Type of Grace in the *Inward*" (11.129). And outwardly, of course, Jack looked very much like Peter, and was often mistaken for him. The narrator reports the opinion of "the famous *Troglodyte* Philosopher":

> *'Tis certain (*said he) *some Grains of Folly are of course annexed, as Part of the Composition of Human Nature, only the Choice is left us, whether we please to wear them* Inlaid *or* Embossed; *And we need not go very far to seek how that is usually determined, when we remember, it is with Human Faculties as with Liquors, the lightest will be ever at the Top.* (10.116)

And beyond all this, the fable of Peter, Martin, and Jack and the digressions of the narrator stand in an unsteady inside-outside relation to each other, one or the other of them being, in theory, the empty container thrown out to the whale to prevent that Leviathan — in a strikingly mixed metaphor — "from laying violent Hands" (Preface, p. 24) on Church and State. The narrator clearly indicates the equivalence of these apparent opposites when he moves blithely from an encomium of madness and the inward generation of delusion (9) to a statement of preference for outward delusion, praising the man who "can with *Epicurus* content his Ideas with the *Films* and *Images* that fly off upon his Senses from the *Superficies* of Things" (9.110). He demonstrates the same thing structurally by the total conflation of fable and digression at the end of the *Tale,* so it is indeed merely a matter of choice whether we read our follies "Inlaid *or* Embossed."

The interaction of outsides and insides furnishes the essential key to reading the *Tale* intelligibly. The narrator understands both physically: outsides are bodies, and insides are more bodies, fragments of bodies, or mechanical causes of motion in bodies. The narrator really thinks he is getting *inside* human beings when he sees a woman flayed or a beau stripped; he believes he is mastering the insides of books when he learns their titles or scans their indexes. For that reason, his own book accumulates a large collection of outsides — title page, epigraphs, lists of other books, "An Apology," "Postscript," the bookseller's dedication, "The

Bookseller to the Reader," "The Epistle Dedicatory to His Royal Highness Prince Posterity," "The Preface " and finally Section I, "The Introduction." Inside all of that is the tale itself, which the narrator constantly goes outside of to give us his theories about criticism, madness, digressions, and so on. All of these he also views physically, as material additions to the magnitude of his work:

> . . . having the *Modern* Inclination to expatiate upon the Beauty of my own Productions, and display the bright Parts of my Discourse; I thought best to do it in the Body of the Work, where, as it now lies, it makes a very considerable Addition to the Bulk of the Volume, *a Circumstance by no means to be neglected by a skilful Writer.* (5.82)

Despite surface appearances, the narrator of *A Tale of a Tub* acts in a reasonably consistent manner toward his book. It essentially offers him another surface to be adorned or another tub to be filled up: whether we regard the *Tale* as an inside or an outside depends entirely upon whether we decide he is adorning a surface or filling a container. He is at least perceptive enough to see that those acts are identical. If Sartorism makes the body an inside and the soul an outside, Peter's actions nevertheless use the coats as surfaces to be adorned — and do so to such a degree that what started as an outside becomes an inside to be uncovered by Martin and Jack in their own diverse fashions. The same paradox is true of human bodies: insides in the tenets of Sartorism, they become for the narrator surfaces to be decorated and at all costs not to be entered. At the extremes, the opposites meet, as Jack and Peter so often do, and the narrator at least sees that "Inlaid *or* Embossed" is our only choice about anything.

As readers, we confront that choice at every paragraph of the *Tale*. The story of Peter, Martin, and Jack is clearly an allegory, a parable, that demands interpretation — demands that we enter into it and examine its contents. How shall we do that? By Peter's method of textual analysis? That method leads the narrator to conclude that critics are asses — which may be true, but is only another metaphoric statement that itself requires further explanation, and, taken in any sense, is hardly comforting to *us*. By Jack's method, then, of total literalism? We are then indeed dealing with a tale of a tub: there's nothing in it. And what of the supposed digressions? Most of them are not genuinely digressive at all. Are they the real point of the *Tale* and the fable only a delusive outside? If that is the case what holds it all together? What structures it and regulates its progress? How are we to get inside the digressions — inside an inside — and uncover their meaning? Or is their meaning, too, all there on the surface?

The answers to all these questions lie in a more precise definition of the kinds of insides and the kinds of outsides we and the narrator are dealing with. Probably the most pertinent place to begin clarifying these matters is with the narrator's use of the traditional metaphor of the mirror of art — a metaphor we have already seen adapted in a similar (I think) manner by Pope in *The Rape of the Lock*. Here, the narrator speaks of the critical mirror particularly. He stresses the superficial nature of the reflection involved: only surfaces are reproduced; the imitation is confined to the material, to the body alone.

> A certain Author, whose Works have many Ages since been entirely lost, does in his fifth Book and eighth Chapter, say of *Criticks,* that *their Writings are the Mirrors of Learning.* This I understand in a literal Sense, and suppose our Author must mean, that whoever designs to be a perfect Writer, must inspect into the Books of *Criticks,* and correct his Invention there as in a Mirror. Now, whoever considers, that the *Mirrors* of the Ancients were made of *Brass,* and *sine Mercurio,* may presently apply the two Principal Qualifications of a *True Modern Critick,* and consequently, must needs conclude that these have always been, and must be for ever the same. For, *Brass* is an Emblem of Duration, and when it is skilfully burnished, will cast *Reflections* from its own *Superficies,* without any Assistance of *Mercury* from behind. All the other Talents of a *Critick* will not require a particular Mention, being included, or easily deducible to these. (3.63)

Let us pass over the narrator's interesting literalism and the possible significations of Mercury and Brass to concentrate on the extremely corporeal version of artistic reflection that Swift here describes. The mirror itself is presented as a solid surface that resists penetration: it lacks physical or metaphorical depths. The image is quite physically thrown back from this superficies. The reflexiveness of this process approximates what took place before Belinda's mirror: the kind of criticism Swift here describes literally creates in its own image or simply repeats its own image, just as Shadwell repeated Flecknoe. But I have talked about this particular process enough in other chapters. Swift's lines are illuminating for another reason: his conception and his language are Lucretian. He is in fact employing here Lucretius's description of the behavior of atoms in the formation of reflected images.[5] These are the same *"Films* and *Images* that fly off . . . from the *Superficies* of Things"* that the narrator assured us contented Epicurus and "a Man truly wise" (9.110; see Lucretius, *De Rerum Natura,* 4.26 ff.).

The narrator behaves as a perfect Lucretian throughout the *Tale.* His epigraph from the *De Rerum Natura* sets him a task equivalent to Lucretius's:

> 'Tis sweet to crop fresh Flow'rs, and get a Crown
> For new and rare Inventions of my own:
> So noble, great, and gen'rous the Design,
> That none of all the mighty *Tuneful Nine*
> Shall grace a Head with Laurels like to mine.
> For first, I teach great Things in lofty Strains,
> And loose Men from *Religion*'s grievous Chains.
>   (1.935–41)[6]

Later he refers to himself as Secretary of the Universe and again quotes lines from the *De Rerum Natura* that level his undertaking with Lucretius's:

> ——— Quemvis preferre laborem
> Suadet, & inducit noctes vigilare serenas.
>   (1.141–42)

> . . . I wake all Night,
> Lab'ring fit Numbers, and fit Words to find,
> To make Things plain, and to instruct your Mind,
> And teach her to direct her curious Eye
> Into coy *Nature's* greatest Privacy.
>
> (1.172–76; see *Tale,* 5.77)

And once again — this time with explicit reference to Jack — he quotes from the same Lucretian passage that provided his epigraph:

> ——·— Mellaeo contingens cuncta Lepore.
>
> (6.89)

Creech somewhat loosely translates as follows (I will give the clauses preceding to make clear the connection between this and what I have already quoted):

> For first, I teach great Things in lofty Strains,
> And loose Men from *Religion's* grievous Chains:
> Next, tho' my Subject's dark, my Verse is clear,
> And sweet, with Fansy flowing ev'ry where.
>
> (1.940–43)

Implicitly, this casts the narrator as the poet-propagandist-disciple Lucretius to Jack's guide-philosopher-exemplar Epicurus; his task, like Lucretius's, is to expound the system of his master. At all events, these explicit parallels and the ubiquity of reference to, and quotation from, *De Rerum Natura* delineate the narrator's role.

The Lucretian materials are certainly not accidental: they form an integral part of the mind and character of the narrator of the *Tale,* and at the very least add a piquant irony to "the *freshest Modern* ['s]" frequent deplorings of the ignorance of the ancients. As we have seen, he conceptualizes vision and the process of mirroring according to the tenets of Lucretian atomic theory. He presents as well an impeccable Lucretian case for the material nature and effects of language, paraphrasing and quoting Lucretius to the effect that air and words are heavy bodies leaving consequently material impressions on implicitly material minds.

> The deepest Account, and the most fairly digested of any I
> have yet met with, is this, That Air being a heavy Body, and
> therefore (according to the System of *Epicurus*) continually
> descending, must needs be more so, when loaden and press'd
> down by Words; which are also Bodies of much Weight and
> Gravity, as it is manifest from those deep *Impressions* they
> make and leave upon us; and therefore must be delivered
> from a due Altitude, or else they will neither carry a good
> Aim, nor fall down with a sufficient Force.

> *Corpoream quoque enim vocem constare fatendum est,*
> *Et sonitum, quoniam possunt impellere Sensus.* Lucr.
> Lib. 4 (1.36)

Creech translates the Latin lines very concisely: "'Tis certain then, that
Voice that thus can wound / Is all *Material: Body* every *Sound*"
(4.545–46). The prose before and after the Latin verse condenses and
paraphrases material from the same section of *De Rerum Natura,*
roughly 4.524 ff. and 4.563 ff. respectively. The Aeolists have not
failed to grasp at least one implication of these ideas; they argue succinctly that *"Words are but Wind; and Learning is nothing but
words;* Ergo, *Learning is nothing but Wind"* (8.97). For the Aeolists,
of course, that is a compliment.

But wind plays a much more fundamental role in Aeolist cosmology
than that quotation indicates. With the kind of literal-mindedness that
characterizes the narrator of the *Tale,* they literalize the *forma infor-
mans* of man, whether it be called *spiritus, animus, afflatus,* or *anima,*
into its etymological and imagistic base, wind alone (8.95). This wind
we already know to be purely material, and according to Aeolist doctrine
it defines the nature of man.

> . . . Since *Wind* had the Master-Share, as well as Operation
> in every Compound, by Consequence, those Beings must be
> of chief Excellence, wherein that *Primordium* appears most
> prominently to abound; and therefore, *Man* is in highest
> Perfection of all created Things, as having by the great

Bounty of Philosophers, been endued with three distinct
Anima's or *Winds,* to which the Sage *Aeolists,* with much
Liberality, have added a fourth of equal Necessity, as well as
Ornament with the other three; by this *quartum Principium,*
taking in the four Corners of the World; which gave Occasion
to that Renowed *Cabbalist, Bumbastus,* of placing the Body
of Man, in due position to the four *Cardinal* Points.

In Consequence of this, their next Principle was, that *Man*
brings with him into the World a peculiar Portion or Grain of
Wind, which may be called a *Quinta essentia,* extracted
from the other four. (7.95–96)

Swift has so managed affairs here that these Aeolist doctrines point by
point parallel and parody Lucretius's explanation of the mortality and
materiality of the spirit and the way in which it causes motion in the
body — a point with obvious relevance to our earlier discussion of the
relation of Aeolism to Hobbes's "principal part within." This passage in
fact parallels in form and function the parody of Hobbes that preceded
the exposition of the tenets of Sartorism. Here is Creech's translation of
part of Lucretius's argument:

'Tis Certain then, the *Seeds,* that frame the Mind,
Are thin, and small, and subtile, and refin'd:
For when the *Mind* is gone, the former Weight
Each *Limb* retains, the Bulk remains as great.
　And yet 'tis *Mixt:* for when *Life's* Pow'rs decay,
A gentle *Breeze* with *Vapour* flies away:
This *Vapour* likewise shews that *Air* is there,
All *Heat* has *Air;* for *Heat,* by Nature rare,
Must still be intermixt with Parts of *Air.*
　Well then: we know the *Mind* and *Soul* comprise
Three Things; yet from all these no *Sense* can rise,
No vig'rous Thought from such a Frame as this.
Then we must add a fourth Thing to this Frame;
And yet that *Fourth,* tho' *Something,* has No *Name:*

Its Parts are smooth, small, subtile, apt to move,
When press'd, or troubl'd by the weakest Shove:
From this comes *Sense*. (3.220-36)

Next, how these four are mix'd, I would rehearse,
How fitly join'd; but now my flowing Verse
The Poorness of the *Latin* Tongue does check:
Yet briefly, and as that permits, I'll speak.
   They all confus'dly move; no diff'rent Space
To each allotted, and no proper Place,
Where this divides, from that, and lies alone;
But all their Pow'rs, conjoin'd, arise as one.
So gen'rally, in ev'ry Piece of *Meat*,
Our Sense discovers *Odour, Savour, Heat;*
The Flesh the same: So *Heat,* and *Air,* and *Wind*
Make up one *Nature* mix'd, and closely join'd
With that *Quick Force,* which makes them move; and whence
Thro' all the *Bodies* Parts springs vig'rous *Sense.*
This *Nature*'s deeply hid; this does possess
The inmost Space, and most remote Recess.
As in our *Limbs,* the *Soul*'s remov'd from View,
Because its *Seeds* are thin, and small, and few;
So this fourth *Nameless Force* within the Soul
Lies hid, its chiefest Part, and rules the Whole.
So likewise must the *Heat,* and *Air,* and *Wind*
Be in convenient Place, and Order join'd:
This must be uppermost, that lower fall,
To make it seem *One Nature,* fram'd of *All:*
Lest *Heat* and *Air,* plac'd sep'rately, distract
The Pow'r of *Sense,* and make it cease to act. (3.250-75)

The three *animae* and the *quartum principium* tally in both texts; the Aeolists' "*Quinta essentia,* extracted from the other four" seems transparently a parodic extension of Lucretius's mysterious blending of his principles into an inexplicable unity. It is somewhat difficult to determine, at this point, whether Swift is using the rationalistic system of Lucretius to debunk the obscurantism of the sects, or the obscurantism of the sects to explode the rationalism of Lucretius, or where either stand in relation to the DNA and RNA of modern corpuscular theory. And Swift substantially complicates the parodic element by using Lucretius's description of an epileptic fit as the vehicle for his own description of an Aeolist rite (8.98; compare Lucretius, 3.487 ff. and Creech's translation, 3.469–85).

The Aeolists — and the narrator, apparently — accept the principle of the correspondence of the microcosm and the macrocosm. The narrator describes Aeolist sages delivering their knowledge by adopting

> a certain Position of Countenance, which gave undoubted Intelligence to what Degree or Proportion, the Spirit agitated the inward Mass. For, after certain Gripings, the *Wind* and Vapours issuing forth; having first by their Turbulence and Convulsions within, caused an Earthquake in Man's little World; distorted the Mouth, bloated the Cheeks, and gave the Eyes a terrible kind of *Relievo*. At which Junctures, all their *Belches* were received for Sacred, the Sourer the better, and swallowed with infinite Consolation by their meager Devotes. (8.97)

This "Earthquake in Man's little World" synopsizes Lucretius's description of the process of eathquake in the great world, with no loss of causal relationships and little change of scenery (*De Rerum Natura*, 6.557 ff.; Creech, 6.540 ff.). And the narrator pursues a similar argument from analogy in tracing the origins and workings of madness:

> For the *upper Region* of Man, is furnished like the *middle Region* of the Air; The materials are formed from Causes of the widest Difference, yet produce at last the same Substance and Effect. Mists arise from the Earth, Steams from Dunghils, Exhalations from the Sea, and Smoak from Fire; yet all Clouds are the same in Composition, as well as Consequences: and the Fumes issuing from a Jakes, will furnish as

comely and useful a Vapor, as Incense from an Altar. Thus
far, I suppose, will easily be granted me; and then it will
follow, that as the Face of Nature never produces Rain, but
when it is overcast and disturbed, so Human Understanding,
seated in the Brain, must be troubled and overspread by
Vapours, ascending from the lower Faculties, to water the
Invention, and render it fruitful. Now, altho' these Vapours
(as it hath been already said) are of as various Original, as
those of the Skies, yet the Crop they produce differs both in
Kind and Degree, meerly according to the Soil. (9.102–3)

This argument, too, seems to be a condensation of Lucretius, though the
point is not important: see *De Rerum Natura,* 6.451 ff. In the para-
graphs immediately following this, the narrator employs the same process to explain how love becomes madness through the conversion of
semen to choler and its ascension to the brain. His language throughout
draws explicitly and implicitly on Lucretius's passage on the causes of
physical desire (*Tale,* 9.103–4; *De Rerum Natura,* 4.103 ff.). In any
event, the reversible proposition, as in man so in the universe, seems as
firmly established for him and the Aeolists as it earlier was for him and
the Sartorists.

   In Swift's parodic system, the Lucretian materials obviously provide a
philosophic base for Aeolism parallel to Sartorism's roots in Hobbes's
works. But Lucretius is more important than that to the narrator, who
sees himself as an avatar of the classical poet-scientist-philosopher, like
him engaged in clarifying *rerum naturam.* The Epicurean atomism
Lucretius expounds subsumes Hobbes's thinking (which was contem-
porarily considered a revival of classical atheistic atomism — of
Epicurus and Lucretius, in short):[7] Hobbes's materialism and
Descartes's vortices (9.105) appear as no more than elaborations of
Lucretius's attempt to explain the workings of the universe materially
and mechanically. These latter qualities the narrator himself singles out
for mention in his brief summation of Epicurus's major tenets:

   Epicurus modestly hoped, that one Time or other, a
   certain Fortuitous Concourse of all Mens Opinions, after

perpetual Justlings, the Sharp with the Smooth, the Light and the Heavy, the Round and the Square, would by certain *Clinamina,* unite in the Notions of *Atoms* and *Void,* as these did in the Originals of all Things. (9.105)

We have already seen the roles of atoms in forming films, images, vapors, the weightiness of speech. The *Clinamina* are, loosely, the angles of incidence, attraction, or attachment of atoms to each other; in classical atomic theory, these and the sizes or qualities of the atoms themselves determine the nature of the body produced. This is also true of the world of the narrator of the *Tale:*

> Now, the former *Postulatum* being held, that it is of no Import from what Originals this *Vapour* proceeds, but either in what *Angles* it strikes and spreads over the Understanding, or upon what *Species* of Brain it ascends; It will be a very delicate Point, to cut the Feather, and divide the several Reasons to a Nice and Curious Reader, how this numerical Difference in the Brain, can produce Effects of so vast a Difference from the same *Vapour,* as to be the sole Point of Individuation between *Alexander the Great, Jack of Leyden,* and Monsieur *Des Cartes.* (9.107)

And since the microcosm mirrors (in what manner we have already seen) the macrocosm, the behavior of atoms becomes the behavior of men:

> But, here the severe Reader may justly tax me as a Writer of short Memory, a Deficiency to which a true *Modern* cannot but of Necessity be a little subject. Because, *Memory* being an employment of the Mind upon things past, is a Faculty, for which the Learned, in our Illustrious Age, have no manner of Occasion, who deal entirely with *Invention,* and strike all Things out of themselves, or at least, by Collision, from each other. . . . (6.84)

And by the same token, the Sartorists argue that what "are vulgarly called *Suits of Clothes,* or *Dresses,* do according to certain Compositions receive different Appellations. . . . If certain Ermins and Furs be placed in a certain Position, we stile them a *Judge,* and so, an apt Conjunction of Lawn and black Sattin, we intitle a *Bishop*" (2.47). And Peter's ability to juxtapose an S, an H, an O, and so on, will at length bring forth the desired shoulder knot. Words become bodies, bodies become words, and both are reducible to randomly colliding atoms. This, in its barest form, is the world inhabited by the narrator of *A Tale of a Tub.*

Swift's latter-day Lucretius has the virtue, for my purposes at least, of making explicit what seems implicit in everyone else. Atomic theory — known to the seventeenth and eighteenth centuries as the "corpuscular theory" — provides the rationale for the insistent process of reification that I have so often remarked on. Hobbes and Descartes do no more than Epicurus and Lucretius in confining human knowledge to the surface of things; Locke's distinction between primary and secondary qualities — between what is really "in" the object and what human perception puts there — merely reinforces the limitation. Atomism explains those bodies and surfaces. I do not mean this in any loose or haphazard way; I mean precisely that the kind of ideas about language, about body, about society, and about the cosmos that I have been discussing were shaped by the premises and implications of what contemporaries knew as the corpuscular theory and what we glibly pass off as the dawn of Western science. Almost from the Restoration onward, some form of atomic theory dominated scientific investigation, banishing older ideas of the nature of bodies and along with them established notions of the relationships of bodies and souls and spirits of all sorts.[8] What we have seen in literature reflects the substitution of the implications of atomism for Aristotelian genera and species or for the Platonic web of relations between physical existence, the ideal, and the One. Atomism makes transcendence impossible; it lops off a whole, previously inhabited dimension of human life. It calls into being a chaotic, purely material world — and this is the shared accusation that Dryden, Pope, and Swift have leveled at all of their villains. What alarms them is the possibility that bad art *can* call into being just such a world, that Flecknoe, Shadwell, the Grub Street hack, Belinda, Dulness and her minions, all can in fact create a cosmos where art is a corpus. Paradoxically, they can only accomplish this because of the shared faith of Dryden, Pope, and Swift in the ability of language to reflect and to affect reality. That is, Dryden's, Pope's, and Swift's fears are based on an acceptance of the microcosm-macrocosm analogy as *ontologically* true: consequently, the conceptualizations of the human mind and the artistic cosmoses that result from them directly affect the greater world. Atomism eliminates all analogies but one, that of random bodies randomly constellating at all levels of existence. Atomism negates all other modes of relationship and replaces them with a new and terrifying absolute: body totally without access to grace, corporeality that excludes all other forms of existence, all other modes of being. This accounts in large part for the peculiar satiric uses of bodies in Augustan literature, from Shadwell's "Tun of Man" to the Yahoos; this same cosmological revolution radically altered the relationship of language and body for Augustan and all subsequent art.

Looked at on a purely literal level, there is no great gulf between Swift's narrator's account of the origin of madness and Bernardus Silvestris's explanation of the formation of the various humors in the human body (see above, pp. 42–43). From any other point of view, the difference is enormous. Although he does not hesitate to use physical language and mechanical conceptions, Bernardus describes a process that is firmly embedded in a world of analogies and in an analogically intelligible world. What happens chemically in the human body also occurs, *mutatis mutandis,* morally and intellectually in the human mind or spirit or may be checked, reversed, negated, or redirected by the mind or spirit. Astrological phenomena and terrestrial phenomena may parallel human actions, but they do not control them. Body may explicate spirit for limited intelligences, but it does not dominate spirit. In the world of *A Tale of a Tub,* body *is* spirit, as the Aeolists so amply prove, and the point of such analogies as remain is their physical necessity. Steam and vapors ascend to the sky and form clouds; vapors ascend to the human brain and form madness. Both universe and human mind obey physical laws. What for Bernardus gave a spiritual dimension to the physical and made things invisible explicable through things visible, for

Swift's narrator eliminates the spiritual entirely and reduces everything to the more or less predictable (if you know the kind of brain and the angle of incidence of the vapors) action of physical agents. The central fact, metaphor, and analogy of the cosmos of the *Tale of a Tub* is the random motion of an atom.

Since individuals also behave like atoms, it follows that any kind of society is impossible save the loose union of those whose madnesses harmonize. Everything else remains fragmentary and haphazard. Exemplary figures are impossible: since conquests and systems are the greatest products of the greatest madnesses, no individual has anything to learn from the career of an Aeneas or a Red Crosse Knight, either literally or metaphorically considered. In that sense, epic too is impossible. Peter's and Jack's interpretations reduce Scripture to chaos; the narrator's emulation and denigration of Homer wreak the same havoc on epic. The really heroic calling, he assures us, is the practice of criticism,

> to travel thro' this vast World of Writings: to pursue and hunt
> those Monstrous Faults bred within them: to drag out the
> lurking Errors like *Cacus* from his Den; to multiply them like
> *Hydra's* Heads; and rake them together like *Augeas's* Dung.
> Or else to drive away a sort of *Dangerous Fowl,* who have a
> perverse Inclination to plunder the best Branches of the *Tree
> of Knowledge,* like those *Stymphalian* Birds that eat up the
> Fruit. (3.58)

Scripture is destroyed when the will becomes an expression of Peter's will; epic is undone when it becomes the mode of the narrator's — or any individual's — madness. In the world of *A Tale of a Tub,* there are only individuals, and mad ones at that.

The absence of genuine society indicates the disappearance of structures of all sorts. Governments and systems of thought are the projections of individual eccentricity, from Odysseus's reconquest of Ithaca to, I suppose, the *Code Napoleon* and Cambodia and Laos. Literary structures are equally beyond the pale, as *A Tale of a Tub* so graphically shows — materials that belong in the preface find their way into the body of the work, tale and digression confusedly intertwine, writing itself only furnishes an opportunity for the narrator to empty his commonplace book. Of the characteristic epic structure we examined earlier, there remains this much: at the center of the book, the narrator shifts our attention from Peter to Jack, (6), from the exponent of the outside to the exponent of the inside, and launches forth in praise of digressions and the discovery of "a *Nut-shell* in an *Iliad*" (7).[9] In the first half of the book, while Peter was busily adorning the outside of his coat, the narrator was just as busily leading us into the penetralia of books, mysteries, signs, and allegories; in the second half, as soon as Jack begins exploring the inner man, the narrator declares his allegiance to excurses, outsides, and "Those Entertainments and Pleasures . . . such as *Dupe* and play the Wag with the Senses" (9.108). After this, insides and outsides change places, as they have so often, and fable becomes excursus, digression the matter of the work: "a *Nut-shell* in an *Iliad*" is only an outside within an outside. Containers contain containers, digressions "inclose Digressions in one another, like a Nest of Boxes" (5.77; the narrator at this point disapproves of the arrangement). Every step of uncovering merely reveals another surface — which is at least one good reason why outsides are preferable to insides.

There is another. The cosmos of the *Tale of a Tub* is Lucretian to the core — and the irony of that is that for Lucretius there is no core. Every seemingly solid body contains the void. Everything, everyone, is a superficies covering nothing. The atoms paper over the hollowness, but the hollowness remains — for, as Lucretius argues, if there were no void, there could be no penetration, no displacement, no motion of any sort (*De Rerum Natura,* 1.329 ff.). So in a Lucretian world, everything is a tale of a tub — everything that exists is a container that contains nothing. All is a series of surfaces, box within box. Sartorist soul and Aeolist spirit are both films flying off the superficies of things, surfaces held forth to divert attention from the void within — so, too, Grub Street fables, so, too, the heroic genealogy of critics. In the same ironic way in which Pope structures chaos, Swift fuses form — or formlessness — and meaning in the *Tale of a Tub*. The fragmentation of the narrative, the constant asides and digressions, the myriad of images and opinions thrown off, the alternations of discourse and narrative, theoretical pronouncement and practical result, the frenzies of Peter and Jack and the alarums and excursions of the narrator's momentary preoccupations — these are not the vehicles of meaning in the *Tale*: these *are* meaning. The *Tale* itself, like the tub whose precise significance escaped the Grand Committee ("The Preface," p. 24), *embodies* meaning in a way that neither Peter, Jack, nor the narrator are capable of grasping; it embodies it by giving it form, by using form — body — as a physical language and language as a formal body and thereby, in a final irony, creating the "artificial man" Hobbes spoke of. The success of that artifice is a uniquely Swiftian triumph: to have shaped a repudiation of Hobbesian and Lucretian materialism exclusively out of the materials of the "corpuscular" philosophy, to have invalidated a whole way of life by giving it existence — this runs close to the borders of logic and the limits of language. It is an act of courage, too, to call into being the very world whose possibility one fears, and perhaps the saddest irony of the *Tale* is its prophetic accuracy. We inhabit the world of *A Tale of a Tub*. It, too, like all other solid bodies, contains the void.

II

The *Discourse Concerning the Mechanical Operation of the Spirit* offers Swift the opportunity for one last fillip: it functions in relation to *A Tale of a Tub* as does the last squirt of seltzer water in a Marx Brothers movie. It virtually ignores the presence of the *Battle of the Books* in its explicit linkings with the *Tale*: imagery, metaphor, subject, treatment, all derive logically from the *Tale*, and either continue and complete what the *Tale* has started or make explicit what to this point has been only implied. In any event, the end product of any or all of these is an outrageous intellectual slapstick.

For example, the opening two sentences:

> It is now a good while since I have had in my Head something, not only very material, but absolutely necessary to my Health, that the World should be informed in. For, to tell you a Secret, I am able to *contain* it no longer. (p. 171)

My reaction to the narrator's inability to *"contain"* anything so "very material" is a mixed one indeed. Consider also his choice of the epistolary form: "Letters to a Friend" are now in vogue, ergo, "having dispatched what I had to say of Forms, or of Business, let me intreat, you will suffer me to proceed upon my Subject; and to pardon me, if I make no farther use of the Epistolary Stile, till I come to conclude" (p. 172). The discursive correspondent blatantly shares the narrator of the *Tale*'s disregard for the consonance of subject, genre, and style. He possesses as well the same fondness for beginning with an allegory, and the one he chooses seems particularly charged: certainly the observant reader cannot take the fable of Mahomet and his ass as simply an allegory of the "Fanatick Auditory" and the "Gifted, or enlightened Teacher" (p. 173) without doubling the complications and amusement by recollection of the Ass-Critic and Ass-Jack from the *Tale*, or Aesop's escape in Ass's form in the *Battle*. The explanation of the mechanical operation of the spirit conforms very neatly with everything we have been told about Aeolist inspiration, from the ascension of vapors to the unfortunate extension of the outer vessel and the system-builder's sad seduction by his lower parts into a ditch. And the basis of both systems is identical: "I am apt to imagine, that the Seed or Principle, which has ever put Men upon *Visions* in Things *Invisible*, is of a Corporeal Nature . . . " (p. 188).

There does not seem to me anything terribly complex about the *Mechanical Operation of the Spirit,* at least not as compared to *A Tale of a Tub.* [10] Its importance seems to me to reside in its final mirroring, across the *Battle of the Books,* of the concerns and attitudes of the *Tale.* The *Tale* concludes *diminuendo,* as the narrator tries to write about nothing; the *Mechanical Operation* repeats once again, even more diminished, a by-now familiar refrain. Even more explicit than the *Tale,* even more fragmented, it still reminds us as the volume dwindles to a close that this is *one* book, that there are connections among the three works, that, in short, *A Tale of a Tub,* the *Battle of the Books,* and the *Mechanical Operation of the Spirit* are to be read as an interconnected and unified work.

To prove that last statement, I will have to show real connections among the three works and especially between the *Battle* and the *Tale*. In an obvious way, of course, the *Battle of the Books* and the *Mechanical Operation of the Spirit* simply separate the twin concerns of the *Tale* — abuses in learning and religion — and treat each of them individually. But there are more meaningful links than that.

The *Battle of the Books* continues the major metaphors that Swift generated in *A Tale of a Tub*. First the simple process of reification, the reduction of intellectual and spiritual concepts to physical bodies, reaches its logical conclusion in the literal battle of the books, and the bookseller's friendly reminder that "when *Virgil* is mentioned, we are not to understand the Person of a famous Poet, . . . but only certain Sheets of Paper, bound up in Leather" (p. 139) merely reinforces that point, as does the goddess Criticism's later adoption of octavo format. Second, both narrators agree about the inefficacy of satire. I quote here the narrator of the *Battle*: "Satyr is a sort of *Glass*, wherein Beholders do generally discover every body's Face but their Own; which is the chief Reason for that kind of Reception it meets in the world, and that so very few are offended with it" ("The Preface of the Author," p. 140). Third, the narrators agree also in their preference of outsides to insides:

> THERE *is a* Brain *that will endure but one* Scumming: *Let the Owner gather it with Discretion, and manage his little Stock with Husbandry; but of all things, let him beware of bringing it under the* Lash *of his* Betters; *because, That will make it all bubble up into Impertinence, and he will find no new Supply: Wit, without knowledge, being a Sort of* Cream, *which gathers in a Night to the Top, and by a skilful Hand, may be soon* whipt *into* Froth; *but once scumm'd away, what appears underneath will be fit for nothing, but to be thrown to the* Hogs.[11] ("Preface," p. 140)

And as for containers — the books themselves are containers, holding the "Spirit" or "*Brutum hominis*" (p. 144) of their authors; the library is a container; the *Full and True Account of the Battle* is itself a container very much like the *Tale of a Tub*, filled with episodes and digressions and, even more like the *Tale*, ultimately composed of several layers of surfaces.

The surfaces I refer to are the several layers of allegory that make up the *Battle of the Books*. In a manner exactly like the beginnings of the *Tale* and the *Discourse,* the *Battle of the Books* opens with an allegory that sets the theme of the narration and/or exposition to follow. In this case, the narrator presents his little fable of the republic of dogs, and proceeds to apply it to affairs in St. James Library, to the advantage of neither group in the dispute. From this point on, the *Battle*'s mode of procedure differs from the *Tale*'s: the narration progresses in a reasonably straightforward manner, with few of the digressions and interruptions of the *Tale*. Those sections — where the narrator speaks *in propria persona*, offering systems, theories, and interpretations — are now largely confined to the *Mechanical Operation of the Spirit.* That is, the process of confusing fable and digression that we saw at the end of the *Tale of a Tub* has now been carried out to its logical conclusion, and fable and digression have now completely changed places: the fable now treats of abuses of learning (*Battle of the Books*), and the digressive essay (*Mechanical Operation of the Spirit*) now concerns itself with abuses of religion. Both subjects have been reduced to a primarily physical mode of existence, and once again separated into unrelated entities: in effect, the narrator of the *Tale* has fully succeeded in his project of secularizing and materializing religion and learning.

That digression will, I hope, be pardoned; I am a victim of my environment.

The *Battle of the Books* proceeds episodically to no conclusion: Bentley's and Wotton's ignominious trussing, like "a Brace of *Woodcocks*" (p. 164), is followed only by a sprinkling of asterisks and a feeble "*Desunt caetera.*" The road thither has led through an explanation of the origins of the quarrel, the steps preliminary to actual hostilities, the encounter of the spider and the bee and its exposition and application by Aesop, the catalogues of the armies, the council in heaven, the visit to, and visit of, the goddess Criticism (a kind of descent to the underworld), the battle itself (a series of individual skirmishes in the Homeric manner), a council of generals with the intrusion of a

Thersites (Bentley), a night expedition and the "deaths" of Bentley and Wotton in a wonderful parody of Virgil's Nisus and Euryalus episode. All of these, except the episode of the spider and the bee, very obviously fit the mock-epic pattern, and it is striking to realize just how much characteristically epic material (at least characteristically Iliadic) Swift has gotten into so short a work. But the exception is what I want to examine.

The fable of the spider and the bee is simple to the point of being transparent, and Aesop's application of it strikes every reader as somewhat spiderishly venomous but perfectly apt. The complications arise from its context. Once again, outsides triumph over insides, and the wide-ranging bee handily humiliates the self-sufficient spider. But after what we have seen of outsides and insides in *A Tale of a Tub*, I for one find it very difficult to take that straightforwardly. And Aesop's allegorization only makes things more confusing; he is, after all, an allegorical figure himself, who provides us, in the middle of an allegory, with another allegory. Then, too, there is the question of genre and decorum, since we are dealing with books in general and epic in particular: what is a beast fable doing in the middle of an epic? Or more generally, what is the relation of the whole spider and bee episode to the rest of the *Battle of the Books?*

The several layers of allegorical surfaces that precede all this provide the answer to that question. The story of the republic of dogs leads the narrator to explain the quarrel between the Ancients and Moderns as centering on possession of the highest peak of Parnassus. In this quarrel, "*Ink* is the great missive Weapon" (p. 143), and the trophies both sides set up in celebration of a victory are books, which are subsequently stored in libraries. In St. James Library, because of accident or mismanagement or mischief, Ancient and Modern books were jumbled together, and that led to their resuming the quarrel. Allegory (republic of dogs) leads to exposition (quarrel about Parnassus) leads to allegory (ink as weapon, books as trophies) leads to exposition (books are stored in libraries, thus, battle of books). Clearly then, the episode of the spider and bee fits the pattern of allegory and explanation set up by the narrator, and the question then becomes one of why the pattern breaks down after this episode. But there are other elements to the pattern as well. The republic of dogs has its roots in fact, not parable — only the application of language drawn from the sphere of government makes it in any way metaphoric, and certainly not genuinely allegorical. What the narrator offers as an application of it, however, is most definitely allegorical — the quarrel about possession of the highest peak of Parnassus — but this is presented to us as fact. Then again, ink as weapon and books as trophies: this is barely metaphor at all; it is hyperbole at best. But the narrator presents it as allegory, and the quarrel in the library among physical books is presented as fact. So, too, the actions of the spider and the bee, which would seem like the doings of the republic of dogs to be rooted in fact, are made allegory by Aesop, whose application or explanation becomes the fact that supplants them. Allegory is more real than reality. Like religion and learning, inside and outside have once more changed places: interpretation is now prior to fact, literature is prior to reality. Books replace men, and "real" occurrences are only materials for allegory at best. We have stepped through the looking glass.

And that is the point of it all, of the inconclusiveness of the *Battle of the Books* and the downbeat ending of the *Tale* and the final emblematic fall that concludes the *Mechanical Operation*. It is when we realize fully the implications of the spider and the bee, that in an allegory we are reading another allegory that is being allegorized for us by an allegorical character, that Swift's simple point emerges in devastating clarity. He is talking about the substitution of literature for life, about the deformation of life by literature — literature in the sense of all letters: theology, philosophy, physics, poetry. What he is talking about is the peculiarly modern temperament that substitutes theorizing about life for living it, or that makes life over to fit the theory. His whole point lies in the tenuous connection between art and reality, between word and thing, and the myriad ways in which that connection can be broken. To make everything words is just as bad as to make everything body, and the simple statement of Swift's whole volume is that we do.

The *Battle of the Books,* in which all that exists becomes literature, stands between *A Tale of a Tub* and the *Mechanical Operation of the Spirit,* in both of which all that exists becomes body. At the center of the

Battle stands the episode of the spider and the bee, which would appear to be the most digressive element in it, but which in every important sense forms the heart of it, revealing just how flesh is made word.[12] Swift inserts it in a mock epic for the same reason that Pope litters clues about *The Rape of the Lock*, to demonstrate that same disjunction of epic manner and epic matter. The *Battle of the Books* has no real connection with epic save through a parody of its surface; the insides of epic are contained, ironically, in *A Tale of a Tub*. There, as in *The Dunciad*, art and philosophy, religion and government are presented in the process of being fragmented, materialized, and destroyed. The narrator of the *Tale* and the sort of mind he embodies are making what later writers would call unity of culture impossible, and with it they are banishing epic, since traditional epic had always been the vehicle for precisely that awareness of the interrelatedness of human life. Aeneas, in Landino's view, had step by step to learn private morality, the virtues and defects of public or civil life, and finally the lessons of philosophy about the *summum bonum*. The narrator of the *Tale* eliminates that tedious process and, like the spider of the *Battle*, spins everything out of himself, either by inspiration or by sounding the harmonizing chord of his madness. In either case, it marks the destruction of traditional epic by substituting private vision for the wisdom of a culture, by making the individual the paradigm for the whole. It is, simply, the substitution of solipsism for society. Swift's playing with allegoresis throughout the volume demonstrates that point again and again: what is the real difference, after all, between what Aesop does to the spider and bee and what the narrator of the *Tale* does to asses, or what the narrator of the *Mechanical Operation* does to Mahomet and his ass? The universal tendency of all the characters in all these works is to impose private visions from without and to claim that they constitute the real insides of the matter. Swift, like Pope, is describing the breakdown of a whole civilization, the moment at which all the energies and aspirations of a culture turn against themselves and bring forth parodies of their ideal. What Scaliger charges to Bentley in the *Battle* can stand equally well as an indictment of Swift's narrators and Pope's dunces: "Miscreant *Prater, said he,* Eloquent only in thine own Eyes, Thou railest without Wit, or Truth, or Discretion. The

Malignity of thy Temper perverteth Nature, Thy *Learning* makes thee
more *Barbarous,* thy Study of *Humanity,* more *Inhuman;* Thy
Converse amongst Poets more *groveling, miry,* and *dull.* All Arts of
civilizing others, render thee *rude* and *intractable; Courts* have taught
thee *ill Manners,* and *polite Conversation* has finished thee a *Pedant"*
(p. 161). Bentley, like Peter and Jack and the narrators, is a man
deformed by letters, a life warped by literature. He is also the wave of the
future, sure proof that art does affect life and alter reality. The narrator of
the *Mechanical Operation* states the proposition succinctly, and his is,
after all, the last word on the subject: " . . . There is many an Operation, which in its *Original,* was purely an *Artifice,* but through a long
Succession of Ages, hath grown to be natural" (p. 175).

III

From the point of view of literature, the volume containing *A Tale of a
Tub,* the *Battle of the Books,* and the *Mechanical Operation of the
Spirit* accomplishes, in prose parody, the overt separation of epic matter
from the epic manner. *Gulliver's Travels* goes on to exploit epic matter
in a prose comic or mock epic without the epic manner. Lemuel Gulliver
explores the metaphoric and ontological cosmos the *Tale* volume has
called into being. Gulliver succeeds the narrator of the *Tale* as map-
maker of this brave new world. Like his predecessor, he straddles
painfully the diverging worlds of body and mind. Confounded by the
total duality of spirit and matter, he can only offer us the latitude and
longitude of his life and ours. Simultaneously failed philosopher and
inadvertent guide, he is the Cartesian cartographer of our schizoid,
unepic universe.

Gulliver's Travels presupposes the world of *A Tale of a Tub.* It is, on
the face of it, a perfectly *reasonable* world. Absent from it are God,
religion, human affection, and any firm standards of judgment. Total
egocentricity and chance replace them. Gulliver exists as a fragmentary
individual, isolated from family and his fellow men both by the illogic of
random events and the shallowness of his own feelings. The simple

sequence of events, the variables of his life, become the determinants of it. His own judgments, conditioned and altered by perspective and vanity, are the only norms. At the same time, they are what is most crucial in the book, what Swift resolutely directs our attention toward. Gulliver is a new kind of protagonist in literature, chosen and developed for his paradoxically peculiar averageness — middle son of a middle-class family from the middlemost county in England, attended university but took no degree, and the university "canting Emmanuel" at that. Gulliver is no extraordinary figure chosen because his life offers a pattern for emulation; his role is rather to represent all of us. He is the hero as synechdoche rather than exemplar. This new Everyman represents us all because he is different from us all, just as we are different from each other; his idiosyncratic vanity and eccentricity link him to us and furnish the bond of our common humanity. These factors in themselves put *Gulliver's Travels* on the road to the novel.

Swift's uses of bodies and clothing indicate in themselves the continuities between *Gulliver* and *A Tale of a Tub*. Bodies are both the expression of reality and the determinants of Gulliver's judgments about it — though his judgments usually invert the value so blatantly displayed before him. The tininess of the Lilliputians betrays their pettiness, their smallness of mind and spirit; Gulliver fails to see it but comes to share it, glorying in the title of Nardac and vigorously defending the honor of the Lilliputian lady with whom he is improbably accused of having an affair. Starting from the proposition that "human Creatures are observed to be more Savage and cruel in Proportion to their Bulk" (2.1.87), he fails to see that the size of the Brobdingnagians reflects their magnanimity, and he carefully suppresses all evidence of his own physical pettiness by resolutely avoiding mirrors — though it still breaks out in his ostentatious triumphs over rats and flies, in his near disasters with rats and monkeys, and — in a more important moral dimension — in his vicious offer to the king of the secret of gunpowder. The bodily deformity of the Laputans clearly tokens their deformity of mind. Theirs is a Cartesian world indeed: the husbands keep their heads, deformed by the total domination of mind and the nature of their studies, quite literally in the clouds, while their comely ladies solace their neglected bodies on the mainland below. The Academy of Lagado derives almost directly from the "Digression on Madness," and the Struldbrugs descend lineally from the unfortunate flayed woman. As for the Houyhnhnms: Gulliver finds it easier to think of himself as quadruped *manqué* than as well-dressed Yahoo, and it is the sexual advances of a female Yahoo that definitely determine the point. As corollaries to all this, Gulliver's clothing in the various adventures sustains the central action and metaphorics: his patchwork garment demonstrates his immersion in the smallness of vision of the Lilliputians; his mouse-skin breeches sustain the Brobdingnagian King's indictment of Gulliver-sized people as "little odious Vermin" (2.6.132). His scientifically made and ill-fitting clothes in Laputa show the depth of the disjunction between mind and body. In Houyhnhnmland, he once again clothes himself in animal skins, including Yahoos'. In a lovely final irony, Swift has Gulliver — the would-be Houyhnhnm who seeks to deny any bond with the Yahoos — make his departure from the Houyhnhnms in a boat made of Yahoo hides, with Yahoo-skin sails, and calked with Yahoo tallow. The body, as Swift would have known from Augustine if from nowhere else, is the ship that transports the soul through the vicissitudes of this life. Deny it as he will, Gulliver must accomplish all his travels in and with a Yahoo body. And ignore it though he does, outsides still embody insides for those with eyes to see.

Swift develops the character of Gulliver with fine consistency from his first adventures to his final misanthropy. Each book, of course, is written as if it were done immediately after the journey described, so that in fact we are dealing with four distinct stages of Gulliver's character as he responds to, and is altered by, the immediately preceding events. Gulliver among the Lilliputians reveals some of the traits that lead him finally to the tranquillity of an English stable. Although he can be very exact and acute about things external to him, including other people, he is obtuse and vague in his knowledge of himself. For example, in the same chapter (1.6) in which he describes Lilliputian law and custom with brevity and precision, and his own clothing and living arrangements somewhat more verbosely, he also protests with deadpan seriousness his innocence of any liaison with a Lilliputian "great Lady." In Brobdingnag, too, although he can tell us in great detail about warts and cancers and how many hogsheads a maid of honor pisses, he manages to delude himself about his own size, with explicitly comic results after his rescue. For all the importance of bodies in determining character and even in defining the knowable, Gulliver suppresses this evidence with amazing ease when it is unsettling to his self-esteem. This, of course, is what he ultimately does vis-à-vis Yahoos and Houyhnhnms. In the first two books, where he encounters the human body telescoped and micro-scoped but essentially undistorted, Gulliver is able to assimilate himself to his surroundings completely and think of himself in the same perspec-tive as the natives. In Laputa and Lagado and among the Struldbrugs, where distortion of body mirrors distortion of mind, he has more diffi-culty but still manages to internalize the "set," the *Weltanschauung,* of his environment: he is unhappy on Laputa because his hosts, busy with airy speculation, pay little attention to him; but in Lagado, he cheerily confesses that "I had myself been a Sort of Projector in my younger days" (3.4.178) and immerses himself in the Academy. The Struldbrugs shock him, because he had been forgetting that the body decays: both the Academy of Lagado and the Flying Island had, in their different ways, been devoted to overcoming or ignoring physical limits, and the Struldbrugs — like Tithonus or the Sybil — are eternal embodiments of exactly that, freed from one great limitation in order to perpetuate all the others. That and the evidence of Glubbdubdrib, where he once more sees the process of decay, from Aristotle to Descartes and from *"English* Yeomen of the old Stamp" (3.8.201) to contemporary politicians, force him to "melancholy Reflections" on the degeneration of the human race. At this point, he begins to conceive of normal humanity in something of the same light that he saw himself — physically, at least — in Brobding-nag. Houyhnhnmland confronts him with the final distortion of body. *Animal rationale* has bifurcated into an irrational animal with a human body and a rational animal with a horse's. Instead of recognizing that he is neither Houyhnhnm nor Yahoo but some third thing between them — *animal rationis capax,* in Swift's phrase — Gulliver embraces both erroneous extremes simultaneously. He has never been able to see himself clearly in relation to others but always had, to the best of his ability, to become others. Here, shocked by the physical proof that he shares at least part of Yahoo nature, he ignores the physical proof that he has no part of Houyhnhnm nature, that the Houyhnhnms are totally alien. Swift has made them horses for the same reason that the Laputans' bodies are distorted: the kind of mind they embody is, simply, not human. The pure rationality of the horses lies as far beyond Gulliver as the pure bestiality of the Yahoos lies beneath him, and it is pointless to argue whether it is an ideal for men or not: human beings, in Swift's view, are simply not capable of it, and that is why he has personified it in totally nonhuman form. Unfortunately, Gulliver does not realize that. Gulliver's self-knowledge breaks down completely when he accepts the logic of "because I am a Yahoo I must be a Houyhnhnm"; from that point, it is a short step to the mad ex-surgeon in the stable talking to horses.

I think we must see *Gulliver's Travels* as a comic *Odyssey*. Not because of particular incidents or analogues, though there are plenty of those — Yahoos and Circe's swine, Glubbdubdrib and the Odyssean descent to hell, and so on — but because of the central importance to the satire of Gulliver's failure to know himself. Odysseus, the man of many turns, always knows who he is, even through he often has to lie about it, as to the Cyclops — but even there the episode closes with his declaration of his identity. His final assumption of his full identity — as Odysseus, son of Laertes, father of Telemachus, husband of Penelope, king of Ithaca — climaxes the poem, and the progression is swift and sure from the seeming beggar's bending of the great bow to Penelope's being convinced by his knowledge of the secret of the bed to his reunion with Telemachus and Laertes. To put it crudely, Odysseus never thinks for a moment that he is a Cyclops; Gulliver does. Gulliver is an obtuse version of the Odysseus of the other tradition, the Ulysses whom Virgil depicted as the arch-liar and whom Dante put in hell for misusing his intellect, for giving false counsel and persuading his followers to leave home again. He has no Athene to guide him and no Penelope to sustain him — only an amorphous wife who seems to go on producing children with or without his presence. But he may be the artificer of Odysseus's greatest trick: the Trojan horse.

> Therefore since my Acquaintance were pleased to think my
> poor Endeavours might not be unacceptable to my Country; I
> imposed on myself as a Maxim, never to be swerved from,
> that I would *strictly adhere to Truth;* neither indeed can I be
> ever under the least Temptation to vary from it, while I retain
> in my Mind the Lectures and Examples of my noble Master,
> and the other illustrious *Houyhnhnms,* of whom I had so
> long the Honour to be an humble Hearer.

> ——— *Nec si miserum Fortuna Sinonem*
> *Finxit, vanum etiam, mendacemque improba finget.*
> (4.12.292–93)

Fortune can make Sinon wretched, but it cannot make him a liar; thus
speaks Ulysses' catspaw, the man who is about to persuade the hapless
and trusting Trojans to welcome the wooden horse into their city, to their
ultimate destruction. Thus quotes the man who has just told a whopping
great falsehood about a race of rational horses. The Houyhnhnms are
Gulliver's wooden horse, and you accept them to your own destruction.
They are the delusive outside that hides the hollow and dangerous core;
they are the external form of Gulliver's own madness.

The literary joke about Guilliver's veracity is complicated somewhat
by the frontispiece that appears in some editions of the *Travels*
(Faulkner's, 1735) depicting Captain Lemuel Gulliver and with the
inscription *"Splendide Mendax. Hor."* On the one hand, this literally
(particularly when coupled with the Sinon allusion) casts Guilliver as
another lying traveler with the usual collection of tall tales; it compounds
the point of the travel book format, in effect. On the other hand, the
phrase comprises Horace's praise of Hypermnestra, the one of the fifty
Danaids who lied to her father and did *not* murder her husband. From the
interplay between these two possibilities and from the seeming con-
tradiction between the Horatian allusion and the Virgilian, I think we can
discern the dimensions of the kind of tension Swift is seeking: not
clear-cut distinctions between lie and truth, but a notion also of a kind of
lie that reveals the truth, of a fiction that gets closer to the truth than fact
does. *Gulliver's Travels* is that kind of beneficial lie; the Houyhnhnms

are not, and Gulliver's quotation of Sinon's lines is one last Odyssean
warning about what is in store for us if we do not look into the horses
carefully. Gulliver is a liar, a mendacious traveler peddling tall tales —
but he has been places we have not and seen true things that only fiction
can express.

Gulliver's Travels is an inverted *Bildungsroman:* it is about the
limitations of knowledge, empiric and speculative, and particularly
about the kinds of limits that body and the mere fact of having one
impose on mind. Laputan males attempting to play along with the music
of the spheres while their wives play with footmen translates into the
grammar and rhetoric of *Gulliver's Travels* the fable of the
"philosopher" of the *Mechanical Operation of the Spirit,* "who, while
his Thoughts and Eyes were fixed upon the *Constellations,* found himself seduced by his *lower Parts* into a *Ditch*" (p. 190). Scatology looms
so large in the book for precisely this reason: it embodies the least common denominator of our corporeal, animal nature. Despite the Lagadan
projectors' attempts to "denature" it, the fecal bond holds firm throughout the book; in its metaphors, the Yahoos' shitting on Gulliver's head
constitutes a claim of kinship with him, just as in Brobdingnag his
landing knee-deep in a cake of cow-dung reminds us of his — and our —
real physical limitations. A man's reach should not exceed his grasp,
unless he is willing to get "filthily bemired" (2.5.124).

Since most things, in the Lockean and Berkleyan view, exist as they
are perceived, the conditions of our knowing form the determinants and
limits of our knowledge. For this reason, the first two books of *Gulliver's
Travels* center primarily on epistemological satire rather than social or
political. The Gulliver who generously refuses to destroy Blefuscu is the
same Gulliver who offers to teach the king of Brobdingnag how to
destroy his subjects: what have changed are the conditions of Gulliver's
position — particularly the direction in which his vanity is engaged. So
Swift's playing with sizes in books 1 and 2 is not simply a juggling with
perspective but a demonstration that how we know determines what we
know and that the process of our knowing is ultimately dependent not on
a calm, free mind formulating clear and distinct ideas but on a very
limited, frail, intimidatable body and a mind open to distortions induced

by fear and pride. It is significant of this that after his return from Lilliput Gulliver does not fear being stepped on, but after returning from Brobdingnag, "I was afraid of trampling on every Traveller I met" (2.8.148). In the same way, Gulliver proudly indulges in a childlike bit of penis display to the Lilliputian soldiers who march between his legs and stare up at his tattered breeches, but in Brobdingnag, where it can have no effect at all, he carefully conceals his genitals when he hides behind a sorrel leaf to urinate. In these terms, the gulf between his mind and the Houyhnhnms' is most succinctly distilled in their inability to understand him when he speaks of "those Parts that Nature taught us to conceal" (4.3.236).

Book 3 turns to examining the limits imposed on speculative and practical knowledge by the interaction of mind and body — speculative most graphically in the Laputans, practical in the Academicians. But the flying island itself is the image that dominates the book. As a heavy body floating in air, it represents the same thing as the Laputans' pretensions to hear the music of the spheres — an attempt to transcend physical limitations, to control nature. But the irony, of course, rests on the fact that the whole power of the island comes from nature, from the inert body of the lodestone, and that its limits are precisely fixed by the effective range of the stone. The famous rebellion episode, which has been so much cited as an instance of political satire, is no more than a demonstration of the impossibility of transcending bodies and physical limitations. Physical laws govern the motion of the island, and physical means control it; and if those four towers mean anything at all specific, it is surely something like the four elements rather than the four *Drapier's Letters*. The Struldbrugs confirm all this: at the close of the book, they explicitly embody all of the limitations that corporeal existence imposes on the human mind. They are witnesses to the ravages of physical decay and petty passion: weak, ignorant, helpless, envious of living and dead alike.

At the end of book 3, nearing his return to England, Gulliver declines the ceremony of "trampling upon the Crucifix" in a chapter (3.11) that contains the only explicit reference to Christianity in all of the *Travels*. The crucifix is, of course, the overt sign of the redemption, the symbol of the fact that man is weak and in need of divine intercession and aid. It is a statement of human limitation, and trampling on it would be a rejection of that notion, a refusal of intercession or aid, and, in the terms of Laputa and Lagado, an implicit statement of human self-sufficiency and non-limitation. At the end of book 3, Gulliver refuses to make that statement; in book 4, he does.

The name Houyhnhnm means "Perfection of Nature" (4.3.235); they are what man would be if he were genuinely definable as *animal rationale*. They are also what man would be if he were perfectly natural. He is, however, none of these things, as "trampling upon the Crucifix" and Gulliver's treatment at the hands of his mutineers are designed to remind us. The Houyhnhnms do not even approximate what man could have been if Adam had not fallen: they are too perfectly rational to feel any emotion other than a rather tepid friendship (contrast Adam's and Eve's feelings in *Paradise Lost*), and one of Swift's master ironies is that it is precisely Gulliver's ego-involvement that leads him to choose them as ideal. Moved toward misanthropy by his experiences at Glubbdubdrib and with the Struldbrugs, confirmed by the treachery of his own crew, the shock of the Yahoos and his identification of them with the rest of humanity force him to recoil to the antithetical, nonhuman extreme of passionless logic — a position he comes to hold with intense passion and prideful contempt for even the exemplary humanity of Pedro de Mendez. Gulliver employs a consistent double-think by accepting both wrong extremes and identifying himself with Yahoo and Houyhnhnm simultaneously. His final failure is the root failure from which he began, his inability to know himself independent of external references. (It is worth noting that here as in Brobdingnag Gulliver avoids sight of himself whenever possible [4.10.278].) The man who stands in the stable talking to horses is certifiably insane: the dream of reason ends in exactly that kind of nightmare.

IV

Gulliver, within the limits of its comic-parodic form, points the way toward the possible prose epic of our now prosaic world. It inversely illuminates the possibility of reaching wisdom without divine guides. For Swift and the writers who follow him — for us — Athene and Raphael are no longer available. What future heroes must discover and map, with their merely human equipment, is not the divine plan for them but the existence and dimensions of the human spirit and the possibility of freeing it from the bind of matter or at least giving it direction over matter. They must learn to live with and beyond their bodies — this lies behind the importance of chastity in *Joseph Andrews* and behind the importance of constancy, both as physical direction (as opposed to random movement) and as physical and emotional chastity, in *Tom Jones*. In a world of flux, of bodies in motion, they will have to seek sanity and stability, to assert once again the possibility of order and of the primacy of a mind that has learned to live in and with the weaknesses of its body as well as with its own limitations — as Captain Booth finally does at the end of *Amelia*.

With all that, it is probably not correct to see *Gulliver's Travels* as the direct antecedent of Fielding's novels. Fielding reverts to the thematic pattern of serious verse epic; Swift's work is firmly grounded in the mock-epic pattern. The former always locates its hero, whatever his personal importance, in a much larger cosmic, historical, or social framework that dwarfs him and reduces his merely human claims to greatness or to pity to their relative proportions. Aeneas is important not for himself but as the founder of Rome, and before those as-yet-unborn generations his purely personal feelings, for Dido or for Troy, must bow.[13] The allegory accentuates this even more, evaporating Aeneas as an individual and replacing him with an Everyman who suffers and achieves as surrogate for all of us. So, too, Fielding's heroes in their commonality — Tom Jones — represent us; so, too, do they locate themselves within the framework of family and society, within a web of relations that diminish their personal importance while enhancing their social and historical stature. But the thematics of mock epic, which constitute Swift's peculiar milieu, are something far different from this. In mock epic, as in spiritual autobiography, the hero is central not just to the story but to the cosmos. Things happen *for* him; everything possesses meaning in relation to him. *Robinson Crusoe,* with its special providences and intensity of focus on the process of the hero's calling and conversion, probably offers the paradigmatic eighteenth-century example of orthodox spiritual biography.[14] In mock epic, the hero possesses the same centrality and importance as he does in spiritual autobiography; and as in the latter, he must also learn to recognize his calling, his election, and his cosmic significance — "Thy own Importance know," Ariel tells Belinda. But in mock epic the hero goes even beyond this: his task becomes the imposition of his *self* upon the cosmos. He becomes the creator-god who remakes the world in his own image. This is the essential narrative-thematic burden of all mock epic, from *MacFlecknoe* through *The Rape of the Lock* and *The Dunciad* to *A Tale of a Tub* and *Gulliver's Travels*. Gulliver's final vision of the world as exclusively divisible into Yahoos and Houyhnhnms is simply the projection of his own schizophrenia, his version of the *Tale's* choice between being a fool or a knave. The novels that spring from *Gulliver's Travels* are the great eccentric novels like *Tristram Shandy* and *Finnegans Wake,* which see in the creation and imposition of a self an act that is at once cosmic and comic. They are the novels of doubleness of vision, the bifocals for the split personality of our age. Their heroes continue Gulliver's work, mapping the unknown islands of our lives — nice places to visit, for the most part, but you wouldn't want to live there.

Neither did Fielding.

1. For this particular point and others about Hobbes's place in *A Tale of a Tub,* see Phillip Harth's *Swift and Anglican Rationalism* (Chicago, 1961). Edward Rosenheim, in his provocative *Swift and the Satirist's Art* (Chicago, 1963), discusses the passage from a different point of view (pp. 124–26). I have drawn several suggestions and much stimulation from both these books.

2. Thomas Hobbes, *Leviathan,* ed. Michael Oakshott (Oxford, n.d.), p. 5.

3. For the importance of these images to literature, see, of course, Rosamund Tuve's *Elizabethan and Metaphysical Imagery* (Chicago, 1947).

4. Wit, too, is frozen by the narrator into object by his strict and literal observance of the unities of "Time, Place, and Person," which results in a jest "that will not pass out of *Covent-Garden;* and such a one, that is no where intelligible but at *Hide-Park* Corner" as well as in his calculating "the Taste of Wit" exactly "for this present Month of *August,* 1697" ("The Preface," p. 26).

5. Cf. *De Rerum Natura*, 4.97 ff. and 4.150 ff. For a differing consideration of the role of Lucretian materials in the *Tale*, see Ronald Paulson, *Theme and Structure in Swift's Tale of a Tub* (New Haven, Conn., 1960).

6. The text of Lucretius that I use throughout is Creech's edition and translation: *Titus Lucretius Carus, of the Nature of Things*, trans. Thomas Creech, 6th ed. (London, 1722). The Lucretian lines in question are 1.930 ff.

7. Again, for an account of the importance of atomism at this time, see Kargon's *Atomism in England*.

8. For a fuller discussion of the banishment of spirit from Western thinking, see Kargon, *Atomism in England*, Dijksterhuis's *Mechanization of the World Picture*, and Bethell's *Cultural Revolution*.

9. As a matter of fact, there *is* great subliminal correspondence of part to part according to the pattern I discussed earlier, but I have no wish to beat a dead horse. Swift no doubt knew what he was doing.

10. This is not to imply that there are not many important areas of the *Discourse* that need clarification: e.g., the "Crowd of little Animals" on page 181.

11. It is important to note, however, that though the preference for outsides remains, outsides here bear different values — as, for instance, the clean surface of the Helicon that flows over "a thick sediment of *Slime* and *Mud*" (p. 162).

12. In terms of the palindromatic structure discussed earlier, the *Battle of the Books* as a whole and the spider and bee episode in particular function as the central mirroring unit.

13. In the same way, Odysseus is always seen in relation to Telemachus and to Laertes (in the Greek text, his patronymic, Laertiades, is ubiquitous); Homer locates him in a web of relationships — father, son, husband, warlord, guest, king, and so on. In an even more explicit manner, Adam and Eve are more important as parents of the human race than in themselves, and many of the heroes of the *Faerie Queene* share the same kind of historical or prototypical significance.

14. For spiritual autobiography in relation to the novel, see George A. Starr's *Defoe and Spiritual Autobiography* (Princeton, N.J., 1965).

PIC'S VARYING FORTUNES fall into a relatively coherent pattern, both formally and materially. Verse epic in the high style is, if we are to take *The Rape of the Lock* seriously, impossible because of disjunction between the fragility of contemporary mores and pursuits and the ponderousness of the vehicle that would have to convey them. *A Tale of a Tub* postulates a further disjunction between the theoretically exemplary epic hero and the fragmented, multiplex society he can no longer adequately represent. Swift's choice of form also demonstrates how great an indecorum would be involved in the use of full-dress verse epic format for the aspirations of Augustan England. In a real sense, the Longinian revival and the attachment of the aesthetics of the sublime to epic criticism should be understood as an attempt to substitute a rhetorical grandeur for what no longer existed in fact. All that this sort of criticism accomplished, however, was to distance epic still further from the real interests of the age, to make it more unreal and irrelevant, just as the gradual elevation of the hero from normal humanity to near divinity, from representative to paragon, accomplished the material cognate of that formal disaster. To be arbitrary and absolute, from the moment of Landino's singling out Aeneas as the man "destined for glory" — as opposed to Bernardus's "dweller in the body," i.e., everyman — poets and critics steadily intensify the virtues and status of the epic hero until the appearance of such bloodless lay figures as Blackmore's Arthur or Fénelon's Télémaque. Only Milton really stands aside from this development, showing in Adam and Eve the possibility of epic scope and heroism in flawed humanity, but that represents a direction epic did *not* take.[1]

Restoration and eighteenth-century readers chose rather to try to assimi-
late *Paradise Lost* to then prevailing notions of epic regularity, and
Milton himself moved into a much more conventional pattern with
Paradise Regained.

All the works we have examined so far have one firm material link with
traditional epic: they have all offered or satirized competing or com-
plementary definitions of wisdom. Wisdom, whether conceived as
knowledge of philosophy or theology, politics or ethics, has been the
core of epic from the Hellenistic allegoresis of Homer forward. Renaissance criticism and practice intensified this element by heavily emphasizing the didactic purpose of epic and fitting it out as a tool to teach
man about, and to help him obtain, felicity: the *summum bonum.*[2]
Usually this end was sought through the medium of allegory, as in Tasso
and Spenser, but subsequent poets tended to be more and more explicit
about the goals of their poetry. Thus Milton deals overtly with the loss
and regaining of felicity, and Fénelon, pursuing a civil virtue rather than
a theological one, puts his Télémaque through a series of explicitly
political lessons. The matter of the allegory tends to replace the matter of
the narrative. Epic is in the process of biting its own tale, of moving
through narrative and allegory back to psychomachy — a process that is
perhaps best illustrated in *The Dunciad* or *A Tale of a Tub*. The process
is complicated further by the shifting definition of wisdom itself, which
was undergoing changes diametrically opposite those of the epic hero.
While he was metamorphosing from everyman to super-hero, wisdom
was moving from divinity to near-worldliness, from an attribute of God
and knowledge of things divine shared by men only through a kind of
divine in-flowing or participation in Christ who was Wisdom, to
philosophical knowledge naturally obtainable, to morality, to
prudence.[3] The epic virtue moves out of the sphere of contemplation and
more and more into the realm of action — like the respective bodies of
knowledge in *The Dunciad* and *A Tale of a Tub* — while the epic hero
performs the contrary motion and becomes more and more actionless —
like David in *Absalom and Achitophel,* or Shadwell in *MacFlecknoe,*
or Cibber in *The Dunciad.* The tension tears epic apart, dividing it
between a series of episodes more and more sensational because they

must provide the interest and a hero who because of his superiority to all circumstances can provide no drama whatever. At least a part of the mock epics we have talked about has been legitimately mockery of the epic: Cibber's inactivity means many things, and that is one of them. The *Tale of a Tub*, too, partakes of that mockery: its alternation of fable and essay and usurpation of fable by essay recapitulates the process by which content destroyed form. These two works embody, for me at least, the nadir of formal epic, epic's own descent to hell. Fielding plays the sybil to lead it back to light. In his works, from *Joseph Andrews* through to *Amelia,* epic meaning is once again welded to epic action, and the internals and externals of epic are made to coincide.

Fielding's three novels deal with increasingly larger and more generous notions of wisdom and with correspondingly greater sweeps of society. Their themes progress from an examination of prudence and constancy in *Joseph Andrews,* where the effects are confined to the relatively small space symbolized by Wilson's home, to the elaboration of a much fuller conception of wisdom in *Tom Jones* and the greater scope represented by the Allworthy and Western estates, to the meticulous investigation of philosphic liberty in *Amelia* and the embryonic regeneration of a whole society. As this thematic growth goes on, Fielding at the same time proceeds to utilize more and more traditional epic material; this culminates in *Amelia,* which, simply, *is* epic. If Renaissance is to be defined or characterized, as Irwin Panofsky suggests, by the rejoining of classical form with classical meaning, then Fielding's novels constitute the Renaissance of epic: by *Amelia,* a classical notion of wisdom has been relinked with a classical notion of epic scope, both articulated over a traditional structure and worked out through the deeds of flawed human beings. Fielding, by discarding the petrified *forms* of epic and rediscovering the human nature of the epic hero, managed to restore epic to the culturally central position that, under the guise of the novel, it has not lost since.

It is probably important at this point to acknowledge that, strictly speaking, it is incorrect to speak of *"the* novel." Novel is not *a* genre but many genres: Fielding's kind derives from the epic and responds best to criticism guided by that knowledge whereas Defoe's kind, for instance, derives from spiritual biography and responds best to examination from that point of view, as Hunter's and Starr's books have shown. Richardson's novels, too, have a different pedigree, and there are undoubtedly many others, but real generic distinctions *can* and *should* be made among them. To refer to them all in a lump as "the novel" is not merely confusing, it is dead wrong.

I

It should be clear from all this that I regard seriously Fielding's claim that *Joseph Andrews* is a comic epic in prose, however unfashionable it may be to do so. Fielding does not obfuscate, however much he may indulge his irony, and his careful establishment of pedigree, his examination of *Joseph Andrews*'s form, action and fable, characters and manners, and diction in the manner Bossu made standard for criticism of epic ("Author's Preface"), his careful distinguishing of "*Joseph Andrews* from the productions of romance writers on the one hand, and burlesque writers on the other" ("Author's Preface") — all these seem clearly designed to guide and shape the reader's expectations from the beginning of the book. I cannot see what value an extended irony at this point would have for an author as concerned about form and the reader's response to it as Fielding consistently shows himself to be. He seriously means that *Joseph Andrews* is "a comic romance," which is in turn the same thing as "a comic epic-poem in prose," and he really means that its non-comic counterpart and predecessor is "the Telemachus of the Archbishop of Cambray" (p. 2) — and behind that, of course, the *Odyssey*.

At just about the halfway point of the novel, Fielding uses Parson Adams to remind us of that opening analysis by having that benevolent Christian express and explain his preference of the *Iliad* to the *Odyssey*, contrary to the opinions of Aristotle and Horace (3.2). Adams employs the same divisions Fielding earlier used: subject, action, manners, sentiments, and diction. To these he subjoins several other considerations — that of "the *Harmatton,* that agreement of his action to his subject"; Homer's excellence in delineating "the pathetic"; and his management of "*Opsis*, or the scenery." Fielding is of course exploiting some obvious ironies here in the kindly parson's taste for the fierceness and cruelty of the *Iliad* while he himself is unknowingly engaged in an *Odyssey,* but that should not distract us from the larger ironic counterpoint between the things Adams praises in Homer's poem and the excellences of Fielding's novel. Certainly Parson Adams's encomium of the richness of Homer's characters and his ability to delineate the passions is designed not merely to remind us simultaneously of Adams's erudite vanity and basic good heart, but also to call forth our assent that these are indeed accomplishments and to direct our attention to just how much Fielding has done in the same vein. And the notion of the *Harmatton* seems crucial to Fielding's own book: its subject is constancy, and its action, like the *Odyssey*'s, a much-interrupted journey home.[4] Adams and Joseph are, in the literal sense, men of as many turns as Odysseus. And for scenery, Fielding offers neither the plains of Troy nor the summits of Ida, Olympus, or Sarnos, but the inns and homes of England, where, as Parson Adams remarked some pages earlier, "he almost began to suspect that he was sojourning in a country inhabited only by Jews and Turks" (2.16).

Fielding frequently strives for this sort of juxtaposition, and he achieves it in a number of ways besides through formal analysis or criticism. A number of quotations from the *Aeneid* are scattered throughout *Joseph Andrews* that serve the immediate function of (usually) allowing Parson Adams vent for his feelings and the ultimate one of briefly juxtaposing moments from *Joseph Andrews* with moments from classical epic. Fielding's occasional burlesques and his more frequent allusions to the high style serve the same ends. Stylistic self-consciousness furnishes one of the most important means by which Fielding can with greater and greater sharpness distinguish what his novel is doing from what it will not even attempt. In distinguishing *Joseph Andrews* from works in the high style, Fielding can make some very precise discriminations about the adequacies and relevance of those styles.

The twelfth chapter of the second book furnishes a fine example of this. Ostensibly, what happens in the course of this chapter is very simple. Adams and Fanny are driven by rain to an ale-house where Fanny hears a man singing in another room and promptly faints; Adams bellows to call help; the singer, responding, turns out to be Joseph Andrews, and a joyous reunion follows. But that synopsis entirely misses the point of the chapter, which is — and is conveyed by — style. Fielding begins with a paragraph, preparatory to his description of Fanny, that concerns itself with the deliciousness of the artifact about to be introduced and invokes several precedents, classical and otherwise, for the danger of infatuation:

> Fanny sat likewise down by the fire; but was much more impatient at the storm. She presently engaged the eyes of the host, his wife, the maid of the house, and the young fellow who was their guide; they all conceived they had never seen anything half so handsome, and indeed, reader, if thou art of an amorous hue, I advise thee to skip over the next paragraph; which, to render our history perfect, we are obliged to set down, humbly hoping that we may escape the fate of Pygmalion; for if it should happen to us, or to thee, to be struck with this picture, we should be perhaps in as helpless a condition as Narcissus, and might say to ourselves, *Quod petis est nusquam.* Or, if the finest features in it should set Lady _____'s image before our eyes, we should be still in as bad situation, and might say to our desires, *Coelum ipsum petimus stultitia.* (2.12)

The description that follows debunks this mock solemnity and showy erudition by its sheer naturalness: Fanny's beauty is unaffected, owes nothing to art, and in fact is not reducible to it: " . . . Add to these a countenance in which, though she was extremely bashful, a sensibility appeared almost incredible; and a sweetness, whenever she smiled, beyond either imitation or description. To conclude all she had a natural gentility, superior to the acquisition of art, and which surprised all who beheld her." Fielding immediately juxtaposes this with Joseph's song, "a voice from an inner room," which is "artistic" in the extreme, filled with Lethes and Narcissus, Graces and Zephyrus, images living in the breast and burning souls. It concludes with an ornate and elegant fornication and an equally elegant joke:

Advances like these made me bold;
    I whisper'd her, "Love, — we're alone";
The rest let immortals unfold:
    No language can tell but their own.
Ah, Chloe, expiring, I cried,
    How long I thy cruelty bore!
Ah! Strephon, she blushing replied,
    You ne'er was so pressing before.

                      (2.12)

The artificiality of language and sentiment masks the extreme natural-ness of the wooer's and lady's behavior — indeed, masks the irony that it is chaste Joseph Andrews who sings this seduction song. Fanny has more reason than the shock of recognition for fainting. Her reaction, of course, immediately deflates the artificiality of the song's reunion of lovers, and their simple exchange — "Are you Joseph Andrews?" "Art thou my Fanny?" — effectively demolishes the ornate style for the purposes of this novel, just as the real chastity of Joseph and Fanny undercuts the literary copulation of Chloe and her swain. The death blow — in many ways — is dealt by Parson Adams, who prances for joy at this renuion, and does not notice that his Aeschylus, like Strephon, is expiring in flames. Adams's Aeschylus is an easy symbol of his harmless vanity and pride in his erudition; equally easily, it embodies the most elaborate form of an ornate and ritualized art, and the first subsidiary genre derived from epic. Fielding is making points about decorum and about natural-ness, and both the stylized lyric and the stylized drama (and I would say, by extension, the stylized epic) are inappropriate as vehicles for what he has to depict, just as the artifice of the Pygmalion simile is inappropriate to the naturalness of Fanny or the sophisticated license of the song is inappropriate to the unaffected modesty of Joseph and Fanny. The high style and the genres and conduct associated with it are no longer an adequate vehicle for the kind of truth Fielding is trying to express. The whole point of the juxtaposition of all these elements in this chapter is to dramatize the necessity, out of reasons of simple decorum, to generate a new form commensurate with these contents.[5] In the same manner, I would also argue that one of the functions of the "Tale of Leonora, or the

Unfortunate Jilt" is to demonstrate the narrative inadequacies of the Richardsonian epistolary form. This is exactly the opposite of the function of the ornate style in *The Rape of the Lock*; here the mock epic is mocking the epic, or at least that portion of it that had been frozen into attitudes and language inappropriate to contemporary reality. One need only compare the reunion of Orestes and Electra in the Aeschylus that Parson Adams discards with the reunion he witnesses to realize the gulf that Fielding's style has crossed.[6]

I do not mean that Fielding created *de novo*, of course, but that he forced a new bloom from the old rootstock, and most of its characteristics can be traced with relative clarity to various components of its ancestry.[7] Fielding's burlesques of the epic are, with the exception of Adams's and Joseph's battle with the hunting squire's dogs, not substantive but stylistic, and the sorts of romances he distinguishes his book from are not *Don Quixote* or *Gierusalemme Liberata* or the *Faerie Queene,* but "such . . . voluminous works commonly called Romances, namely, *Clelia, Cleopatra, Astraea, Cassandra,* the *Grand Cyrus,* and innumerable others, which contain, as I apprehend, very little instruction or entertainment" ("Author's Preface"). I want to suggest that in establishing a structure for this book, his first try at "this species of writing, . . . hitherto unattempted in our language" ("Author's Preface"), Fielding consciously or unconsciously, with or without knowledge, recreated the form of the prime example of the "grave romance" in English, Spenser's *Faerie Queene.* Let me make clear at the outset that I am not trying to argue that Fielding in any detailed sense used a particular book of *The Faerie Queene* as a model; rather, I want to suggest that in Spenser he could find a versatile structural pattern used to embody a subject matter very similar to what he himself had in hand (*The Faerie Queene* is not the only place he could find it, of course, but it is one of the most proximate). He could also find in *The Faerie Queene,* seriously treated, the chivalric materials *Don Quixote* burlesques, which would be in itself an advantage to his "Imitation of the Manner of Cervantes" without burlesque. That is, *The Faerie Queene* is the major English work that stands in the same relation to *Joseph Andrews* as the continental chivalric romances do to *Don*

Quixote. For these reasons I will attempt to use Spenser's poem to clarify Fielding's novel (which may be darkness heaped on darkness); for the sake of simplicity and because of the consonance of subject matter, I will confine my discussion to the Britomart episodes of *The Faerie Queene.* Again, I will not be arguing that Fielding "followed" Spenser; I am only trying to show the place that the comic materials of *Joseph Andrews* already held in the epic tradition and to locate them against the background of serious meaning another writer in that tradition utilized. The underlying assumption I am making is that epic as genre possesses a kind of autonomy that in and of itself bends its practitioners into paths already blazed within its confines. Something like this notion seems to me to lurk not very far behind the eighteenth century's respect for genre and decorum; the very violations of decorum to which so much of my discussion thus far has been attentive seem in themselves to point to an organic relation among form, content, and style of which it would be folly to assume a writer as sensitive to such matters as Fielding was unaware. For all of these *a priori* reasons, I find it useful to consider *Joseph Andrews* in the light of *The Faerie Queene; my ex post facto* reason is that it works.

   Although it is undeniably true that Joseph Andrews in the course of his wanderings acquires the kind of prudence that will enable him to survive in the world and that Parson Adams so delightfully lacks, it is neverthe-less not true that this is the point of the novel. If it were, I doubt anyone would read it or that a man as imprudent as Henry Fielding would have written it. It has always struck me that in making *Joseph Andrews* into a tract on prudence we act as if it were written by Blifil. The simple virtue or compound of virtues that *Joseph Andrews* genuinely displays, how-ever, and that impels the major actions of the story, from Joseph's first refusal of Lady Booby's bed to his final escape from her hand and house, can be subsumed briefly under the name of constancy — the constancy of Joseph to Fanny that informs his chastity and enables him to scorn the lure of wealth and position, her constancy to him, Parson Adams's constancy to his parishioners and his own benevolence, even, in both the physical and metaphorical senses, the constancy of their homeward journeys. This more generous and humane virtue is the real core of

Fielding's novel; for it, Joseph and Fanny are rewarded — "A minute carried him into her arms, where we shall leave this happy couple to enjoy the private rewards of their constancy" (4.16) — and to it, prudence, circumspection, and all narrower virtues are clearly subservient.

Britomart's quest for Artegal spans books 3 and 4 of *The Faerie Queene,* the books of chastity and friendship respectively; and the idea of constancy provides the unifying element for the diverse episodes of these books in the same manner that constancy in Fielding's novel holds to a single point the diverse pulls of chastity, love, and friendship among Joseph, Fanny, and Adams. The sexual roles are, of course, reversed, and Joseph plays Britomart's part as exemplar of chastity, impelled by love and constantly seeking union with his beloved. However, he is like Artegal in that he is a changeling. Fanny seems more like Amoret — lovely, timorous, chaste, faithful to her lover, a foundling also, and incessantly subject to attack, abduction, and near rape, from which she is rescued by Britomart. Fielding conflates all of the diverse love pursuits of *Faerie Queene* 3 and 4 into a single tale of chaste love aided by friendship. But the importance of the *Faerie Queene* to *Joseph Andrews* is not through specific characters, though there are many correspondences — the blood-and-thunder gentleman who descants to Adams about bravery and flees at the first alarm is a lineal descendant of Braggadochio, for instance — but through the broad structural pattern I discussed in connection with *The Rape of the Lock* and through certain narrative particulars Spenser uses in association with it.

Joseph Andrews employs the same basic epic grammar as the other works we have thus far discussed. Books 1 and 4 answer each other with perfect symmetry in every major factor. The discovery of Joseph's real birth and family in 4 parallels the account of his supposed birth and family at the very beginning of the book. Lady Booby's and Slipslop's comic attempts to seduce him correspond to Didapper's inept attempt at Fanny and Adams's innocent sojourns in Slipslop's and Fanny's beds (in Joseph's discovery of him in the latter, Fielding also gives us a reprise of Mrs. Towwouse's discovery of her husband in the arms of Betty the chambermaid). Joseph dismissed, robbed, stripped, and abandoned is recapitulated and reversed by Joseph freed from trial, dressed, and welcomed as brother into the Booby family. Books 2 and 3 are more intricately intertwined and paralleled, in a manner reminiscent of Spenser's overall management of his books 3 and 4. Here Fielding multiplies incidents astonishingly, and the correspondences abound, ranging from the repetitive loss and recovery of Adams's horse and his preference of the "pedestrian" mode to the "equestrian," through symmetrical fights at inns, to counterpointed rescues of Fanny from rape. The cowardly hunting squire of book 2 anticipates the vicious hunting squire of book 3. The troubles Adams's Aeschylus and his vanity about his learning lead him into at his trial in book 2 foreshadow the similar troubles raised by his readiness to read a sermon and play Socrates in the hunting squire's prank. The first meeting of Joseph, Fanny, and Adams is matched by their reunion near the end of book 3. The argument Adams has with the innkeeper, at the end of 2, about practical and speculative knowledge is perfectly paralleled by a similar argument, near the beginning of 3, with Joseph about public and private education. Over this basic grammar, of course, Fielding has fashioned a structural rhetoric of his own, which works itself out through an intricate series of repetitions and modifications of thematic situations involving religion (Barnabas, Trulliber, Adams himself), law (the quarreling lawyers, Adams and Fanny's trial, Wilson's story, Lawyer Scout, Joseph and Fanny's trial), active good works, love and sex, interpolated stories, and so on. Wilson's story is obviously central to this rhetoric since it provides links forward and backward to almost every major theme in the story, including the crucial one of Joseph's and Fanny's real identities.

The Wilson episode functions too as a comic version of the typical Spenserian "house of recognition," which usually schools the hero about himself and matters pertaining to the theme of the particular book. Such are the House of Holiness in book one of the *Faerie Queene,* the Castle of Alma in book 2, the Temple of Isis in book 5, and less typically but more relevant here, Belphoebe's dwelling ("a dainty, place . . . As it an earthly Paradize had beene . . ." [3.5.40]) and the Garden of Adonis (3.6), both the symbolic loci of chaste and fertile love, like Wilson's house and gardens, which Adams, ignoring the intrusion of reality in the young squire's cruel shooting of the spaniel (as death, too, mars the perfection of the Garden of Adonis), declares "was the manner in which the people lived in the golden age" (3.4).

Characteristically Spenserian, too, is Fielding's use of houses of recognition — or perhaps more properly, houses of temptation — at the beginning and end of his book. In book 3 of the *Faerie Queene,* these are the Castle Joyous, where Malecasta attempts to seduce Britomart, taking her for a man, and the House of Busirane, where Britomart frees the faithful Amoret from her captivity to lust; in *Joseph Andrews,* they are the town and country homes of Lady Booby. Malecasta tempts to simple lust, from which pitfall Britomart is effectively saved by the naturalness of her inclinations and their being already fixed on Artegal. Nevertheless, she is somewhat taken in by Malecasta's "strong extremitie" (3.1.53) and as a result sustains a slight wound from Gardante (3.1.65), that is, lust of the eyes. Lady Booby's own "strong extremitie" subjects Joseph Andrews to the same trial, which he comically passes through the strength of his virtue ("Your virtue! . . . I shall never survive it." [1.8]) and, as we discover later, of his love for Fanny. Nevertheless, he too is touched: "But I am glad she turned me out of the chamber as she did: for I had once almost forgotten every word Parson Adams had ever said to me" (1.10). The temptation posed in the House of Busirane is far more complex, and Britomart, to emerge safely from it and save Amoret, must draw on everything she has learned in the course of the book about love, chastity, and constancy. She must, in effect, see through the whole Masque of Cupid and distinguish lust in all its disguises. Then she must reject not merely lust as an end, but lust as a means to power, position, wealth, and so on. At Booby-Hall, Joseph undergoes this complex of temptations as, with shifting clarity, it becomes apparent that he is no longer a footman and as marriage to Lady Booby becomes a more and more real possibility. He is no longer tempted to simple lust (in that respect he is exactly like Britomart in the House of Busirane, fighting not for his own chastity but for another's) but rather to inconstancy, self-aggrandizement (self-improvement, Pamela would say), and loveless marriage: he can, if he wishes, use Lady Booby's lust as a means to his own ends. Lady Booby is of course no longer the simple lay figure for sexual desire and hypocrisy that she was in book 1; she, too, is now presented as a far more complex creature, alternately driven and distracted by her desires, even to the point that, like Busirane, she would sooner destroy her beloved than lose him.

To pass this test, Joseph must balance his own love and fidelity against the demands of a fickle and inconstant world and the kind of prudence, which, to this point, has been the *sine qua non* of survival in the world. That is, at the crucial point in the novel and his fortunes, he has to turn his back on the world and opt for impracticality and improvidence — for Parson Adams, in short, rather than Lady Booby. The choice is not easy, particularly when Joseph finds Adams and Fanny in bed together: after all that has happened in the novel, it requires a very impractical act of faith to believe that Adams does not know "whether she is a man or a woman" (4.14). If the momentary disclosure that Joseph and Fanny are brother and sister exposes the limitations of prudence as a governor of human conduct (there being no possible prudential step that could prevent their ignorant incest, and the unpredictable appearance and chance information of the pedlar being the basis of the episode), then Joseph's final choices with regard to Lady Booby and Parson Adams show the absolute necessity of transcending it. Lady Booby is prudential, and at the end of the novel Lady Booby is alone. It is a nice touch, I think, that Fielding casts this last test for his heroes in the form of Britomart's first. In that episode, her manly appearance in full armor led Malecasta to think her a man and subsequently to steal into her bed; discovering the intrusion, Britomart grabbed her sword and Malecasta shrieked in fright, rousing the household, thus revealing Britomart's sex and finally forcing Britomart and the Red Crosse Knight to fight their way out of the Castle. The compound of mistaken identities and genders that speeds *Joseph Andrews* to its conclusion is loosely drawn on this same pattern: Parson Adams, responding to a cry for help, mistakes the sexes of assailer and assailed, releases Didapper (who had already mistaken his target) and pummels Slipslop, whose sex he only discovers when Lady Booby arrives with light. Embarrassed but exonerated, he beats an erroneous retreat to Fanny's bed, where he is discovered by Joseph soon after, unable to explain his presence and protesting

— with some justice, after his run-in with Slipslop and Didapper — that "As I am a Christian, I know not whether she is a man or woman" (4.14). In that denial lies the real comic resolution of *Joseph Andrews;* coupled with Joseph's and Fanny's acceptance of it, that narrative moment graphs both the limitations of prudence and the limits of chastity, as well as the absolute necessity for constancy, love, and friendship to transcend them. What is at stake here is a virtue in which prudence, chastity, love, friendship, and constancy are all rooted — self-knowledge, the simple fact of one's own identity. In the terms of *Joseph Andrews,* to know who you are is to know what you are; for this reason the novel climaxes in its plethora of mistaken identities and final sortings-out of relation, all of which are comically encapsulated in Parson Adams's nocturnal misadventures. Vanity prevents one from seeing himself and others clearly, and from that vice only Joseph and Fanny are free, though the vanity of others has made the two of them the victims of misunderstanding and misinterpretation throughout their adventures. Their final appearance before the justice (4.5) dramatizes this: treated as vagrants and criminals because of Lady Booby's vanity, they are freed and reappraised because of her nephew's familial pride. No one sees them in themselves, only in relation to a complex of factors engaging or endangering their own pride and self-esteem. Adams and Fanny's early appearance before a justice almost overtly states this: (2.11) the issue of the hearing becomes Adams's identity, and to the query "What's your name?" Adams, answering another challenge to his vanity and not the relevant question, responds, "It is Aeschylus, and I will maintain it." Vanity, as Fielding insists throughout the book, fogs the mind and the perceptions, makes us see ourselves and others falsely — and the only viable correctives to vanity are self-knowledge, constancy, and active charity joined together. Prudence merely serves vanity, and the others disjunct are powerless against it, as is Joseph by himself — discharged, robbed, and beaten — or Fanny — deceived and nearly raped — or Adams — deceived, put upon, made a butt of. Together they triumph in the novel's understated and inevitable denouement when, in one of Fielding's moments of crystallized significance, Parson Adams marries Joseph and Fanny.

Again let me insist that I do not mean to imply that Fielding is in any way alluding to Spenser. I do not think that an awareness of the presence of Spenserian elements is important to understanding *Joseph Andrews*. The reasons I mention Spenser at all in connection with Fielding are three: first, the *Faerie Queene* shows the place Fielding's thematic materials already held in "serious romance" (not entirely serious either; there are many comic elements already in the *Faerie Queene,* and many more capable of comedy); second, Fielding could find in Spenser a usable pattern for structuring his narrative; and third and most important, he could find in Spenser the techniques for making that narrative *be* meaning, rather than *bear* meaning. Plot in novels or epics is usually talked about as a separable value: it is nice, neat, well-rounded, or it is loose, uneven, disjointed, and so on. It is never discussed as if the plot — the simple movement of the characters from place to place, episode to episode — in itself meant anything. It does. This does not refer to situational symbolism, intermittent allegory, or anything of that sort, but to a pervasive use of the literal statement of the plot as significant, intelligible, in itself; not the vehicle of meaning, but meaning itself.

All love, the Renaissance knew, moves toward fulfillment, and the kind of motion it performs defines it. Rational motion is like the motion of the planets, circular, from east through west and back to east again. Animal appetite is centrifugal, a straight line breaking out of the rational circle; love is centripetal, a straight line breaking through the ring of rationality. Constancy guides these motions, holds them to their goal, and bends the straight lines of appetite and love into the circles of reason.[8] That set of motions furnishes Fielding's "*Harmatton,* that agreement of his action to his subject" (3.2); his subjects are love, lust, and constancy; his action is a homeward wandering — a straight line that the conclusion of the novel curves into a circle. So the journey itself is not symbolic. It is not the vehicle of meaning; it *is* meaning. We are not dealing with a system of substitutions here, with things standing for other things, but rather with a system of equations: love is motion, motion is a journey, love is a journey, and every step and episode of that journey exist and mean in precisely that way. This is not exactly allegory, and it is certainly not metaphor; but whatever you call it, it works. Consider, for example, Parson Adams asleep and unknowing by Fanny's side: the meaning of that episode is contained perfectly in the action — or inaction — of it. It is not that it does not mean anything — it means, and means profoundly, in the context of *Joseph Andrews* — but that its meaning is perfectly crystallized in its narrative statement. Fielding has achieved, at this moment, and in the wedding, and in a few others in *Joseph Andrews,* a perfect consonance between form and content so that his subject is embodied with perfect clarity, with unimpeded translucence, in his action.

This notion of Harmatton, the congruence of tenor and vehicle, seems as central to Fielding's conception of his book as Adams implies it is to epic, and Fielding's manipulation of it and the narrative manner that develops from it are thoroughly Spenserian. This means, I think, that the novel proceeds by a kind of quasi-allegoresis: quasi because the process is, as I said before, not one whereby one thing stands for or represents another but rather a process of embodiment or equation. My critical vocabulary is inadequate to what I am trying to express here: what is at stake, as clearly as I can put it, is the articulation, the enunciation, of the figurative not through but *in* the literal — in the terms I have used elsewhere in this book, it is, metaphorically, the rejoining of spirit and letter, theologically, making the word flesh.

I can only clarify by examples. Fielding often in *Joseph Andrews* forces us to appraise the *littera* of his text by juxtapositions that push us to awareness of the value of sameness and difference. Early in the novel, Slipslop's awkward attempt on Joseph neatly counterpoints Lady Booby's more elegant try. Later in the book, in two supposedly simultaneous actions, Joseph and Adams, tied to the bedpost, argue about giving vent to the emotions, while a poet and a player argue about the state of the drama (3.10,11). Poet and player pass from decrying the poorness of the stage and blaming it, respectively, on players and poets to excluding each other from the general condemnation to quarreling about which was responsible for the failure of their last endeavor. In the parallel chapter, Joseph bemoans the loss of Fanny, and Parson Adams comforts him in such a fashion that he is even more grieved. Joseph admits his obligation to accept the dispensations of Providence, but denies he is capable of performing it; Adams further lectures him in the same vein, until Joseph bursts out with a snatch of Shakespeare. The whole final paragraph deserves quotation:

> They remained some time in silence; and groans and sighs issued from them both; at length Joseph burst out into the following soliloquy:
>
> > Yes, I will bear my sorrows like a man,
> > But I must also feel them as a man.
> > I cannot but remember such things were,
> > And were most dear to me. —
>
> Adams asked him what stuff that was he repeated? — To which he answered, they were some lines he had gotten by heart out of a play. — "Ay, there is nothing but heathenism to be learned from plays," replied he. — "I never heard of any plays fit for a Christian to read, but *Cato* and the *Conscious Lovers;* and, I must own, in the latter there are some things almost solemn enough for a sermon." But we shall now leave them a little, and inquire after the subject of their conversation. (3.11)

The sequence apparently takes its point from the ancient metaphor of the world as stage or the stage as world; the two chapters simply juxtapose the two terms of the metaphor, leaving the reader to choose for himself whatever relation of tenor to vehicle he likes while pushing him to see the mutual equality of both.[9] The two cases are not so much allegories of each other as they are parallels: both are concerned directly with the problems raised by a difficult part; both revolve around the expression of emotion. But the poet and the player argue because the emotion — the distress — was, either in the writing or the saying, expressed inadequately; the distress was not done justice. Adams and Joseph, on the other hand, argue because Joseph *is* expressing distress, despite the fact that the latter doesn't "endeavour to grieve." Adams preaches a harsh and highly erudite Stoicism to Joseph that seems not only inappropriate to the moment but pretty well beyond the powers of a human being. The stage appears more real(istic?) — certainly more human — than life; life, as expounded and exemplified by Adams, has all the artificiality, the role-playing, of the stage. Adams makes life into formal declamation and the striking of pose, like the two highly rhetorical and attitudinizing plays he cites, *Cato* and *The Conscious Lovers,* "in the latter" of which "there are some things almost solemn enough for a sermon." Joseph breaks the deadlock — for the reader, if not for Parson Adams — by appealing out of life to high art, out of the unfeeling life that Adams at this point expounds to the rich humanity of Shakespeare. He merges life and art in the moment when artistic utterance becomes the only valid expression of what he really feels; although Parson Adams damns the play, Joseph does the distress of it justice. How you handle life and how you handle a role are the questions of the two chapters, and humanly is Shakespeare's and Joseph's and Fielding's answer. Parson Adams's assertions that "there is nothing but heathenism to be learned from plays" and that he "never heard of any plays fit for a Christian to read, but *Cato* and the *Conscious Lovers*" sound more than odd from one whose prize possession has been an edition of Aeschylus, and we may very well wonder what it all means. The tension in Adams between theory and practice, between the formulaic demands of his erudition and the spontaneity of his own feelings, remains unresolved in *Joseph Andrews;* Adams is still at the end of the novel a schizoid figure who cannot rationally master, as he knows he ought, what he so passionately feels. He appeals to the wrong authorities, to the aloofness of Stoicism and the ritual of Aeschylus to order and restrain a life that resists both. Joseph's turning to Shakespeare shows the inadequacy of that kind of art to contain real life just as Adams's throwing his Aeschylus in the fire out of joyous excitement dramatizes the same thing. The richness, diversity, and irregularity of Shakespeare offer the only adequate merging of art and life, the only adequate vehicle for the actions of real people in a real world. As opposed to Adams's Aeschylus, Seneca, Cicero, and Homer, Shakespeare is well within the reach and capacity of Fielding's "mere English reader." In the bedroom farce that moves the novel to its final unraveling, Adams can only call upon the *deus ex machina* of witchcraft, whereas Joseph can recognize a wrong turning. That, and these two chapters, are not allegories for something else: like Shakespeare's plays, they are the thing itself.

Parson Adams provides the formulaic center of the novel, the man who generates theories to explain what is going on around him. The fact that his theories are always inadequate to explain, much less to control, the events of the book aligns him in conception and function with Gulliver and the narrator of *A Tale of a Tub* and with the yet unborn Walter Shandy — which is one very clear reason why Parson Adams is not and cannot be the hero of the book. He shows in himself the irrelevance of theory to reality, the futility of trying to force life into a mold rather than looking at it clearly. For this reason, I think, Fielding has equipped him with a harsh theoretical Stoicism that contradicts directly the warmth of his own feelings as well as a "masterpiece" against vanity that must underscore his own very real vanity about his pastoral and pedagogic abilities. Similarly, Wilson appears in his own story in the same way; he is a man who has tried all of the theoretical approaches to life, from sensuality to reason to literature, from activity to retirement, from public to private, from gentleman to imprisoned debtor, from the fixity of reason to total commitment to fortune. His story functions in the novel as a succinct *Rasselas,* exploring all of the possible choices of ways of life according to eighteenth-century preconceptions or theories. Fielding uses the Wilson episode as a comic descent to hell in parodic relation to the *Aeneid:* Adams, Joseph, and Fanny, frightened by what they take to be ghosts, flee down a steep hill and across a river, enter the house of a man who is in fact Joseph's father, hear from him an autobiography that is a paradigm of the knowledge needful for survival in the world and that contains the essential clues to Joseph's identity. Joseph, however, sleeps through it all, and all practical knowledge is wasted on Parson Adams. What *we* eventually learn from it, however, is who Joseph is and what he must become: we see in it the inadequacy of Parson Adams's theory of private education, the ludicrousness of his system of physiognomy, and the irrelevance of his "book traveling" to form a man capable of dealing with reality. We understand, simply, what the protagonists of mock epic never learn, that you cannot substitute theory for life. Parson Adams's pronouncement that Wilson's life is Edenic, despite the vicious neighboring squire and the killing of the spaniel, simply confirms him as a mock-epic figure and an inadequate guide, an earthly Anchises from whose erroneous tutelage Joseph must break free.[10]

Fanny's role in the novel illustrates in a similar way this process by which Fielding realizes the figurative in the literal. Since Fanny provides the main impetus for Joseph's single major act (leaving London for the country) and many subsequent lesser ones, she is obviously a crucial figure in our understanding of the novel (though you might not be able to judge that from the dearth of readers' comments about her). Physically, Fielding describes her as the female counterpart of Joseph: they are obviously, in a meaningful phrase, made for each other. It would be simplest merely to juxtapose the two descriptions.

> Mr. Joseph Andrews was now in the one-and-twentieth year of his age. He was of the highest degree of middle stature. His limbs were put together with great elegance and no less strength. His legs and thighs were formed in the exactest proportion. His shoulders were broad and brawny; but yet his arms hung so easily, that he had all the symptoms of strength without the least clumsiness. His hair was of a nut-brown colour, and was displayed in wanton ringlets down his back. His forehead was high, his eyes dark, and as full of sweetness as of fire. His nose a little inclined to the Roman. His teeth white and even. His lips full, red, and soft. His beard was only rough on his chin and upper lip; but his cheeks, in which his blood glowed, were overspread with a thick down. His countenance had a tenderness joined with a sensibility inexpressible. Add to this the most perfect neatness in his dress, and an air which, to those who have not seen many noblemen, would give an idea of nobility. (1.8)

> Fanny was now in the nineteenth year of her age; she was tall, and delicately shaped; but not one of those slender young women who seem rather intended to hang up in the hall of an anatomist than for any other purpose. On the contrary, she was so plump that she seemed bursting through her tight stays, especially in the part which confined her swelling breasts. Nor did her hips want the assistance of a hoop to

extend them. The exact shape of her arms denoted the form of those limbs which she concealed; and though they were a little reddened by her labour, yet, if her sleeve slipt above her elbow, or her handkerchief discovered any part of her neck, a whiteness appeared which the finest Italian paint would be unable to reach. Her hair was of a chestnut brown, and nature had been extremely lavish to her of it, which she had cut, and on Sundays used to curl down her neck in the modern fashion. Her forehead was high, her eyebrows arched, and rather full than otherwise. Her eyes black and sparkling; her nose just inclining to the Roman; her lips red and moist, and her underlip, according to the opinion of the ladies, too pouting. Her teeth were white, but not exactly even. The small-pox had left one only mark on her chin, which was so large, it might have been mistaken for a dimple, had not her left cheek produced one so near a neighbour to it, that the former served only for a foil to the latter. Her complexion was fair, a little injured by the sun, but overspread with such a bloom that the finest ladies would have exchanged all their white for it; add to these a countenance in which, though she was extremely bashful, a sensibility appeared almost incredible; and a sweetness, whenever she smiled, beyond either imitation or description. To conclude all, she had a natural gentility, superior to the acquisition of art, and which surprised all who beheld her. (2.12)

This physical similarity, of course, matches a general moral similarity: both are pure, honest, devoted to each other, and acquiescent to their lot in life. But there are other differences as well as those that spring from gender and the roles and limitations that imposes. Fanny is shy, retiring, sparing of speech (even when she does talk, Fielding tends to report it indirectly rather than by direct quotation), normally undemonstrative, and quite unassertive. She is also illiterate — which is more than a sardonic comment on Pamela's epistolary prolixity. Despite the fact that she is a strapping country girl, she remains the essentially helpless and passive target for a series of would-be rapists and molesters that includes the diminutive Didapper. While being hurried off "towards the squire's house, where [she] was to be offered up a sacrifice to the lust of a ravisher," she alternately weeps, implores aid from passersby, and protests most improbably against the captain's references to Joseph as "that pitiful fellow" and to her own "fondness for men." Clearly, she embodies more than the object of Joseph's love; she stands in a relation of total dependence to him, not just for her safety but even for activity, for speech, for literacy. Except for her original move to join Joseph, Fanny does nothing in the book that is not impelled directly by another, and even that is motivated by her concern for him. Joseph is her active principle, she his goal and source of direction. The full dimensions of her role are perhaps signaled by her surname, Goodwill, though I do not take this in any rigorous sense. Peter Pounce, shortly after rescuing her, modifies Parson Adams's definition of charity — "a generous disposition to relieve the distressed" — to "not so much consist in the act as in the disposition to do it" (3.13). Fanny is something like that, well-disposed but in herself powerless to act, though able to generate action in others. She is the mainspring of Joseph's virtues as she is of many others' basenesses — as object, morally neutral, though capable of exciting to either good or evil; as subject, disposed to good though impotent to do it. She plays the "unmoved mover" of the novel, the source of constancy and goal of love, toward which still point Joseph Andrews and the novel inexorably move. Fielding ludicrously hyperbolizes this in a comic reprise of his implicit comparison of her to Galatea and himself to Pygmalion (2.12), where he has Joseph frozen and fixed by the sight of Fanny's bosom, which "was more capable of converting a man into a statue than of being imitated by the greatest master of that art" (4.7). So, too, when they are wed: "She was soon undrest; for she had no jewels to deposit in their caskets, nor fine laces to fold with the nicest exactness. Undressing to her was properly discovering, not putting off, ornaments: for, as all her charms were the gifts of nature, she could divest herself of none. . . . Joseph no sooner heard she was in bed than he fled with the utmost eagerness to her. A minute carried him into her arms, where we shall leave this happy couple to enjoy the private rewards of their constancy. . . ." Shortly after, Joseph and Fanny join the Wilsons in their retirement, rounding the physical journey of the novel into its perfected circle and returning Joseph to his true home. The prominence of vicissitude, inconstancy, changes of fortune, and even the fickle goddess herself in Wilson's history make his home a haven of stability and permanence and a refuge from change and bustle. To this stillness Joseph and Fanny, immediately fertile in their union, retire. The novel closes with quiet insistence on this sabbath from change, the permanence of the achieved stillness after motion:

> Joseph remains blest with his Fanny, whom he doats on with the utmost tenderness, which is all returned on her side. The happiness of this couple is a perpetual fountain of pleasure to their fond parents; and, what is particularly remarkable, he declares he will imitate them in their retirement; nor will be prevailed on by any booksellers, or their authors, to makes his appearance in high-life. (4.16)

II

In *Tom Jones,* Fielding moves much closer to the traditional epic. The novel's much-remarked-upon plot falls with almost perfect symmetry into the ancient palindrome.[11] Tom, in his pursuit and attainment of Sophia, emulates literally and allegorically both Aeneas and Odysseus; Fielding's epigraph reinforces these correspondences; *"Mores hominum multorum vidit."* Sophia herself amalgamates into her role portions of Penelope — fidelity; Athena — the wisdom for which she is named; Venus — the love she feels and inspires; and Lavinia — the wife and prize. An outline of the plot of *Tom Jones* is the skeleton of epic, from the strange birth of the hero through his exile and labors to his triumphant return. *Tom Jones* manages to be comic epic in both Dante's sense and *Joseph Andrews*'s sense. In so being, it redefines and re-creates epic as genre in a new, complex, and viable manner, with a vitality that Fielding could never again reach, despite the richness and penetration he was later to bring to *Amelia.*

Fielding continues the constancy theme of *Joseph Andrews* in the plot of *Tom Jones,* making of it the nub of Tom's relations with Sophia. Here the concept and its handling are far more complex than they were in the earlier novel. Even on the simplest literal level, Tom violates constancy in his amours with Molly Seagrim and Jenny Waters and Lady

Bellaston as Joseph never does; and if Tom *is* constant as he claims to be, he must be constant to something beyond Sophia's physical form. The great reconciliation scene between the two plays intriguingly with these notions. [12] After the withdrawal of Squires Allworthy and Western, Jones asks Sophia to forgive him: she responds by appealing to his own justice "to pass sentence on your own conduct" (18.12). She then accuses him of inconstancy: "What happiness can I assure myself of with a man capable of so much inconstancy?" Tom in turn protests that his love is sincere, that had he possessed the slightest hope of her, "it would not have been in the power of any other woman to have inspired a thought which the severest chastity could have condemned. Inconstancy to you!" Sophia responds to this by saying that only time will give proof of the sincerity of his repentance: "After what is past, sir, can you expect I should take you upon your word?" The central dialogue of the whole scene follows, for which we need the exact words of the text:

> He replied, "Don't believe me upon my word; I have a better security, a pledge for my constancy, which it is impossible to see and to doubt." — "What is that?" said Sophia, a little surprised. — "I will show you, my charming angel," cried Jones, seizing her hand and carrying her to the glass. "There, behold it there in that lovely figure, in that face, that shape, those eyes, that mind which shines through these eyes. Can the man who shall be in possession of these be inconstant? Impossible! my Sophia; they would fix a Dorimant, a Lord Rochester. You could not doubt it, if you could see yourself with any eyes but your own." — Sophia blushed and half smiled; but, forcing again her brow into a frown — "If I am to judge," said she, "of the future by the past, my image will no more remain in your heart when I am out of your sight, than it will in this glass when I am out of the room." — "By Heaven, by all that is sacred!" said Jones, "it never was out of my heart. The delicacy of your sex cannot conceive the grossness of ours, nor how little one sort of amour has to do with the heart." — "I will never marry a man," replied Sophia, very gravely, "who shall not learn refinement enough to be as incapable as I am myself of making such a distinc-

tion." — "I will learn it," said Jones. "I have learnt it already. The first moment of hope that my Sophia might be my wife taught it me at once; and all the rest of her sex from that moment became as little the objects of desire to my sense as of passion to my heart." — "Well," said Sophia, "the proof of this must be from time. Your situation, Mr. Jones, is now altered, and I assure you I have great satisfaction in the alteration. You will now want no opportunity of being near me, and convincing me that your mind is altered too." (18.12)

Sophia promises that she will eventually, after this probationary period, marry Tom: he ecstatically kisses her, and they are interrupted by Squire Western's explosion into the room demanding an immediate wedding, to which importunate parental directive Sophia becomingly agrees. The chapter closes with general joy and congratulations.

Tom appeals to the idea of Sophia as proof of his constancy — to her image in the glass (with all that that should mean to us after the long history of the image itself and of reflective relationships in mock epic and epic), to the mind that her physical form manifests, to her image in his heart. His plea explicitly distinguishes between the physical Sophia and the idea of Sophia, between his own physical errancies and his spiritual constancy: for Sophia, that distinction is not valid, and Tom must learn that his physical fidelity must reflect his spiritual devotion just as Sophia's physical existence mirrors her spiritual perfections. One of the first facts Fielding told us about Sophia constitutes almost the last lesson Tom must master in the novel: to merge totally the flesh and the spirit.

> ————Her pure and eloquent blood
> Spoke in her cheeks, and so distinctly wrought
> That one might almost say her body thought.
>
> (4.2)

As Sophia is, so must Tom become, body mirroring mind, both embodying and enacting the virtues Sophia possesses and Tom pursues. At the very end of the novel, Fielding assures us that he has done this: "Whatever in the nature of Jones had a tendency to vice, has been corrected by continual conversation with [Squire Allworthy], and by his union with the lovely and virtuous Sophia" (18.13). Tom Jones must become the permanent mirror of Sophia's perfections, and the constancy he must develop is fidelity to that elaborate amalgam of virtues: that alone will wed him to Sophia and transform him from mere Tom Jones into Tom Allworthy.

Fielding rediscovered one basic fact about epic that guaranteed him a place in any history of epic or any other literature: the key to its complexity is its total simplicity; the entrance into myth and universality is through uniqueness and individuality. One can safely postulate, without the benefit of very much statistical research, that there were not very many foundlings in eighteenth-century England who were adopted by wealthy landowners or who married the prize catch of the county; yet for all that, Tom — to borrow a phrase from a later book in this same tradition — "is one of us." So the woman he loves, loses, leaves, pursues, and ultimately weds is Sophia. The sheer directness of that quasi-allegorical, "gothick" conception diverts attention from what Fielding is actually doing, just as the bland simplicity of Fielding's earlier citation of "the celebrated Dr. Donne['s]" description of *his* version of the female Wisdom figure (the verses quoted above, from *The Anniversaries*) masks the equation he is there making. Is Sophia wisdom? Certainly, or Fielding would not have called her that; but how she is wisdom and in what sense she is wisdom are questions far more problematical. She certainly does not appear to be wisdom in the same sense that Una is holiness: it is not her primary level of existence or signification in the novel. Rather, she *becomes* wisdom by what she does and by what is done about her; even more than in *Joseph Andrews,* the narrative events provide the mode for significance. Static symbols have little place in Fielding's novel except among the minor characters — Thwackum, for instance. For the reader, Tom's relationship with Sophia begins when Blifil releases the pet bird Tom had given her (4.3-4). The episode, ending with Tom's falling from a tree into the canal and the bird's falling to a hawk, provides a comic miniature centered in problems of justice and mercy, liberty and confinement, real and dissembled motive. The discussion among Thwackum, Square, a lawyer, and the two squires that follows it makes two facets of the situation clear: no one sees Blifil's real motive for his action (Thwackum and Square are blinded by devotion to their own theories of conduct, Allworthy by his softheartedness, and neither Western nor the lawyer are interested in motive, only in results), and the rather ponderous ethical issue at stake in this trivial event is justice. The law of nature legislates freedom for all creatures as the highest good; Christian equity demands that we do as we would be done to. Human law is silent in the case, since it is *nullius in bono.* All of this is true, but it takes Squire Western's simplicity to put it in perspective.

> "Well," says the squire, "if it be *nullus bonus,* let us drink about, and talk a little of the state of the nation, or some such discourse that we all understand; for I am sure I don't understand a word of this. It may be learning and sense for aught I know; but you shall never persuade me into it. Pox! you have neither of you mentioned a word of that poor lad who deserves to be commended: to venture breaking his neck to oblige my girl was a generous-spirited action: I have learning enough to see that. D--n me, here's Tom's health! I shall love the boy for it the longest day I have to live." (4.4)

The trouble with all the views expressed is that they are all partial ones, all singling out one aspect of justice and offering that as the whole, whereas justice itself, the crown of the virtues, embraces a whole gamut of considerations, from prudence and self-knowledge through to the duties owing to society and to God. The practice of justice is wisdom in its highest form, as any reader of Charron's *De la Sagesse* would have known.[13] Sophia is already being linked with wisdom in this sense by the predictive analogue of this episode: Blifil's machinations in the name of justice "free" and ultimately destroy an object of Sophia's affection, a small bird not accidentally named Tommy, and set up for the rest of the novel both narrative problems about the human Tom's fate and thematic problems of definition about justice, liberty, and confinement. These are the central concerns of the novel itself that will reach their climax in the parallel actions of Tom freed from prison and — the scene discussed before — Tom distinguishing apparent from real motive before Sophia's mirror. Sophia *becomes* wisdom by being inextricably involved in Tom's progress through these concerns; she is wisdom in the sense that the attainment of wisdom involves the practice of justice and mercy, "the natural beauty of virtue" and "the divine power of grace" (3.3), liberty and confinement, truth and self-knowledge. That is to say, the wisdom Fielding concerns himself with in *Tom Jones* is not mere prudence but a much larger virtue composed of speculative and practical, theological and profane elements. It is, in short, much more closely allied with the wisdom of the epic tradition than it is with the practicality of *Moll Flanders*: Fielding's Sophia derives from the same complex of ideas as does Bernardus's or Landino's explanation of Venus, or Pope's parodic goddess Dulness. Fielding leaves no doubt about the richness of the figure he is drawing: in the middle of his elaborate introduction of her (4.2), sandwiched between a quotation from Suckling and a quotation from Horace, he quotes from, and compares her directly to, the heroine of Donne's *Anniversaries,* that complex "she" who can only be understood as Donne's version of the traditional wisdom figure.[14] Fielding very deliberately and very explicitly places himself and his creatures in the mainstream of epic tradition: "this heroic, historical, prosaic poem" (4.1) domesticates epic in England as it had never been before.

The complexity of Sophia's role and Tom's relation to it does not demand that she *be* specific things but that she *do* certain things, that, for instance, she have the intelligence to refuse both Blifil and Fellamar, and the courage to do it; that she free herself from the confinement and restriction her father, her aunt, and Lady Bellaston seek to impose on her; that at Upton she remind Tom of what he is losing and spur him to seek it. She enables Tom to discover himself, not only in that through his pursuit of her he finds himself to be Allworthy's nephew, but also in that through her he becomes aware that what he does defines him and consequently seeks to change his actions. In their climactic interview, Sophia gives Tom a lesson in the whole gamut of virtues — justice, mercy, honor, constancy, temperance — before both are moved by the purely appetitive and unreflecting Squire Western to the union that both desire but which an ambiguous prudence inhibits. Like *Joseph Andrews, Tom Jones* ends with the transcending of prudence. Tom and

Sophia at the end of the novel re-create very closely the conditions of the icon of wisdom that prefaces Charron's *De la Sagesse:*

> *Sagesse* is represented as a beautiful woman, naked, *quia puram naturam sequitur,* and standing firmly on the cube of Justice. Her face is healthy, joyful, and radiantly imposing. On her head are branches of laurel and olive, symbolizing the fruits of wisdom: victorious self-mastery and tranquillity. Around her is the empty space of sapiential liberty. Her arms are crossed as though she were embracing herself. This signifies the wise man's independence and self-sufficiency. Like *Sapientia* in the *Wisdom and Fortune* which illustrates Bovillus' *De sapiente,* she is looking at herself in a mirror, "because she always looks at and knows herself." To her right we read the device, *Je ne scay;* to the left, *Paix et peu.* Chained below her feet are four women: Passion, her face in a hideous grimace; wild-eyed Opinion, supported by the heads of the fickle and inconstant mob; Superstition, her hands clasped like a kitchen maid, trembling with fear; and Science, artificial, acquired, pedantic, and arrogant, the archenemy of wisdom, who reads in a book the words *ouy* and *non* — dogmatic knowledge crushed by the laughing skepticism of the wise *homme de bien.* This is Charron's wisdom, an imitation of nature whose imperatives are skepticism and *preud'hommie,* whose cause and obligation is man's own nature, whose method is the active practice of justice, whose fruits are constancy, tranquillity, and an imperturbable virtue. [15]

Most of what is present there iconographically is present in *Tom Jones* narratively and dramatically. The handsome Tom and lovely Sophia are both freed from the restraints and confinements that have plagued them throughout the novel. Both of them have attained literal and figurative self-knowledge, most emphatically displayed in the mirror scene we have been discussing. Tom has achieved mastery over his passions (dramatized in his prudent retreat from Mrs. Fitzpatrick's transparent hints). Both have triumphed over opinion, jointly in the persistence of their love for each other, singly in Sophia's separation from her maid,

Honour, who has joined Lady Bellaston, with whom honor resides in London, and in Tom's graduation from the several inadequate notions of honor exemplified by such groups as the soldiers with whom he originally joined and the gypsies. He has conquered superstition in the graphic form of Partridge, whose faults he now sees clearly; in its larger manifestation as ignorance, he has been combatting it throughout the book. The capitulation of arrogant and pedantic science is marked by Square's letter of retraction and Allworthy's finally seeing through the viciousness of Thwackum, as well as political Aunt Western's withdrawal from the action of the novel. The marriage of Tom and Sophia conforms to the dictates of nature in almost every conceivable sense of the phrase; and Fielding presents it in the novel as almost coincident with Tom's final distribution of justice and mercy to Blifil, Thwackum, Lawyer Dowling, Partridge, Jenny Waters, and the Seagrim family. For the remainder of Charron's attributes, the final paragraph of the novel speaks for itself:

> To conclude, as there are not to be found a worthier man and woman, than this fond couple, so neither can any be imagined more happy. They preserve the purest and tenderest affection for each other, an affection daily increased and confirmed by mutual endearments, and mutual esteem. Nor is their conduct towards their relations and friends less amiable than towards one another. And such is their condescension, their indulgence, and their beneficence to those below them, that there is not a neighbor, a tenant, or a servant, who doth not most gratefully bless the day when Mr. Jones was married to his Sophia. (18.13)

The mirror scene illustrates perfectly Fielding's ability to realize the figurative in the literal. Sophia, for all her spirit, functions to restrain Tom (during the period in which their love ripened, Tom was partially confined to bed and much restricted in his activities by a broken arm acquired in Sophia's service), to confine and channel his energies, sexual and otherwise. When unrestrained by Sophia, Tom has been limited by his own ignorance of himself and by his own passions, up until the moment of his literal confinement in prison, when the true nature of his follies is borne in upon him. Sophia herself, of course, though free of Tom's limitations, has been the victim of many physical confinements and quasi-imprisonments throughout the book. The whole ambiguity of liberty and confinement was early encapsulated in the novel by Blifil's release of the bird: confined it was safe; free, it perished. The core question obviously becomes: confinement for what? and freedom for what? For Tom and Sophia, true liberty and proper confinement are clearly simultaneously defined as the fulfillment of their mutual love. But they are both restrained from achieving that by prudence, until Squire Western breaks the deadlock for them. Squire Western has throughout the novel acted something like pure, undirected will, reaching out for one object after another, but chiefly preoccupied with the hunt, the bottle, and the bed; he traced an erratic path in his pursuit of Sophia and was easily diverted by foxes and by hospitality. Most of Sophia's acts are traceable to her acceptance or rejection of his willfulness. So then, are we to understand, when she at Western's urging agrees to marry Tom, that we have just seen an allegory of the will and the judgment, or of appetite and wisdom, or some such thing? Perhaps. Why not? That is, after all, what happens on the literal level of the story — but that is exactly why, I think, we *cannot* say that *Tom Jones* is an allegory. Sophia is not judgment or wisdom, though she does embody and enact both of those, and we do not come to understand this scene or any in the book by extrapolating from fixed values but rather by evaluating the dynamic interactions of very fluid characters. What the characters are is what they do (and vice versa): Sophia proceeds straight from Somerset to London according to a preconceived and thought-out plan with a known end; Tom wanders aimlessly, trying out one scheme after another until Sophia recalls him to himself and provides him with a goal and a direction; Squire Western begins with a goal but loses both his way and his interest in short order. That requires no allegorization to understand: it is clear both literally and figuratively at the same time. You have only to compare this with, say, the episode of the Red Crosse Knight's leaving the road to seek shelter from a rainstorm in a wood to see the differences between allegorical method and Fielding's mode of figurative narration. On the simple literal level, the Red Crosse Knight acts in a perfectly normal and morally neutral manner; there is nothing wrong with sheltering oneself from the rain. But our full understanding of that act is conditioned and dictated by our knowledge of the *static* allegorical correspondences: this is the Red Crosse Knight, that is, Holiness, and holiness is leaving *the* path, that is, deviating from the plain way of truth into error. This is what the episode means in the allegory; and though it is not incompatible with the narrative, it is not coincident with it. Rather, it is prior to the narrative, directs its shape, and dictates its meaning. In Fielding, such a situation almost never occurs: there are practically no static symbolic or allegorical characters to impose fixed meanings, and we are never called upon to reinterpret a scene in the light of its figurative sense because the figurative and the literal almost always coincide. Epic allegoresis, whatever form it takes — Bernardus's, Landino's, Spenser's — operates out of and within a fixed value system, a cosmos well-regulated enough to provide unchanging reference points from which writer and reader could triangulate the significance of any unknowns. Fielding has divorced himself from that; in effect, he has accepted the challenge of *MacFlecknoe*, of *A Tale of A Tub*, of *The Dunciad*. He has confronted the problems of subjectively generated significance, of the cosmos understood as flux, of pervasive corporeality, all of which overwhelmed traditional epic, and answered them with a mode of figurative narration that takes dynamic flux as its base of meaning and out of the interplay of events generates objective significance, while at the same time wedding that meaning to the body of language. The overall narrative technique that generates meaning out of plot essentially duplicates the technique by which individual characters — Sophia for instance — come to embody meaning. He achieves linguistically the kind of proper incarnation of thing-in-word and word-in-thing that has been the implicit property of epic from at least Virgil forward; he achieves literarily the adaptation of epic, with most of its appurtenances intact, to the unmapped new world of change and flow. It is an act of cultural reclamation almost without parallel in literature or any other art. (Not the least striking aspect of Fielding's achievement is the success with which he translated large quantities of characteristically epic exegesis into the overt narration of his revitalized form. There is not time or space to catalogue all of these things, but a few examples are in order: the childhood and adolescence of his hero realize, on the literal level, what the ages-of-man theory had seen on the allegorical; Paradise Hall, Black George, and Tom's expulsion therefrom recapitulate mythically both the Eden story of Milton and the Troy episodes of the *Aeneid* as understood by the commentators; the movement from country to city back to country explicitly captures the thought-action-contemplation or retirement-activity-retirement pattern of the commentators' explanations.)

As I said before, the plot of *Tom Jones* forms an almost perfect paradigm of epic, especially as understood and elaborated by the kinds of commentators we have discussed. Fielding manages to bring under control the tendency of the allegorical explanation to supplant the epic tale by overtly incorporating aspects of what would normally be the allegory into his narrative — Tom's childhood, for instance, and his ability to withstand the contradictorily erroneous teachings of Thwackum and Square, while his doppelgänger Blifil, in fine mock-epic fashion, steers a parodic mean between their doctrines. (As with Parson Adams's role in *Joseph Andrews*, Fielding in *Tom Jones* manages to employ and to counterpoint epic and mock-epic patterns.) The novel moves as Bernardus's *Aeneid* moves, from childhood to maturity and knowledge, and also as Landino's *Aeneid* moves, from an ambiguous home where the hero is unproductively at rest in the flesh out into the active world and at last to a real home and the possession of wisdom. It is important to realize that Fielding remains faithful to the core of the epic tradition and antipathetic to contemporary notions of wisdom and prudence (as active, practical, and pragmatic virtue)[16] in allowing his hero to pass through the active life to come to rest in retirement and contemplation. The whole point of the *Aeneid* and the *Odyssey* (even, in an ironic mode, of the *Iliad*) lies in the achievement of order, the reestablishment of stability: rest after motion is the goal of epic, whether it be in the narrative or the allegory, public or private, individual or social.

Tom Jones contrives to achieve that rest in almost all its aspects. Tom, Sophia, Squire Western, and Squire Allworthy retire to the country and lives of personal tranquillity, abandoning the city, which the popular town-country opposition had made the locus of the active life. Epic tradition made cities both that and the locus of temptation — Troy, the city of the flesh; Carthage, both the active life and the temptation of Dido — and Milton's treatment in particular made cities almost one of the direct results of the Fall and the chief site of human misery, next to which the country seemed still at least slightly Edenic. *Tom Jones,* in these senses, plays itself out across a properly epic landscape: Paradise Hall, badly misnamed, is its Troy, an *earthly* paradise at best, where despite a benign but by no means omniscient or infallible Squire Allworthy, vanity, pettiness, greed, lust, and jealousy provide the basic motivations for most of the characters. For Tom to remain here is for Tom to remain ignorant, passive, sterile: he does not know who or what he is, who acts upon him or why, what the real state of the world is. He is a stranger in his own home, different from its other inhabitants — more potent than Allworthy, better than all the rest. So his expulsion from the false familial order of Paradise Hall becomes an entrance into the possibility of other orders to which, potentially or hypothetically, he may belong. His acquisition of his putative father Partridge is a sign of that, though like Aeneas and Anchises he will not find his real home until that "father" is removed. He tries or sees a number of societies, all with varying social codes based in one way or another on the slippery concept of honor, and all insufficient: the navy (he initially plans to go to sea), the army, the gypsies, the *beau monde* of London itself, as personified by Lady Bellaston.[17] It is obviously not mere chance that Lord Fellamar's plans for Tom should involve fulfillment of his own original plan (Fellamar means to have him taken by a press gang and sent to sea); that they are frustrated by Tom's arrest and imprisonment is no irony, but a literal working-out of Tom's true state. Without wisdom, without self-knowledge, he is in prison and has been in prison all along. The real irony is that *in* prison — in a forced state of rest, his motion stopped — Tom becomes free: in prison he discovers both his paternity and his own nature; at rest, he discovers his capacity for action.[18] After this his attainment of Sophia is ensured: starting with real self-knowledge (literally the knowledge that he is Allworthy's nephew and Blifil's half-brother) he can proceed to the acquisition and execution of justice and mercy and from here, by virtue of marriage to Sophia, to the constancy he has so desperately needed. His retirement to the country is a withdrawal from activity to rest, from change to constancy, from confusion to clarity. There, in limited realm of his family and estate — in private, as the eighteenth century would have said — he practices the virtues he has acquired and exorcises the vices he was born with.

Although the action of *Tom Jones* is confined to a few individuals and families, the scope of the novel is much greater than that. I don't mean by this the common notion of Fielding's amazing spectrum of types and panorama of England and English life. Rather, I am referring to the intricate use Fielding has made of the historical fact of the 1745 uprising on behalf of Prince Charles Edward, "the young Pretender." Fielding uses this as an ambivalent analogue to his main action. First mention of the '45 occurs with the arrival of political Aunt Western, and it coincides with the initial confusion among Sophia, Squire Western, and his sister as to whom Sophia loves and who is to pay court to her. At this point, Tom is apparently the Pretender, seeking Sophia's hand and her father's estate, and his exile soon after seems to confirm this. But we, the readers, although ignorant of Tom's true birth, also know that Blifil certainly pretends to Sophia's affections and that *his* goal really is her father's estate. Once on the road, of course, the complications multiply: Tom attempts to join a troop of soldiers going to fight for the crown; the Jacobite Partridge believes he plans to support the Pretender; the Man on the Hill gives them an account of his unfortunate involvement in an earlier rebellion; Sophia is mistaken for the Pretender's mistress, Jenny Cameron. Insofar as she loves Tom, she *is* the Pretender's mistress; insofar as her family obliges her to Blifil, she is also the Pretender's mistress. Aunt Western, with her basic political and social differences from her Jacobite brother and her constant political turn of phrase, serves as the convenient crossover point from the political analogue to the main plot: by her constant use of words like alliances, treaties, tactics, and so on, she makes the public disturbances and the private ones metaphors for each other, synecdoche and metonymy for the same basic attempt at usurpation. The predictive value of our knowledge of the outcome of the rebellion would seem to doom Tom — he was, after all, "born to be hanged" — until the point at which he and we learn who he really is and , consequently, who the Pretender and usurper really is. So the defeat of the Pretender and the restoration of public order under what Fielding felt a rightful monarch parallels exactly the restoration of private order under the rightful heir. The cause of justice and English liberties — public and personal — triumph over the pretensions of absolutism — political and moral. Tom's and Sophia's "condescension, their indulgence, and their beneficence to those below them" (18.13), which close the novel, are the private models of those virtues restored to English public life. For this reason, in what seems to me a casual masterstroke of significance, Tom does not return to Paradise Hall but settles rather on the neighboring estate of Squire Western, which the old foxhunter abdicates to him — Tom, who has played Aeneas to Blifil's Turnus in their struggle for Lavinia (Sophia) attains his Hesperia, the Western lands that were Aeneas's fated goal, and yet another Troy-novant rises on English soil. In that marvelous understated moment, classical epic makes a home in English literature. At least one phase of the *translatio studii* has achieved its own rest from wandering.

III

With *Amelia,* Fielding moves on to the logical culmination of his work; after the comic romance of *Joseph Andrews* and the comic epic of *Tom Jones,* he here attempts the serious epic in prose with Virgil's *Aeneid* as his confessed model.[19] Overt parallels between the two works abound, in terms of both character and situation. Miss Matthews corresponds to Dido, Colonel James to Turnus, Amelia at different points to both Creusa and Lavinia. Booth's recitation of his past to Miss Matthews approximates Aeneas's similar recounting to Dido. The sea journey and Gibralter adventures relate closely to the battles at Troy and Aeneas's wanderings; in these and in Booth's subsequent mishaps the unselfish Atkinson plays "fides Achates" to his Aeneas. Fielding also shifts emphases, carefully using the *Aeneid* as a foil. The threatened duel between Booth and Colonel James, which would furnish a climax and a demonstration of the hero's individual *virtus* in the manner of Aeneas's battle with Turnus, never takes place, but much examination of the whole ethic of dueling does. Book 4 of *Amelia* ought, because of parallels already established, to correspond to book 4 of the *Aeneid;* but although Miss Matthews does early and easily seduce Booth, most of the book is taken up by Booth's reunion with Amelia and problems with Colonel James (raised by Miss Matthews, to be sure) and by the ominous introduction of the Noble Lord. Far from being the slothful hero luxuriating in his mistress's love and recalled to duty only by a divine messenger, Booth's conscience quickly and thoroughly discomforts him for his one week of inconstancy. Indeed, even the metamorphosis of Mercury into Dr. Harrison's letter warning Booth against vanity and improvidence is part of this playing-off of Fielding's creation against Virgil's paradigm. [20]

Equally important to an understanding of Fielding's accomplishment in *Amelia,* however, is an awareness that he has also employed Milton's *Paradise Lost* as a foil in a similar manner. From Booth's first entry into the "not improperly called infernal" (1.10) region of Newgate to the point at which, as Dr. Harrison phrases it, "the devil hath thought proper to set you free" (12.5), Fielding has set up a network of correspondences and counterpoints between his own work and Milton's epic. As these are somewhat elaborate and affect directly the development and meaning of the novel, it would be best to discuss the most important ones sequentially and in detail. Fielding is constructing *Amelia* out of the materials of the epic tradition, and he is relying on our recognition of the materials themselves, the uses he has put them to, and the relations those uses set up with the tradition to make his points. He innovates traditionally, and by what he does changes both the epic tradition and our angle of sight upon it.

The opening sequence of events in *Amelia* indicates the complex use Fielding intends to make of *Paradise Lost.* Milton's poem opens with the fall of Satan and the confinement of the devils in Hell; Fielding's novel begins with Booth's apparently unjust imprisonment (he is committed essentially because he is poor) in Newgate, which is, as Fielding says here (1.10) and elsewhere, Hell. The Council of Demons in Pandemonium and the difficulty of breaking the bonds of Hell are aptly parodied and re-created in the dinner conversation in Miss Matthews's quarters (1.10), and the roles of Miss Matthews and Colonel James (grudging and indirect, to be sure) in effecting Booth's release comically miniaturize the actions of Sin and Death in freeing Satan from Hell. One of the greater ironies of Fielding's treatment of Booth lies in the fact that this process of parallelism identifies him with Satan, or at least, as Dr. Harrison's previously quoted remark indicates, one of his agents or victims. However gross the miscarriage of justice that committed Booth to Newgate in the first place, in the ethical system of the novel he belongs there. He is one of the devils, not because of his subsequent liaison with Miss Matthews, but because of the radical intellectual flaw that permits him to indulge that mere weakness of the flesh. Booth "did not absolutely deny the existence of a God, yet he entirely denied His providence"; he believes "that every man acted merely from the force of that passion which was uppermost in his mind, and could do no otherwise" (1.3). Booth's conversations with Robinson (from which the remarks above are taken) about "the necessity arising from the impulse of fate, and the necessity arising from the impulse of passion" (1.3) and with the Methodist pickpocket about grace and crime accomplish two things in the novel. By parodying the songs and disputations of Milton's demons, who "complain[ed] that Fate / Free Virtue should enthrall to Force or Chance" (2.550–51) and "reason'd high / Of Providence, Foreknowledge, Will, and Fate / . . . / Vain Wisdom all, and false Philosophie" (2.558–59, 565), they confirm the linking of Booth and Satan. In addition, they define the terms of the novel and the scope of its concerns: fate and free will, fortune and ruling passion, liberty of action and the moral neutrality or merit of those actions furnish the central themes of *Amelia,* from its exordium (1.1), which like the invocation of *Paradise Lost* raises basic questions about Fortune, Fate, Free Will, and Providence, right down to Booth's final liberation from prison and repayment of all his debts. Booth is in prison because he thinks he is in prison; he must obey his dominant passion. His good actions produce no effect, because, as he later tells Dr. Harrison, "as men appeared to me to act entirely from their passions, their actions would have neither merit nor demerit" (12.5). Booth is a kind of secular Methodist, denying the worth of works and lacking a redeeming faith. Throughout the novel, he remains in prison, either literally or confined within the Verge of Court or within his own mind. His own sense of "honor" will not allow him to confess his derelictions to Amelia and repent; neither will it allow him to act efficaciously. The prison is the central symbol of *Amelia* and the arena of its action.[21] Because Booth's will is malformed, he is imprisoned; when, by reading Barrow's sermons, his will is reformed, he is freed — and not accidentally, the tamperings with Mrs. Harris's will are discovered and corrected. Booth and Amelia have been thrall to that will all through the novel, locked in poverty by its forged deformation just as they have been locked in failure and futility by Booth's deformed will and his sensitive "honor": the one is the external correlative of the other, and correcting both of them are cognate acts. Booth converted and freed, Amelia prepared for good fortune and for her rightful inheritance are Fielding's version of Adam and Eve repentant and resigned, awaiting the redemption that is their promised heritage. The Booths' escape from the prison of London into the semi-Edenic countryside ironically recapitulates the banishment from Paradise that made all the Londons possible.

Booth is Satanic in the novel insofar as he is his own hell and his own prisoner; other characters are Satanic in much more primary ways. Miss Matthews, for instance, and the Noble Lord both assail the Booths and attempt to break up their marriage, as do Mrs. Ellison and Colonel James. Even Dr. Harrison attempts briefly to separate Booth from Amelia, and to that extent becomes a tool villain. One of the central episodes in the novel defines what is really at stake in the marriage of the Booths and why, consequently, so many of the forces of Hell are bent on destroying that marriage. Mrs. Ellison offers Amelia a masquerade ticket for the Noble Lord; Booth, whose suspicions have been aroused by comments from Colonel and Mrs. James, peremptorily forbids her to accept it. Amelia complies, and Mrs. Ellison leaves. In the chapter that follows (6.6), Booth explains his reasons for this prohibition and Amelia defends herself from what she takes to be demeaning implications about her virtue and intelligence — "Good Heavens! did I ever expect to hear this? I can appeal to Heaven, nay, I will appeal to yourself, Mr. Booth, if I have ever done anything to deserve such a suspicion. If ever any action of mine; nay, if ever any thought, had stained the innocence of my soul, I could be contented." "O, Mr. Booth! Mr. Booth! you must well know that a woman's virtue is always her sufficient guard. No husband, without suspecting that, can suspect any danger from those snares you mention. . . ." "What is it you fear? — you mention not force, but snares. Is not this to confess, at least, that you have some doubt of my understanding? do you then really imagine me so weak as to be cheated of my virtue? — am I to be deceived into an affection for a man before I perceive the least inward hint of my danger? No, Mr. Booth, believe me, a woman must be a fool indeed who can have in earnest such an excuse for her actions. I have not, I think, any very high opinion of my judgment, but so far I shall rely upon it, that no man breathing could have any such designs as you have apprehended without my immediately seeing them; and how I should then act I hope my whole conduct to you hath sufficiently declared." This domestic drama to modern ears borders on soap opera, but its point is far more serious than that. Fielding's situation recreates exactly what happens in the climactic ninth book of *Paradise Lost,* when Eve proposes to Adam that they work apart: Adam objects, and dialogue very like that between Booth and Amelia ensues. I will quote only one passage of Eve's arguments; the similarity to Amelia's will, I hope, be quite evident:

> Offspring of Heav'n and Earth, and all Earth's Lord,
> That such an Enemy we have, who seeks
> Our ruin, both by thee inform'd I learn,
> And from the parting Angel over-heard
> As in a shady nook I stood behind,
> Just then return'd at shut of Ev'ning Flow'rs.
> But that thou shouldst my firmness therefore doubt
> To God or thee, because we have a foe
> My tempt it, I expected not to hear.
> His violence thou fear'st not, being such,
> As wee, not capable of death or pain,
> Can either not receive, or can repel.
> His fraud is then thy fear, which plain infers
> Thy equal fear that my firm Faith and Love

Can by his fraud be shak'n or seduc't;
Thoughts, which how found they harbor in thy breast,
Adam, misthought of her to thee so dear?

(9.273–89)

The immediate result of both episodes is identical: both Adam and Booth
capitulate; Eve goes to work alone, and Amelia accepts the masquerade
ticket. The disastrous effects that follow in *Paradise Lost* are averted in
Amelia by the intervention of Mrs. Bennet, whose tale of her own
seduction in like circumstances sufficiently warns Amelia of her danger.
But the use of *Paradise Lost* as foil for this episode alters the dimensions
of the drama. It is not merely that *Paradise Lost* provides, in some of its
scenes, a model for domestic epic, but that the marriage of the Booths
comes to share some of the importance of the marriage of Adam and Eve.
With all these mighty engines, with Satan himself (through his human
agents, with whom Mrs. Bennet identifies him [7.7]) engaged in attack-
ing it, there must be more involved than the happiness of two individuals, however handsome and admirable.

What appears to be involved is something analogous to the establishment of Rome in the *Aeneid* or the providential plan for humanity
revealed in the last two books of *Paradise Lost.* Through the Booths and
the values they embody, Fielding directly deals with the problem of the
Christian commonwealth: through Booth and Amelia and Dr. Harrison,
he delineates all the difficulties incident to practicing real Christianity in
a world of real evil. The novel opens with an episode of law and justice,
both crudely and cruelly applied, and ends with the Booths at last freed
from the law and given true justice: between those points Fielding tackles
directly the questions of freedom and law, merit and justice, forgiveness
and revenge, as they apply both to the individual and to the commonwealth. Captain Booth himself is the focal point for all this, since as
private individual — Amelia's husband — and as public official — an
officer in the service of the crown — he must balance and adjudicate the
welter of responsibilities that fall to him. Booth fails initially precisely
because, for all his good intentions, his theory of the dominant passion
makes him incapable of assuming responsibility. His actions in his own

eyes always remain morally neutral, and their outcome is determined only by chance. For the greater part of the novel, Booth is literally a Soldier of Fortune (so his penchant for gambling) and not a Christian Soldier. Only when Barrow's sermons convert him to true belief does he break free from the wheel of fortune and into a world of individual responsibility and consequently of causation and effect, where Providence, as Dr. Harrison remarks (12.7), "hath done you the justice at last which it will, one day or other, render to all men." Immediately before this, Booth has sunk to his lowest ebb — imprisoned once again, almost destitute, pitifully dependent that his giving his last fifty pounds to a political functionary will win him a commission. "Thus did this poor man support his hopes by a dependence on that ticket which he had so dearly purchased of one who pretended to manage the wheels in the great state lottery of preferment. A lottery, indeed, which hath this to recommend it — that many poor wretches feed their imaginations with the prospect of a prize during their whole lives, and never discover that they have drawn a blank." (12.2). The "great state lottery of preferment" enmeshes all of society in its turnings, from the Captain Trents and old lieutenants through to the lawyer Murphys and the sister Bettys — and there is no Lady Philosophy here to rescue Booth as there was to save Wilson. The governmental system so based obviously operates amorally — law and justice are hollow concepts, cards to be played to gain advantages over others. Merit, as a nobleman makes clear to Dr. Harrison, furnishes no recommendation for office or promotion, and his passionate defense of a commonwealth based on strict justice and the rewarding of merit produces only the following supercilious retort: "This is all mere Utopia," cries His Lordship, "the chimerical system of Plato's commonwealth, with which we amused ourselves at the university; politics which are inconsistent with the state of human affairs." (11.2). I think it is significant of the extent to which Fielding's reformist thought had gone that, in response to this and other of the lord's declarations of the impossibility of preferring men by merit, he has Dr. Harrison cite honorifically the example of Oliver Cromwell — "and it was chiefly owing to the avoiding this error that Oliver Cromwell carried the reputation of England higher than it ever was at any other time"

(11.2). Coupled with Dr. Harrison's earlier remarks about the role of the clergy and the importance of the example of their lives (9.9–10), as well as with Dr. Harrison's own crucial role in managing and unraveling the lives and fortunes of the Booths, these sentiments seem to point strongly in the directions of republicanism, reform, and something that smacks of theocracy. Dr. Harrison's Christianity is radical — at least in the context of *Amelia* — in that he accepts literally the biblical injunction to "love your enemies" and has consequently recast, in his own mind at least, the whole concept of law:

> "But if this be the meaning," cries the son, "there must be an end of all law and justice, for I do not see how any man can prosecute his enemy in a court of justice."
> "Pardon me, sir," cries the doctor. "Indeed, as an enemy merely, and from a spirit of revenge, he cannot, and he ought not to prosecute him; but as an offender against the laws of his country he may, and it is his duty to do so. Is there any spirit of revenge in the magistrates or officers of justice when they punish criminals? Why do such, ordinarily I mean, concern themselves in inflicting punishments, but because it is their duty? and why may not a private man deliver an offender into the hands of justice, from the same laudable motive? Revenge, indeed, of all kinds is strictly prohibited; wherefore, as we are not to execute it with our own hands, so neither are we to make use of the law as the instrument of private malice, and to worry each other with inveteracy and rancor. And where is the great difficulty in obeying this wise, this generous, this noble precept?" (9.8)

Law such as Harrison envisions constitutes a total antithesis to law as seen and practiced by the other characters of the novel, and one of the signs in the book of the triumph of his views can be found in Captain Booth's and Amelia's joining him in the actual practice of such law — I refer, of course, to their joint distribution of justice and mercy to Murphy, Robinson, and Miss Harris at the end of the book. That is doubly significant in that it marks both the efficacy of Booth's conversion and a partial purgation of a corrupt society. The estate of the Booths and their posterity both typifies and promises the completion of that regeneration: Booth and Amelia, like Adam and Eve, have learned of, and been reconciled to, God's providential plan, and have taken their places in it as progenitors of a regenerate race. Their family is the nucleus and prototype of Dr. Harrison's Christian commonwealth; he is the spiritual father of their incipient "mere Utopia."

Behind all this lies a fundamental concept that gives form to the novel. As I remarked before, Captain Booth is a kind of secular Methodist, and his early encounters in prison with the free-thinking Robinson and the Methodist pickpocket (1.3–5) set up some of the moral terms of the novel — the law, under which they all are bound; the meritoriousness of works, which Booth disbelieves; faith, which Booth must acquire; justification, which can only flow from the latter two; and freedom, which is a consequence of justification. Not surprisingly, given Fielding's long-standing concern with Methodism and what he considered the pernicious doctrine of justification by faith alone (for which, in *Amelia,* he makes the hypocritical pickpocket the spokesman), these are all catchwords and concerns of Saint Paul's Epistle to the Romans, which provided the central document in the quarrel of orthodoxy with Methodism. Fielding's concern with these issues here, however, ranges far beyond his earlier concentration on active charity, just as his use of constancy in *Amelia* as part of a large complex of virtues transcends his earlier, straightforward treatment of it. Like Dr. Harrison's radically literal understanding of Christ's commands, Fielding undertakes a similarly literal exploration of the Pauline epistle, whose meaning, in his view, Methodism and contemporary English mores have narrowed and perverted. Saint Paul talks of freedom from the law and transcendence of it in Christian liberty, and this is the core of Fielding's novel. English law, as misapplied by a heathen society, becomes the eighteenth-century manifestation of Mosaic law, and the true Christian must free himself from bondage to it. The law works only to awaken consciousness of sin, which it does for Booth, but no man is saved by the law. The law leads only to death, as it does for lawyer Murphy. Not accidentally, one of the novel's few enthusiasts for "the constitution, that is the law and liberty" (8.2) is the despicable bailiff Bondum, into whose hands Booth is often conveyed and under whose notion of law and 'liberty Booth suffers. Booth is confined by other kinds of law too, the law of honor for one, which "a man of honor wears . . . by his side" according to Colonel Bath (9.3). Fielding devotes a good portion of *Amelia* to extricating Booth from the trap of this concept of honor, which seems to embody aspects of trial by combat, the law of Talion, and simple unchristian vengeance. Appropriately, Colonel Bath, who lives by the sword, dies by the sword. He is beset as well by "the laws of nature," which he encounters at the very beginning of the novel in the person of Justice Thrasher, who, "if he was ignorant of the laws of England, . . . perfectly well understood that fundamental principle . . . by which the duty of self-love is so strongly enforced, and every man is taught to consider himself as the centre of gravity, and to attract all things thither" (1.2). That law, of course, commits Booth to Newgate in the first place. Varying ideas of freedom correspond to these different notions of law. Primarily, freedom is bought, in this society, by wealth or position or power; and it is freedom in terms of the society — that is, freedom to acquire greater wealth, position, and power, and to manipulate and exploit those who want them. That, too, is a kind of bondage, as is the freedom offered by the Methodist, the freedom of election, which makes a rhetorical distinction between "the days of sin and the days of grace," but which neither affects his conduct nor effects his release from Newgate or from corruption. Finally, Stoicism — in the person of the philosophic debtor (8.10) — purports to offer freedom from the vicissitudes of fortune; but all it can really accomplish is to make imprisonment more endurable, and the emotional and intellectual detachment that even that little requires Fielding quickly shows to be humanly impossible for the debtor, just as it was for Parson Adams. The only real release from the pervasive corruption of society and the doom of the law lies in acceptance of a radically anarchic Christian liberty that transcends Mosaic law and all the ephemeral human laws that furnish its avatars and incarnations. "For the law of the Spirit of life in Christ Jesus hath made me free from the law of sin and death" (Romans 13:2). " . . . The creature itself also shall be delivered from the bondage of corruption into the glorious liberty of the children of God" (Romans 8:21). That liberty is achieved, according to Paul, only through the faith that Booth acquires by reading Barrow's sermons and by what Paul calls "the Spirit of adoption" (Romans 8:14), whereby "we are the children of God: And if children, then heirs; heirs of God, and joint-heirs with Christ" (Romans 8:16–17). Dr. Harrison accomplishes the necessary adoption by his constant references to, and treatment of, Amelia as his daughter, of which practice he makes an elaborate explanation to his visiting friend and clergyman son (9.8), and by referring to Booth for the first time, shortly after his conversion, as "My child" (12.7). At that same time, he announces to Booth that "your sufferings are all at an end, and Providence hath done you the justice at last which it will, one day or other, render to all men. You will hear all presently; but I can now only tell you that your sister is discovered and the estate is your own." What follows in the novel confirms this: Amelia very shortly receives her inheritance, and subsequently (almost at the end of the novel) Dr. Harrison declares "that he will leave his whole fortune, except some few charities, among Amelia's children" (12.9).

All this constitutes the same kind of realization of the figurative in the literal that I have argued was Fielding's technique in *Joseph Andrews* and *Tom Jones*. Here he has specifically worked with literalizations of the metaphors of the Epistle to the Romans — which, being canonical, Fielding and many other pious readers would be likely to treat as more than metaphoric anyway. He has given them in his fiction the same kind of efficacy they have in Scripture, where they function simultaneously as facts and metaphors, literally true statements and images for other things. By so doing, he breaks epic free of the trap of allegory and restores to it literarily the kind of autonomy and validity it had been steadily losing to the omnivorous habit of abstraction. For himself, he accomplishes a perfect fusion of his humane concerns and his religious consciousness. The reforming London magistrate and the serious Christian unite to form the story of man saved from the corruption of society and the bondage of sin to live, not in Somerset or Hesperia, but in Paradise Regained. Fielding's vision in this last novel is radical and millennial: society from top to bottom stinks with corruption, and its only hope of salvation rests with the Booths and Amelias, with the regenerate few whose families are the seedbed and nucleus for a new society of love. He has adopted what we would call now a radical position: implicitly, facing a society where, as *Amelia* insists, law means bondage, sin, and death, he has become a Christian anarchist urging the withdrawal of the few — into what we would now call communes — outside the law and above the law, outside of society and antithetical to it. Like Adam and Eve, Booth and Amelia must populate the earth anew with the inheritors of the promised redemption.

Such an understanding of *Amelia* is dictated by Fielding's careful manipulation of the traditional palindromatic structure of epic. He does not use merely the general pattern, but specifically the intricate interlocking sort of pattern Milton employed in *Paradise Lost*. And *use* is not the right verb: in *Amelia,* as in *Paradise Lost,* the structure embodies the argument. Its symmetries disclose Providence. At the center of the novel, in books 6 and 7, stand the masquerade at Ranelagh and its concomitants, the threat of seduction by the Noble Lord and the destruction of the Booths' marriage as Mrs. Bennet's had been destroyed. Around this central Satanic attempt and failure to separate and seduce Fielding's Augustan Adam and Eve, the other events of the novel circle, concentric rings of events around that dramatic core:[22]

Book 5	*Book 8*
A. Warning about Noble Lord's designs	A. Warning about James's designs
B. Booth's scuffle with Bailiff	B. Booth's duel with Colonel Bath
C. Reconciliation with Colonel James	C. Reconciliation with Dr. Harrison
Book 4	*Book 9*
A. Booth seduced by Miss Matthews	A. James's designs on Amelia
B. Booth freed from prison and rejoined to Amelia	B. Booth freed from prison and rejoined to Amelia.
C. Harrison's censure of Booth's conduct in the country	C. Harrison's censure of Booth's conduct in the city

D. James promises help in obtaining a commission

E. Visit from Mrs. James

F. The oratorio and the strange man

G. Mrs. Ellison's hypocrisy

D. James promises help in obtaining a commission

E. Visit from Mrs. James

F. Vauxhall and the bucks

G. Harrison's friends' hypocrisy

Book 3

A. Atkinson promoted to sergeant

B. Amelia's honor: Bath and Bagillard

C. Booth's imprudence as farmer

D. Marriage of James and Bath's sister

Book 10

A. Atkinson promoted to Captain

B. Amelia's honor: Bath, Harrison, James

C. Booth's imprudence in card game

D. Letter about adultery and marriage to James

Book 2

A. Harrison Booth's champion

B. Booth abnegates self to Amelia

C. Hebbers dying and recovering

Book 11

A. Harrison Booth's champion

B. Booth confesses to Amelia

C. Atkinson dying and recovering

Book 1

A. Miss Matthews and Hebbers

B. Robinson

C. Imprisonment

D. Justice Thrasher

Book 12

A. Sister Betty and Lawyer Murphy

B. Robinson

C. Freedom

D. Justice of Providence

Amelia moves, like *Paradise Lost,* from imprisonment, sin, and hell to the freedom of a providentially ordered world, from the inhumanity of the law and the predatory creatures of it to the newly won humanity of its chastened and strengthened hero and heroine. Amelia is no more a paragon than her husband: a daughter of Eve, she shares Eve's vanities and Eve's weaknesses, and she avoids Eve's sin only through the actions of her surrogate, Mrs. Bennet.[23] Like Captain Booth, she both watches and plays in a complex drama that hell and heaven stage for them and around them, a human comedy for them, a divine tragedy for many others. Fielding has reached back through the abstractions and rationalizations that had accumulated around epic to the living core of the tradition and set in motion once more a human Aeneas, a human Eve, fallible and vulnerable, to work out their destinies among real people rather than cardboard personae. In the radical simplicity of his vision of the family as the seedbed of society and of the bond of love between one man and one woman as its nurturing force, he approached the kind of luminous regularity that makes the works of Homer and Virgil and Dante so all-encompassing. *Amelia* is domestic drama, but all the world is in it, just as all the world was enfolded in the domestic drama of Adam and Eve.

> Life may as properly be called an art as any other; and the great incidents in it are no more to be considered as mere accidents than the several members of a fine statue or a noble poem. The critics in all these are not content with seeing anything to be great without knowing why and how it came to be so. By examining carefully the several gradations which conduce to bring every model to perfection, we learn truly to know that science in which the model is formed: as histories of this kind, therefore, may properly be called models of *Human Life*, so, by observing minutely the several incidents which tend to the catastrophe or completion of the whole, and the minute causes whence those incidents are produced, we shall best be instructed in this most useful of all arts, which I call the *Art of Life*. (1.1)

The "Art of Life" is what the epic had always been and what Fielding made it again — a handbook for life, and a poem made of life. It is just that simple, and just that complex. The heart of epic, and the heart of *Amelia,* is the simultaneous everything-and-nothing of suffering and triumphant humanity, the joyous freedom hidden in the dark of the prison, the single small act of the single small will that alters the shape of the cosmos. That is what *Amelia,* and epic, are all about.

IV

In the course of his discussion of Milton in *The Descent from Heaven,* Thomas Greene enumerates three causes of the demise of epic.

> In thus fulfilling the seventeenth-century tendency to shift the political medium from violence to morality, Milton implicitly rejected, it seems to me, part of the basis of epic itself — the balance of objective and subjective action, the balance of executive and deliberative. In the closing books of *Paradise Lost,* the books which define human heroism, the executive episodes almost disappear. This rejection need not in itself involve grounds for criticism. But it is important to see how the last of the great poems in conventional epic dress contained within itself, not accidently but essentially, the seeds of the genre's destruction. One of these seeds was the internalization of action, the preference for things invisible. A second was the questioning of the hero's independence; a third was the detaching of heroism from the community, the City of man in this world. (p. 407)

As should be clear from the earlier chapters of this book, I agree substantially about the nature of these destructive elements, although I think their seeds were well planted in the genre long before Milton. What I want to emphasize here is how, particuarly in *Amelia,* Fielding has nullified these elements, how he has in effect jumped back over this malignant growth within epic itself to an earlier and sounder understanding of the genre. Fielding has restored a sense of community to epic, and has certainly returned epic to the community: for all of the diabolical engines turned to encompass the Booths' ruin, the action of *Amelia* plays itself out in the very heart of "the City of man in this world" — and even if the novel concludes with an escape from that city, it is a withdrawal that contains the promise of a future salvation for that city and that world. So, too, with Fielding's treatment of "things invisible": the novel fully *embodies* anything that properly fits that category in things very visible indeed — the prison, the Court, the Noble Lord. The question of the hero's independence furnishes the whole point of the novel; it is Booth's discovery of that that constitutes its resolution. Booth's conversion restores epic firmly and finally to the world of living men: no angels enlighten him, even though "an angel might be thought to guide the pen" (12.5) of Dr. Barrow: no "Almighty, nodding, gave Consent; / [or] Peals of Thunder shook the Firmament" (*Absalom and Achitophel,* 1026–27) to ratify his resolution. Booth's change of heart and mind antithesizes David's final stand in *Absalom and Achitophel:* there "Godlike David" conformed himself to the immutability of the God whose image he bore to promulgate divine law; in *Amelia* a very human Captain Booth realizes his own freedom in order to escape from disastrously human law. As the figurative manifests itself in the literal in Fielding's novels, so does the divine incarnate itself in the human. Booth's conversion is his acceptance of *human* responsibility, of his own accountability for his acts: after this, epic heroes and novel heroes can blame neither God nor fate for what they do. Fielding has newly recreated the epic hero as a responsible agent, freely choosing and shaping his own life amidst the anarchic liberty of a universe of flux and change. The gods of epic have withdrawn, and a human world, at last, lies all before us.

1. See Hägin, *The Epic Hero.*

2. In this and some of what follows, I am indebted to John M. Steadman's excellent "Felicity and End in Renaissance Epic and Ethics," *JHI* 23 (1962): 117–32.

3. See Eugene Rice's *The Renaissance Idea of Wisdom* (Cambridge, Mass., 1958).

4. This will be discussed below.

5. A somewhat similar understanding of this scene has been suggested by Maurice Johnson: *Fielding's Art of Fiction* (Philadelphia, 1961), pp. 53–55 and pp. 61–62.

6. The two scenes have interesting similarities: in both the woman is "on stage," the man "off," though in *The Libation Bearers* the male overhears the female rather than vice versa. Electra finds clues (lock of hair, footprints) that lead her to hope Orestes is near; but when he appears, she greets him with mixed elation and skepticism, culminating in her asking directly if he is Orestes. The scene climaxes in Orestes' identifying himself and formally naming Electra and claiming her as his sister. If Fielding is playing with the similarities at all, the whole scene becomes delightfully ironic in the light of the later momentary revelation that Fanny and Joseph are sister and brother.

7. See for example Homer Goldberg's fine study of Fielding's assimilation of previous

continental fiction, *The Art of Joseph Andrews* (Chicago. 1969). Goldberg's description of the continental background of Fielding's first novel seems to me perfectly compatible with my claim for its epic genealogy, first because both sets of materials have already passed through the common experience of romance and second because most of the changes Fielding makes in his adaptations of the continental materials work to re-align them with traditional epic materials.

8. See John Freccero's "Donne's 'Valediction: Forbidding Mourning'," *ELH* 30 (1963): 335–76; and A. R. Cirillo, "Spenser's Myth of Love: A Study of the *Faerie Queene,* Books III and IV," Ph.D. diss., The Johns Hopkins University, 1964.

9. Maurice Johnson discusses the chapters in a slightly different fashion than what follows: see *Fielding's Art of Fiction,* pp. 61–71.

10. Landino so understands Anchises: he is the father of Aeneas's body, and his understanding is fleshly. Thus when Aeneas is told by Apollo to seek his ancient mother, Anchises takes this to mean Crete, which Landino identifies as the physical origin of the Trojans, rather than Italy, which is their spiritual origin. Thus Aeneas wanders aimlessly until he celebrates the funeral games in Anchises' honor, which signifies the burial of sensuality in himself; after that he proceeds directly to his goal.

11. The structural parallels break down loosely as follows:

1	18
Discovery of Tom; Allworthy raises him as his own. Blifil marries Bridget; his brother banished.	Discovery of Tom's parents and his real relation to Allworthy. Blifil banished. Tom marries Sophia.
2	17
False accusation of Partridge	False accusation of Tom
3	16
Tom aids Black George. Thwackum and Square woo Bridget. First mention of Sophia.	Black George aids Tom. Fellamar and Blifil woo Sophia. Sophia breaks with Tom.
4	15
Tom's involvement with Molly Seagrim.	Tom's involvement with Lady Bellaston.
5	14
Sophia tends Tom during illness. Molly's pregnancy and Tom's love for Sophia.	Lady Bellaston visits Tom during feigned illness. Nancy's pregnancy and Nightingale's betrothal.
6	13
Aunt Western confuses Tom and Blifil; Sophia in her charge.	Mrs. Fitzpatrick confuses Tom and Blifil. Sophia in Lady Bellaston's charge.
7	12
Tom loses way. Army and rebels: army and honor. Partridge and gypsy woman	Squire Western had lost his way. Puppets and rebels. Gypsies and honor.
8	11
Man of the Hill's story. Tom joined by Partridge.	Mrs. Fitzpatrick's story. Sophia joined by Mrs. Fitzpatrick and Irish Lord.

9	10
Upton: Mrs. Waters; fray. Arrival of lady and maid.	Upton: Mrs. Waters; fray. Arrival of Sophia and Honour.

Like other epic structures I have described, *Tom Jones* also falls into three large units:

First Six Books	Second Six Books	Third Six Books
Tom's putative parents	Partridge and Mrs. Waters	Tom's true parents
Tom's education	Various societies; the Man of the Hill	Lady Bellaston, Nightingale, the Andersons
Sophia and Molly	Sophia and Mrs. Waters	Sophia and Lady Bellaston
Home and dismissal	Exile and wanderings	End of wanderings; reacceptance; return home.

12. In my discussion of Sophia's role in *Tom Jones*, I have utilized many suggestions from Martin Battestin's important essay, "Fielding's Definition of Wisdom: Some Functions of Ambiguity and Emblem in *Tom Jones*," *ELH* 35 (1968): 188–217. The principal differences between our readings of the book, however, derive directly from our differing understandings of Fielding's concept of wisdom.

13. For a full discussion of the importance of Charron's work and of the relation of wisdom and justice, see Rice's *The Renaissance Idea of Wisdom*, especially pp. 178 ff.

14. For information about Donne's treatment of the figure, see the introduction to Frank Manley's *John Donne: The Anniversaries* (Baltimore, 1963), pp. 10–50.

15. Quoted from Rice, *The Renaissance Idea of Wisdom*, pp. 206–7.

16. It is on this point that I most fundamentally disagree with Battestin's article.

17. For a fuller discussion of this aspect of the novel, see Jessie Rhodes Chambers, "The Allegorical Journey in *Joseph Andrews* and *Tom Jones*." (Ph.D. diss., The Johns Hopkins University, 1960).

18. Fielding will exploit the *locus* and the symbol of the prison much more thoroughly in *Amelia*, to be discussed below.

19. See *The Covent Garden Journal*, No. 8.28 January 1752, ed. G. E. Jensen, 2 vols. (New York, 1964)' 1:186.

20. These parallels and their significance are discussed in George Sherburn's "Fielding's *Amelia:* An Interpretation," *ELH* 3 (1936), and most importantly, in L. H. Rowen's "The Influence of the *Aeneid* on Fielding's *Amelia*," *MLN* 71 (1956): 330–36.

21. For an excellent discussion of this aspect of the novel, see Peter V. Le Page, "The Prison and the Dark Beauty of 'Amelia,' " *Criticism* 9 (1967): 337–54.

22. Also, like *Paradise Lost*, *Amelia*, has subsidiary palindromes within this large framework: the two units of six books are similarly symmetrical within themselves, as are also the yet smaller units of three books each.

23. Mrs. Bennet is her surrogate not only in this respect but also by marrying Atkinson, who loves Amelia, and also by sharing some of Eve's traits — most notably, the desire for intellectual superiority to her husband. In this same respect, she also seems to approximate the arrogance of Charron's *scientia*, which the wise man repudiates.

LIST OF TEXTS CITED

The Poems of John Dryden, ed. James Kinsley (Oxford, 1958), 4 vols.

The Works of Henry Fielding, ed. Edmund Gosse (Westminster and New York, 1898), 12 vols.

John Milton: Complete Poems and Major Prose, ed. Merritt Y. Hughes (New York, 1957).

Poems of Alexander Pope, ed. John Butt (London and New Haven, Conn., 1939–69), 11 vols.

Spenser's Faerie Queene, ed. J. C. Smith (Oxford, 1909), 2 vols.

The Prose Writing of Jonathan Swift, ed. Herbert Davis (Oxford, 1957–68), 14 vols.

Any translations not otherwise indicated are my own and are probably tendentious.

INDEX